Form No. 98.

MIDLOTHIAN
COUNTY LIBRARIES

This Book is due to be returned to
the Library on :—

a

THE SCOTTISH BURGHS

THE
SCOTTISH BURGHS

AN EXPANDED VERSION OF
THE RHIND LECTURES IN ARCHAEOLOGY
FOR 1945

BY

WILLIAM MACKAY MACKENZIE

M.A., D.Litt., H.R.S.A.

OLIVER AND BOYD

EDINBURGH: TWEEDDALE COURT
LONDON: 98 GREAT RUSSELL STREET, W.C.

1949

FIRST PUBLISHED . . . 1949

PRINTED AND PUBLISHED IN GREAT BRITAIN BY
OLIVER AND BOYD LTD., EDINBURGH

PREFACE

THIS book, an expanded version of the Rhind Lectures in Archæology in 1945, has for its aim an account, within moderate compass, of the burgh organisation of Scotland in origin and operation, presented in a view which does not allow the wood to be obscured by the trees. The incommoding fact is that, as in England (see p. 196), every town has really a history of its own, so that individual peculiarities, if the main pattern is to be kept clear, must be relegated to a subordinate position or even, on occasion, disregarded.

It is perhaps proper that here a tribute should be paid to the able and industrious scholars whose work on burgh records must arouse the gratitude and admiration of all labourers in this field.

I have to thank the Carnegie Universities Trust for a grant towards the cost of publication.

W. MACKAY MACKENZIE

ABBREVIATED REFERENCES

A.P.S.   Acts of the Parliament of Scotland.
B.B.C.   British Borough Charters.
R.C.B.   Records of the Convention of Burghs.
R.M.S.   *Registrum Magni Sigilli*, Register of the Great Seal.
R.P.C.   Register of the Privy Council.
R.S.   Rolls Series.
s.d.   *sub data*, under date.
S.H.R.   Scottish Historical Review.
S.H.S.   Scottish History Society.

CONTENTS

CONTENTS

EARLY TOWN PLANS

CHAPTER I

ORIGIN OF BURGHS

In early free towns? Growth at castles and monasteries? In agricultural
communities? Creation not growth.

IT was only as late as 1846 that Parliament passed an "Act
for the abolition of the exclusive Privilege of trading in
Burghs of Scotland," making it "lawful for any person to
carry on or deal in merchandise, and to carry on or exercise
any trade or handicraft, in any burgh or elsewhere in Scotland,
without being a burgess of such burgh, or a guild brother,
or a member of any guild, craft, or incorporation." No
doubt this "exclusive privilege of trading," under pressure
of general economic expansion, had been already falling
into desuetude, and was in practice moribund ; yet it was
still the law, and, in the judgment of the Royal Commissioners
of 1833-35 on the Municipal Corporations in Scotland, the
courts of justice even then "could not refuse giving effect
to it." [1] Business monopolies constituted one side of the
burghal system. The other was their mode of self-government
in which a "close system" of "electing the common councils
and magistrates" of royal burghs had resulted in "much
loss, inconvenience, and discontent" ; while "the mode of
electing such magistracies and councils" as existed in non-
royal burghs was "defective." For these "inconvenient"
conditions a remedy was provided in the Municipal Reform
Acts of 1833,[2] of which one transferred the right of electing
magistrates and councils in royal burghs to those qualified
by the recent Reform Act to vote for a member of Parliament,
and the other extended the same provision to such non-royal
burghs as were now entitled to share in Parliamentary
representation. The Act of 1846 completed the transformation
of the urban framework of Scotland, which had had its

[1] *General Report*, 1835, p. 77.
[2] Quotations above from the Acts.

1   A

beginning over seven hundred years before. The Scottish case, however, was but one variation in an international urban system of which it has been written that " The mediæval towns had created the most consistent, vigorous and long-lived system of economic policy that has ever existed, the most important parts of which were the gild system and the internal regulation of industry in general, and the organisation of foreign trade and commerce." [1]

How then, at whose instance, did this venerable form of social organisation first take shape in Scotland ? Or did it arise spontaneously ? On this problem of origin our authorities speak with varying, even discordant voices. " The burghs emerge silently," says the latest writer on the subject.[2] What lies behind this figure of speech is the signal fact that the term *burgus* for a particular place appears first for certain in charters of the reign of David I.[3] But it may be asked, could not the thing have existed before it found a place on record ? May there not have been burghs in fact before in name ? For us, town-bred or at least town-minded, it is hard to think of a country without towns or of a town as not a natural growth like a tree. There is, indeed, an ambiguity in the use of the term town. Waverley, in the novel of that name, found that in Scotland " a single house was called a town," while " the farm-steading of Charlie's-hope " in *Guy Mannering* "'in the language of the country " was " the Town." We have it, too, for a casual group of buildings in Kirk-ton, Mil[l]ton and such like ; this having been also an English usage. These, however, are just rural units answering to the Pictish " pit " or " pet " and its Gaelic equivalent " baile," prefixed as in Pitfour and Balfour.[4] They are native in a rural economy. But the " burrowis-toun " was another

---

[1] Eli F. Heckscher in *Economic History Review*, vii (1936-7), 46.

[2] *Early Burgh Organisation in Scotland*, David Murray, LL.D., ii, 312. *Cf.* on German towns, pp. 3, 46 *n.*

[3] Ignoring the mention of burghs at Berwick and Roxburgh in the late copy of a foundation charter to the monastery at Selkirk by David as Earl, which displays some questionable features. (*Cf.* Lawrie's *Early Scottish Charters*, No. xxxv and notes.) The confirming charter to Kelso by David as King appears to Lawrie to be " spurious." (*Ibid.*, p. 411.)

[4] See Watson, *Celtic Place-names of Scotland*, p. 407.

matter. With its street lay-out, its facilities for marketing, its professional traders, and its self-government, it is an urban unit, a burgh or town in our sense. Countries have been able to subsist without such units,[1] which therefore in their origin suggest something of method or artifice.

Thus even in countries in which Roman cities had once flourished the rise of the later burghs has been the subject of close investigation and of different theories.[2] No one now holds to the idea that the burghs derived from the old Roman municipalities. These perished or changed character in the lingering decline and parcelling out among invaders of the Roman Empire in the west : " throughout both West and East numbers of still flourishing towns disappeared never to rise again." [3] In England " the decaying civil life of the Roman province was certainly swept away." [4] Of Roman Germany we are told that, after the first invasions, " Many centuries pass before a German town-life comes in sight. Then once more to all appearance it is suddenly there. In the eleventh century we find all at once German towns, German citizens. Now appears documentarily the expression ' burgess.' Now privileges are conferred on towns." [5] The language here and the century bring us near to what is to be said of the Scottish burghs, also sudden in record early in the century following and also then gifted with privileges. For England there is debate as to the degree of continuity between the burghs before and those after the Norman Conquest. Like " town " the term " burh " or " burg "

---

[1] Professor Tait speaks of " the town-hating Angles and Saxons " in contrast with " these latter days, when five-sixths of the population of Great Britain are massed upon pavements " (*Mediæval English Borough*, p. 358).

[2] For a summary of these, see H. Pirenne in *Revue historique*, t. 53, pp. 52-83 ; Carl Stephenson, *Borough and Town*, pp. 3 ff.

[3] *Life and Work in Mediæval Europe*, P. Boissonnade (translation), p. 26 ; *Cf.* C. Seignobos, *The Rise of European Civilization* (trans. 1939), p. 80.

[4] R. R. Darlington in *History*, xxiii (1938), 142.

[5] Es währt lange Jahrhunderte bis ein deutsches Städtewesen hervortritt. Dann aber ist es dem Auscheine nach plötzlich da. Im elften Jahrhundert finden wir mit einem Male deutsche Städte, deutsche Bürgerschaften, etc. (*Das ältere deutsche Städtewesen und Bürgertum*, Georg von Below (1925), p. 2.) *Cf.* here p. 46 *n.*

has a shifting history. In origin, here and on the Continent, it meant a fortified residence or any primitive stronghold. For the tenth century kings of the house of King Alfred it " seems to have meant . . . a fortified enclosure, which may sometimes have been intended only, like those on the Roman wall, for an armed camp." [1] By analogy it was extended to a fortified " ton " or " town." This feature of fortification, so far as it affects Scotland, will be dealt with later.[2] Meanwhile it is significant to find it said for England that " It was not till the twelfth century that our boroughs began to have an independent municipal history." [3] The twelfth century, the time of David I and William the Lion, was a renaissance period in mediæval life.

In Scotland one of the different theories or explanations of the appearance of burghs postulates for them a high antiquity. This was formulated by an eminent scholar in these terms : " From the earliest period of our history, free burghs, with certain privileges of trade and other immunities, had existed in Scotland, and from the days of David I at least, two combinations of these burghs appear." [4] And again, even more emphatically, that " towns and trading communities existed among us as early as we can pretend to speculate upon our history." [5] The combinations referred to in the first version are the *ansus* or " hanse " of the northern burghs, and " the Court of the Four Burghs " in the south— Berwick, Roxburgh, Edinburgh, and Stirling A later historian takes the same line in a more expansive mood, writing, in his account of the reign of David I, that " Free towns in con-

[1] J. H. Round in *Eng. Hist. Rev.*, xxvii (1912), 546.
[2] See pp. 39-44.
[3] Mrs Green, *Town Life in the Fifteenth Century*, i, 11.
[4] Cosmo Innes, *Legal Antiquities*, etc., pp. 113-4. There would seem to be a contradiction in what the same scholar says in another work : " The reign of William is the era of the rise of free burghs in Scotland " (*Sketches of Early Scotch History*, p. 35), that reign not being " the earliest period of our history." One might cavil, too, at the use of the term " free burgh " (*liber burgus*), an expression not found in England before the beginning of the thirteenth century, when it first occurs in a charter of King John (*cf.* p. 14). " Free " then meant " privileged." In later Scotland it denoted a royal burgh in contrast with an " unfree " or baronial burgh.
[5] *Scotland in the Middle Ages*, p. 158.

siderable numbers must already have existed both to the north and south of the Tweed," and that " even before the reign of David such burghs must already have been in existence," his " immediate predecessors " having " doubtless found it in their interest to foster the growth of towns within their kingdom." [1] Apart from his " immediate predecessor " Alexander I, it is hard to see, from their record, any of the others finding their interest in this employment. Nevertheless the idea has the support of a professorial brother, who affirms that " The Scottish burgh . . . goes well back into Celtic times." [2]

Advocates of this continuity of the burghs from early and obscure times make much of the northern and southern groups already specified. Professor Hume Brown introduces the former of these as follows : " Before the time of David, indeed, certain towns beyond the Mounth had actually formed a *hanse* or league for the advancement and defence of their common interests." This account rests upon the terms of a solitary document in the archives of Aberdeen, in which King William grants to all his burgesses of Aberdeen, Moray, and north of the Mounth their free " hanse " (*liberum Ansum*), to be held where and when they wished, as their predecessors had done in the time of King David, his grandfather. There is nothing in the language of the document to warrant the inference that these conditions existed, as is claimed, " before the time of David." The nature of the *ansus*, too, except as some kind of function or assembly, is left vague, and there is no agreement as to the more precise significance to be given

[1] P. Hume Brown, *History of Scotland*, i, 91, 92.

[2] Professor James Mackinnon, *Social and Industrial History of Scotland*, p. 61. Miss I. F. Grant is even more generous : " There had been towns in Scotland long before the eleventh century, especially in the district centreing about the head of the Firth of Tay, and by the time of David I they had evidently reached a considerable degree of development " (*Social and Economic Development of Scotland* (1930), p. 121). The authority cited resolves itself into the details from Ptolemy, the geographer of the second century A.D., and a reference to Brechin as a *civitas* near the end of the tenth century, whatever *civitas* may mean. On the record of Brechin as a town, see pp. 91-2. A previous historian would have none of this. " It is evident," he writes, " that the Celtic inhabitants of the country were averse to settle or congregate in towns " (P. Fraser Tytler, *History of Scotland* (ed. 1864), i, 268).

to the word.[1] Further, the differentiation between burgesses in Moray and those north of the Mounth is odd, since the latter area would include Moray. There is no record of any action in terms of the charter, and the whole matter, like the birth of Mr Yellowplush, is " wrapped up in a mistry."

The second group is introduced by the same historian as " the association of the Four Burghs " already named [2] which, he says, by their " deliberations " produced the code known as the Burgh Laws, professedly " ordained " (constitute) by David I. This, however, is another issue, and the matter as a whole will come up for consideration hereafter.

To the question how and whence these ancient " free burghs " acquired their " privileges of trade and other immunities," the only sort of answer is contained in the statement as to burghs in general that " their laws and privileges were largely copied from English models, and

[1] Of this document the Royal Commission of 1835 say that " the individuals in whose favour it was conceived, could not have been united into a single burghal community, in the present meaning of the terms," but that it may be regarded as proving " that to the north of the Grampian mountains, there existed a set of hanse towns, whose alliance, and whose common privileges and immunities had been recognised and protected as early as the reign of David I " (General Report, p. 11). Cosmo Innes, whose conviction as to ancient " free burghs " has been considered above, was one of the commissioners. Mr Gross's judgment is that the document was " more probably intended, either as a general grant of the Gild Merchant, or as a grant of the right to impose the hanse tribute upon merchants " (Gild Merchant, i, 197). Mrs Green notes that " in 1227 a charter of Henry the Third seems for the first time to enact that burgesses must not only dwell in the borough, hold land, and pay lot and scot, but must also ' be in the Merchant Guild and Hanse ' " (Town Life in the Fifteenth Century, ii, 194). Mrs Pagan refers to " a confederation of burghs in the north " as a theory based on the Aberdeen charter with " no other evidence in support of this theory " (The Convention of the Royal Burghs of Scotland, pp. 25-6). In the reign of Edward III it was claimed for a Welsh borough that all " who wished to enjoy its privileges should . . . contribute a certain custom called ' hanse ' towards the common weal of the burgh " (The Mediæval Boroughs of Snowdonia, E. A. Lewis, p. 166).

[2] The editor of Exchequer Rolls, i, however, would allot to Berwick and some other places " an existence before feudal times as places of foreign trade," while Edinburgh, Stirling, Roxburgh, Ayr, etc., " seem to have sprung up at a later stage of our history " round royal castles (p. lxxix). On Ayr, see pp. 33-4. This analysis would detract from the evidential value of the Four Burghs for the pre-feudal origin of such institutions.

English and Flemings were in many cases their leading citizens " ; [1] or, as another historian puts it more precisely and emphatically, " Scottish burghs were founded on English precedents, and the whole system of burghal law and custom was derived from English models." [2] These statements do not quite concur in expression, though their details are based on a common source in charters of David I [3] and William the Lion. Their bearing on the question of origin will be made clear at a later stage.

What we have been considering, indeed, is not so much a theory as an effort to rationalise the sudden and unprepared appearance of the burghs, how they, " emerge silently," as it has been phrased. The explanation then offered and repeated is that they " must already have been in existence." " Must " simply means that there appears to be no other way of accounting for David's burghs but by descent. It is a term of necessity, what Huxley, in another connection, described as " an empty shadow of my own mind's throwing." " A lang pedigree " was always a thing admired in Scotland. Still, this explanation did not recommend itself to every student. For one thing it gave no clue to a beginning, though such is implied in the conferring of " privileges " and " immunities." Another approach to the problem was therefore found in the idea of growth. A learned exponent has put the case thus : " the little village communities which grew around Royal and Baronial Castles and Religious Houses, or on sites otherwise suitable, cultivated . . . such scanty trade as was then practicable. . . . They were probably in a position of absolute villenage, and had no rights or privileges save such as the policy or caprice of their lords allowed. . . . But in process of time the Sovereign and the more powerful nobles came to recognise it to be their interest to encourage the

---

[1] Hume Brown, as cited, i, 95.

[2] *Scotland*, Sir Robert Rait and George S. Pryde, p. 12.

[3] " David may be regarded unquestionably as the founder of the Scottish burghs " (E. W. Robertson, *Scotland under her Early Kings*, i, 441). The claim made for Prestwick in the charter of 1600 (*R.M.S.*, s.d., No. 1042) for an antiquity of 617 years as a burgh cannot be taken seriously, any more than that Aberdeen was made a royal burgh by King Gregorius, A.D. 893. (*Memorialls for . . . the Royall Burghs*, 1685, " Philopoliteius " (Alexander Skene), pp. 223, 230.) Skene was a bailie of Aberdeen.

development of the little trading communities which had sprung up around them, and this they did by the concession of privileges largely of monopolies and exclusive dealing." [1] The intermediate stages are filled in by an earlier historian, who traces to such an origin at castles, royal and baronial, the " first appearance of towns in Scotland," and pictures " the hamlet growing into the village ; the village into the petty town ; and this last into the privileged and opulent burgh." [2] Then, having eliminated the Celtic inhabitants, he attributes this progress to manufacturers and traders drawn from the " lower orders " of " the more industrious race of the Saxons and the Anglo-Normans," which, so far as it is true, is no more here than conjecture. But as he starts with the protection of a castle or monastery, the whole process comes to be something of a tight fit ; the burgh is on us before the hamlet has well begun. · The same general idea governs a comparatively modern exposition, where we read how burghs " sprung up " round royal castles, or " had sprung out of villages or settlements " in a barony.[3] All of which obviously cancels out the proposition as to pre-existing free towns.

An origin on " suitable sites " or in " village communities " will be considered presently. Meantime we may examine the part usually attributed in this connection to castles and monasteries, as what in logic may be called " material causes."

The prime difficulty is that in Scotland between the introduction of monasteries and castles and the appearance of burghs there was scarcely time for this process of settlement and growth. The same is true of cathedrals : before David's time St Andrews was the only bishopric in Scotland proper ; he added six or more probably eight. The earliest religious houses were those of Scone and Inchcolm, both established by David's brother Alexander I, and the only ones till David

---

[1] Sir James Marwick, *Scot. Hist. Rev.*, i, 123. Adopted in *Edinburgh 1329-1929*, p. 234.

[2] P. Fraser Tytler, *History of Scotland* (ed. 1864), i, 268, 269.

[3] George Burnett, ed. *Exchequer Rolls*, i, p. lxxx. The following definition stands alone : " In origin, then, the burgh was a thanage, barony, or manor, whose inhabitants possessed a monopoly of trade " (George Law, in *Juridical Review*, xi (1899), 304). Actually this is a statement of the things a burgh was not.

himself could be credited with ten or eleven.[1] But neither Scone nor Inchcolm gave rise to a burgh. Further, if the monasteries had played so formative a part in burgh foundations by attracting settlers to their neighbourhood, then we should expect the older and greater houses to provide correspondingly good examples. It is not the case. Kelso Abbey, " the first and perhaps the richest of the Sainted David's monasteries," [2] had from King William only a special privilege for its men in the adjoining hamlet as to buying and selling, and its later burghal history is erratic.[3] Holyrood had an early burgh in Canongate, but that was not the result of an accumulation of settlers at the Abbey gates or of growth ; it was a foundation by charter from King David on unoccupied land. So indifferent were the relations of monasteries and towns. In one order indeed they were hostile. The greater number of Benedictine houses in Scotland was Cistercian, and for these there was no question of having a settlement grow up in their neighbourhood ; rather would they destroy anything of the sort already there, being committed to absolute exclusion from human intercourse outside the cloister. No hamlet or town could thus find a footing near a Cistercian monastery, until in course of time the order had relaxed its original rigidity. It was thus and very late that Culross could become a royal burgh, Melrose a burgh or barony, and the village of New Abbey come into being, these being Cistercian sites. Monasteries from their very nature could be no great fosterers of town life. The same has been remarked of the Continent, where, it is pointed out, certain of the largest and most influential abbeys, such as Cluny and Citeaux, and others of most ancient origin, whether in France or Germany, never acquired any dependency that could properly be called a town.[4]

Much the same analysis applies to castles as parents of burghs. The first record of a castle (*castellum*) in Scotland,

---

[1] Fordun's *Chronica*, v, cap. xxxviii ; *Scotich.*, v, p. xlviii. The latter source adds Dunfermline. Sir David Lindsay attributes fifteen abbeys to David (*The Monarche*, line 4429).

[2] C. Innes, *Sketches of Early Scotch History*, p. 159.

[3] See pp. 79 *n*, 80, 81, 91.

[4] H. Pirenne, *Revue historique*, t. 57 (1895), p. 65.

as of a burgh, is of David's time in that king's charter of Annandale to Robert de Brus. In early days we do find a burgh attached to a royal castle, but not necessarily by way of attractive or parasitic growth ; the burghs of Ayr and Dumbarton are as deliberately and newly founded as the castles themselves, albeit there was an already existent community (*villa*) in the neighbourhood of Ayr at least ; but this community had no part in the burgh. Nor indeed was every early royal burgh sponsored by a castle ; it was not the case at Inverkeithing or Haddington. In respect of burghs baronial castles had little to contribute. Before the middle of the fifteenth century, when the multiplication of burghs in barony began,[1] the very few places of this kind were almost all attached to ecclesiastical establishments. The communities neighbouring a baronial castle, the " castle-tons," were normal accessories, rural pertinents in domain, and, if they became burghs at a late stage, it was not necessarily from any relation to the castle. The mere presence of population need not foreshadow a burgh.

Account must now be made of the latest hypothesis of burgh origins, which differs radically from those that have just been considered. It is included in two exhaustive volumes by a profusely learned author on a group of western burghs,[2] but some of the briefer and more precise utterances will suffice for its exposition. In contrast with what has already been said, it is here affirmed that " In Scotland few burghs owed their origin to castles and monasteries," indeed that " in many cases where a town clustered round a castle or an abbey the burgh was itself of earlier origin "[3] Thus a much favoured derivation of burghs is substantially written off. Then contrary to the assumption of " free towns " or " free burghs " before David I, which are simply continued into a later time, we are now instructed that " The early burgh was not a trading community," and " trading was not the basis of the burgh constitution."[4] That, it is conceded, may be its " modern acceptation," but " In early times the word merely denoted a certain municipal organization—a com-

[1] See p. 79.
[2] *Early Burgh Organisation in Scotland*, David Murray, LL.D.
[3] *Ibid.*, ii, 374.   [4] *Ibid.*, i, 12, 13 ; *cf.* ii, 282.

munity of self-governing freemen founded on a community of property " in land.[1] Thus we start with what are arbitrarily called " burghs of the primitive or agricultural type," [2] which were " ancient institutions in the time " of David I.[3] What " may have been," our author continues, " in the mind " of that king and " what King William aimed at . . . was probably the creation of trade centres " in these agricultural burghs : given a burgh of this type " what King William endeavoured to do . . . was to direct its energies towards trade. He did not touch the constitution." [4] As a result of these royal attentions, we are told, " The original type of burgh was fading away ; the burgh was ceasing to be a cultivating community." [5] A charter was merely the " conferring of trade privileges upon an existing burgh." [6]

These propositions may be challenged as in no particular supported by evidence, but that becomes unnecessary, since the author in his summing up admits this shortcoming and, after so much positive assertion, concludes in what is surely an anticlimax, pleading only that the organised communities which " existed long prior to . . . burghs " were " *probably* self-governing " ; that " it may *reasonably be assumed* that the

[1] *Early Burgh Organisation in Scotland*, i, 12 ; ii, 475. *Cf.* as to England and " the doctrines which would fill England with free landowning village communities. Here we enter a misty region where arguments suggested by what are thought to be ' survivals ' and inferences drawn from other climes or other ages take the place of documents. We are among guesses and little has as yet been proved " (F. W. Maitland, *Domesday Book and Beyond*, p. 340). All this applies even more strongly to Scotland.

[2] *Ibid.*, ii, 375. [3] *Ibid.*, ii, 321.

[4] *Ibid.*, ii, 374-5. According to Pirenne such direction was impossible in the economic circumstances of the time : " La renaissance du commerce et de l'industrie au moyen age a si profondement modifie les conditions de la vie economique qu'il est impossible d'expliquer les constitutions urbaines par l'organisme primitif de la commune rurale " (*Rev. hist.*, t. 53, p. 73). *Cf.* For Germany " The new towns, on the other hand, general economic conditions having meanwhile begun to undergo a marked change, were founded with the intention of establishing centres of trade . . . The settlers invited were merchants (*mercatores personali*) and handicraftsmen " (Art. *Commune, Mediæval*, by F. Keutgen in *Ency. Brit.*, ed. xi). It may be noted, too, that a merchant handling goods would have to be to some extent literate, able to deal with measures and costs, a qualification not then probable in agricultural communities.

[5] *Ibid.*, ii, 432. [6] *Ibid.*, ii, 308.

burgh was a development of an older type " ; and that
" How this came about we know not, but there is *no reason
to suppose* that it did so otherwise than by . . . gradual
evolution " [1]—evolution, which, as Lord Morley has said,
" is the most overworked word in all the languages of the
hour." [2] Anyhow, evolution is the name for a process ; it is
not a factor.

Such, then, are the proffered originals or precursors of
what in the time of David began to be known as burghs :
(1) " free towns " undefined and unaccounted for ; (2) village
communities at particular sites doing a little trade but in a
state of villenage towards their lords ; (3) agricultural
communities municipally organised but ignorant of trade
until directed that way by the kings. Obviously all these
characteristics cannot be true of the same subject at the
same stage ; they embody antagonistic ideas, each cancelling
out the others. Only some fundamental fallacy can lead to
reasoned results so divergent.

There may be dissent from these solutions and yet a
prejudice or conviction left in favour of some nucleus or
root from which the burgh developed or grew. This indeed
was the principle of a German school of specialists, who
postulated such a nucleus in some earlier Roman site or
round a stronghold, and where these failed in some sort of
village settlement.[3] A pre-existing datum there had to be,

---

[1] *Ibid.*, i, 599-600. The italics are mine.

[2] *Politics and History*, pp. 54-5. It does some hard work in the following
passage : " The canoes and other objects fashioned and used by man,
found in and around Glasgow, are evidence that there was a settled community upon the spot at least twelve centuries before Glasgow appears
as a burgh. There can be no doubt that the descendants of the people
who occupied the site of Glasgow became by evolution the community
which we find existing as the burgh of Glasgow in the twelfth century "
(Murray, as cited, i, 599).

[3] Allzeit setzte jedoch die Gründing einer Stadt eine bereits bestehende
Ortschaft voraus oder es musste, wo dieses nicht der Fall war, mit der
Stadtanlage zu gleicher Zeit eine dorfartige Ansiedelung verbunden werden.
" Always, however, the founding of a town presupposed an already existing
inhabited locality or, if this was not the case, a village-like settlement
would at the same time be combined with the lay-out of the town "
(G. L. von Maurer, *Geschichte der Städteverfassung in Deutschland* i, 30-1,
cf. p. 44).

something to give a beginning. From this source the authoritative English scholar, William Stubbs, took his theory of the burgh in England as developed from the village community,[1] and that has been widely followed. But when a later German protagonist of this theory had to confess that he had estimated the number of towns directly due to rural communities as considerably (*erheblich*) higher than he now would,[2] the theory was dead. If burghs could arise without any preceding community, such a beginning was no longer imperative. We shall see examples in Scotland without any prelude of the kind—Canongate being projected on an unoccupied site contemporaneously with the Abbey ; Nairn castle and burgh going up together on a new site acquired for the purpose ; and other burghs being founded in disregard of any earlier settlement, as at Ayr and Dumbarton.

The prevailing error is in the idea of growth or size as the genesis of a burgh, from which it would follow that there must be something to grow. But, as a distinguished English scholar in this field has put it : " In the Middle Ages towns did not ' grow ' but were made. A village, just because it was a large one, could not gradually come to be called a borough any more than it can now-a-days. A definite legal act was necessary. . . . Wherever we can go back to the beginning, this formal act of creation can be traced." [3] Or as expressed in another quarter : " It is not a slow evolution, it is a formal act, which gives it this place apart, and which makes of the word borough a technical term corresponding to a definite legal conception." [4] We can also go beyond " making " in a legal sense to the material fact, as how King Richard, when he determined to build (*edificare*) Portsmouth, let out sites (*placeas*) to many men who should build upon these ; [5] or as King John started Liverpool when, having

---

[1] *Const. Hist.*, i, 99. " The ' burh ' of the Anglo-Saxon period was simply a more strictly organised form of township." *Cf.* 53 ff., 438. Also Maitland in *Domesday Book and Beyond* : " A borough belongs to the genus villa (tún)," p. 216, *cf.* p. 173 ff.

[2] Passage cited from von Below, *Probleme der Wirtschaftsgeschichte* (1920) in Stephenson, *Borough and Town*, p. 10, note 3.

[3] Mary Bateson, *Mediæval England*, p. 125.

[4] *Studies and Notes, &c.*, Ch. Petit-Dutaillis and Georges Lefebvre, p. 69.

[5] *Curia Regis Rolls*, p. 305 ; *Abbrevatio Placitorum*, p. 85.

acquired the manor, he granted to all who should take (*ceperint*) burgages in the *villa* there the liberties of any free burgh by the sea.[1] Not much later than this time William the Lion and Alexander II, as we shall see, were similarly laying out burghs at Ayr and Dumbarton respectively. Indeed, it has been pointed out that in England " from the earliest times we have to account for boroughs which were artificially created, and were not village communities which had acquired a burghal status." [2]

On these lines we reach a different point of view. The focus is not on growth but on a creative act, and that not merely in giving " an impulse towards their development " [3] or " a new impulse . . . towards trade," [4] or anything so vague, but at least in formally conferring upon a place a legal status unlike that of any other political unit, and even, it may be, in the sense of taking the initiative, laying the foundation of what was to be a burgh. From this latter consideration it follows that it is not necessarily the case that every burgh should have a forerunner in kind, or even, if there were a local preoccupant, make use of it. To identify or postulate the presence of a population group is one thing ; to account for a burgh is quite another ; and the former is not the sole begetter of the second. The key-word to the burgh is creation, not growth.

[1] *Rotuli Litterarum Patentium*, i, pt. i, 75. The date is 1207 and this is an early use of *liber burgus*. On which *cf.* p. 4 *n.*

[2] Ballard, *British Borough Charters*, i, p. xci.

[3] Hume Brown, i, 92.

[4] Murray, as cited, ii, 375.

CHAPTER II

ON CHARTERS AND THE BURGH LAWS

Grants by "word of mouth." St Andrews. Canongate. Problem of the Burgh Laws.

THAT the term "burgus" is not found in documentary use before the time of David I is surely a fact of cardinal significance. Another is that "Although money in one form or another is pre-urban, coined money is a town improvement," [1] and our first Scottish coins also date from the same reign. What we do lack are charters of that king to the burghs he names. On this absence of foundation charters and claims to the existence of burghs in any case before their charters were granted, a sweeping conclusion has been based. A burgh could exist without or before a charter. Therefore the charter was only incidental, a form of recognition or encouragement. [2] Therefore burghs existed before being formally recognised as such. Therefore neither the absence nor the presence of a charter of erection is an argument against the pre-existence of burghs. [3] Charters of privileges

---

[1] Professor N. S. B. Gras, in *The Legacy of the Middle Ages*, p. 441. So, too, the standard weights and measures were associated with towns, as the Lanark pound troy, the Linlithgow firlot, Stirling pint, Edinburgh ell. So in 1709 Banff had a new outfit of weights from Lanark, wet measures from Stirling, dry measures from Linlithgow (*Annals of Banff*, New Spalding Club, i, 180).

[2] See p. 5, "a confirmation of something already existing." Murray, ii, 313 : "Its object was rather to confer privileges or franchises on the burgesses beyond those implied in the existence of a burgh." i, 11, *cf.* p. 44.

[3] Thus William the Lion granted to the Bishop of Glasgow and his successors that they should have a burgh at Glasgow (*ut burgum habeant apud Glasgu*). This, it is pointed out, " may suggest that the burgh was not then existing ; but the facts indicate otherwise, and it would seem that on the contrary there was an existing burgh which the charter recognised " (Murray, as cited, i, 292). *Habeant* is then appropriately translated as " maintain," *cf.* pp. 32-3.

to burghs simply "favoured their development." [1] Therefore the burgh itself was not constituted by such means.

What is mistakenly assumed in all this reasoning is that the written charter was the only way of expressing a royal grant. As regards the period before King David an English writer emphasises "the fact that the practice of grants in military tenure was to a large extent conducted by ceremonial feoffment without any charter. . . . It was, in fact, the necessary outcome of the requirements of alienation in an age and in a society which were not much conversant with writing, and had to rely on public declarations and on the memory of witnesses to keep up the validity and the legal tradition of acts." [2] The charter, indeed, came into existence as a convenient record of an act in a more primitive form.[3] All this applied even more strongly to Scotland, where in the twelfth century charters were still a novelty, and particularly so where burghs, themselves a novelty, were concerned. "Scottish lawyers," it has been said by an eminent member of the profession, "had no definite ideas of the terms in which burgh privileges ought to be expressed." [4] Therefore recourse had to be made to models in England, where again there was some uncertainty, so that the charter to one burgh might be constituted by reference to some other already in existence. So obvious is the debt of Scotland to English examples of this class that the Scottish legal writer just referred to can picture William the Lion as having "no doubt carried home with him transcripts of the Winchester charters" to serve as models.[5]

More generally we have the position of the charter authoritatively put thus : "It is unnecessary that this expression of the donor's will should take the form of a

---

[1] Hume Brown, *History*, i, 108.

[2] *English Society in the Eleventh Century*, P. Vinogradoff, p. 227.

[3] "A charter is essentially . . . the confirmation of an act which already lies in the past. Its object is to provide testimony more permanent than that of mortal witnesses" (F. M. Stenton, *Transcripts of Charters relating to Gilbertine Houses*, Lincoln Record Socy., vol. 13, p. xvii).

[4] Murray, *Early Burgh Organization*, ii, 430.

[5] *Ibid.*, p. 429. "The Winchester charters may indeed have been used in drafting the charter of Ayr, as in some respects the one is the echo of the other," p. 431.

written document. It is, to say the least, very doubtful whether the great Norman barons of the first generation, the companions of the Conqueror, had charters to show for their wide lands, and even in Edward I's day men will make feoffments, nay settlements, without charter. Furthermore the charter of feoffment, if there be one, will, at all events in the thirteenth century and thenceforward, be upon its face an evidentiary, not a dispositive document. Its language will be not ' I hereby give,' but ' Know ye that I have given.' The feoffor's intent then may be expressed by word of mouth." [1]

It can now be understood how it is claimed for England in the period 1042-1216 that, since there are but a " few examples of the creation of burghs by charter, we are driven to conclude that during this period many boroughs were created by word of mouth." [2] So, too, it has been held by another Scottish lawyer that " it seems impossible to resist the conclusion that in Scotland also burghs at first were created by oral authority of the King." [3] For England it has been maintained that the sheriff could say : " This place is a borough because it has always been treated as such." [4] Further, " Some of the greatest towns on the Continent flourished for centuries with no charter at all." [5]

That a burgh, therefore, could be in existence before it received a charter is true ; that it could do so without a royal act of nomination or recognition or some fiat of creation equivalent to the later and more sophisticated written document does not follow. The charter of course simplified any issue. The Scottish king, Alexander II, had occasion to determine a trading dispute between Glasgow and Dumbarton and rested his decision on the fact that Glasgow had the

[1] *History of English Law*, Pollock and Maitland, ii, 82. *Cf.* " that the ceremony of investiture and actual possession formed the essence of transmission ; and if these were capable of being proved by witnesses, or in any other satisfactory manner, writing was not then, nor for ages afterwards, essentially necessary " (*Lectures on the Law of Scotland*, Walter Ross, ii, 123).

[2] Ballard, *British Borough Charters*, i, p. xli.

[3] J. T. T. Brown, *Scot. Hist. Rev.*, xxii (1926), 45.

[4] *Hist. of Eng. Law*, ii, 635.

[5] Carl Stephenson, *Borough and Town*, p. 29.

B

right in question before he had founded "any burgh"
(*aliquem burgum*) at Dumbarton.[1] This relation in time could
be established only by the dates of their respective charters,
to which therefore these burghs owed their existence. Similarly
the charter of Alexander is accepted in a confirming charter
of 1609 as "the first erection of the foresaid burgh of
Dumbarton into ane free and royal burgh."[2] These
judgments exclude the contention that the charter or its
equivalent had no relation to the actual coming into existence
of a burgh.[3] That of course is a simple case, but it establishes
the creative significance of the charter where such exists,
and therefore of the corresponding earlier action which did
not reach written record at the time. What has proved
difficult is the fact that "not one of the seventeen or
eighteen Scottish burghs which claim David as founder,
is able to produce a scrap of twelfth century evidence to
show it was erected by charter."[4] Hence, on one hand, the
disparagement of the charter as not primarily important,
and, on the other, recognition of the part played by earlier
procedure.

We may now turn to the documentary references to
burghs that can be assigned to the time of David I.
These, for the most part, are found as dispositions to
religious houses of a building site or homestead ("toft,"
mansura), the qualification of a burgess, described as in the
King's burgh (*in meo burgo*) ; in one case as a yearly payment
from "the revenue (*firma*) of my burgh and the waters of
Elgin."[5] In just a few cases do we have the King brought
into a more direct association with a burgh. For example,
it is the Bishop of St Andrews who announces that with the
licence of King David I he had founded (*nos statuisse*) a burgh
at St Andrews and, with the royal consent and in the King's

[1] *Reg. Epis. Glasg.*, i, 148-9.

[2] *R.M.S.*, s.d. 1609, No. 190.

[3] See p. 15. Murray claims that Glasgow and Dumbarton "although
not described as burghs in King David's reign, must . . . have had
burghal constitutions and usages," *E.B.O.*, i, 7.

[4] Brown, as cited.

[5] On these see Lawrie's *Early Scottish Charters*, passim. Even
charters which can be spoken of as doubtful or spurious can serve on
this point.

firm peace, had appointed Mainard, a Fleming, to be prefect,[1] granting to him and his heirs three building sites (*toftas*) at apparently a favourable rent, because he had been among the first (*ex prioribus*) in beginning to build and equip (*instaurare*) the burgh. The town—*villa* used in this clause, as in other cases we find it substituted for burgh—is described as a free charitable gift (*elemosina*) of the blessed King, and Mainard as having been the King's own burgess (*proprius burgensis*) in Berwick.

On the face of it we have here a record of the beginning of the burgh of St Andrews, which was thus not a growth round the monastery, the foundation of which (1144) was the work of the same Bishop, but his creation by authority delegated from the King, who is thus postulated as the ultimate source for such an institution. Basing, however, on the word *instaurare*, translated in its classical use as " to renew," it is claimed that no more is meant than the renewal, in some unspecified fashion, of a pre-existing town.[2] But *staurum* in mediæval use was just " store," and *instaurare* to furnish a castle or other place with stores or equipment.[3] St Andrews was no doubt an ancient ecclesiastical site, and seems to have been, even in this twelfth century, a known port of communication with the Continent,[4] all which may have contributed, but the burgh was the foundation of Bishop Robert,[5] as aforesaid, with Mainard the Fleming as the foremost of its first constructors.

Another case is that embodied in the charter of Holyrood Abbey, where David grants to the canons the right to institute a burgh between their church and the King's burgh (*meum*

---

[1] *præfectum* : usually translated " provost," as indeed it means in the charter of 1601 to Irvine, *R.M.S.*, s.d., No. 1171.

[2] Murray, as cited, i, 71.

[3] *E.g.* comportantes frumentum et caetera necessaria ad instaurandum castella sua. Walsingham, *Historia Anglicana* (R.S.), i, 389. *Cf.* Knighton, *Chronicon* (R.S.), i, 477.

[4] See *Vita Oswini*, chap. xxxi, in *Miscellanea Biographica* (Surtees Society) ; *Alia Miracula S. Johannis Episcopi*, in " Historians of the Church of York " (R.S.), i, 308.

[5] " When Bishop John [should be Robert] of St Andrews was desirous of erecting a burgh at his episcopal see, the King granted him the site etc. . . . Such was the beginning of the city of St Andrews as a trading burgh " (C. Innes, *Scotland in the Middle Ages*, p. 159).

burgum) at Edinburgh,[1] the burgesses to share the right of
buying and selling in the King's market there and to be
free of toll and customs on what they buy and sell in all royal
burghs over the whole kingdom.[2] The burgh thereafter
constituted on these terms was known as Canongate and
from the whole circumstances of its site as part, or in the
immediate neighbourhood, of what had been royal hunting
ground, was waste or unoccupied land.[3] Canongate was, so
to speak, a creation *ex nihilo* ; it had no predecessor or nucleus
of any kind.

Possibly a significance for *herbergare* and *instaurare* may be
extracted from David's charter to Baldwin his " officer " or
" sergeant " (*clienti*) holding a toft in Perth,[4] whereby Baldwin
is exempted from all service of the burgh except watch and
ward (*vigilia*) and the enclosing (*claustura*) of the burgh to
the extent of his property. The idea of enclosure may lurk
behind the obscure terms (*herbergare* ; *instaurare*) from Holyrood
and St Andrews, but this will be considered later. Baldwin

---

[1] The word here translated as " institute " is the most unusual one,
herbergare, which is commonly translated " to build " or by Lawrie, as
cited, p. 386, " to build and create," indicating a perception that something not quite so simple as " build " is implied. We find Malcolm IV
giving permission to the Prior and monks of Coldingham to bring, according
to their will, their men on their land *ad herbergandum* the vill of Coldingham
(*Chartulary of Coldingham*, p. 14), where Lord Hailes translates as " to inhabit
or people." This, too, is not quite satisfactory and would certainly not
apply in the Holyrood case. Possibly we have the word in the vernacular
" herbery," frequent in later vernacular for " shelter or lodge," sub-
stantive and verb, which has been referred to A.S. *herebeorga*, " shelter for
an army " (Skeat). Maitland thought *Herbergare* was " the ancient
name " of Canongate (*Hist. of Edinb.*, p. 148).

[2] Lawrie, as cited, No. cliii.

[3] *Lib. Cart. Sancte Crucis*, p. lxxxvii : " allanerlie woddis and wildernes,"
as " knawin the inspectioun of historeis."

[4] There is a grant by King William *c.* 1165 of a toft in " my new burgh
of Perth," while, Dr Murray points out, what " has been regarded as its
charter of erection was not granted until 1210," though it is seen figuring
as a burgh " at least thirty years earlier ". His conclusion, therefore,
is that the creation of a burgh by charter, as William " professes to have
done at Ayr," is not to be interpreted strictly (*Early Burgh Organ.*, etc.,
ii, 308). But the Commissioners of 1835 had the charter of 1210 before
them and " found strong reasons for doubting its authenticity," relying
on two such members as Cosmo Innes and Robert Hunter (*List of Markets
and Fairs*, Sir James Marwick (1890), p. 96).

is to have the further privileges of being subject only to the
king's courts and of retiring from the burgh when he wished
and selling his house and toft as burgage.[1] This term, too,
necessarily dates from the records of King David, tenure by
burgage being peculiar to burghs and exempt from the
ordinary feudal obligations, bearing only such as arose from
their relation to the burgh.[2] Of these, as we see, sharing in
the burgh " watch " or policing was one.

II

Other burghal material attributed to David's time does
not now meet with complete acceptance. This consists of
what is introduced as the " Laws and Customs of the Four
Burghs "—Edinburgh, Roxburgh, Berwick and Stirling—as
ordained (*constitute*) by King David. An early authoritative
pronouncement was that " no other body of burgh laws and
customs, so ancient and well authenticated, exists in the
world," [3] and as for that reason is " the real and proud distinction of Scotland " in contrast with " the borrowed plumes
of the *Regiam Majestatem*," [4] a production also assigned to the
time of David I as prepared by his command, but by this time
recognised as only a Scottish adaptation of a later English
treatise on feudal law. These Laws are then cited as " evidence
that burghal communities had grown up and taken shape
long prior to David's time," they being, as they claim, due
to that King " with some additions of later date." Indeed

---

[1] It may be that otherwise he would have been restricted by *le retrait
lignager*, whereby his relatives had certain claims on the manner of disposal
of the burghal property. See *The Retrait Lignager in Scotland*, D. Baird
Smith, *Scot. Hist. Rev.*, xxi (1923-4), 194-5. The proper procedure in
such a case is given in *Reg. Mon. de Passelet*, p. 382 (A.D. 1283), and *Reg.
Ep. Gl.*, i, 197, No. 236 (1280-90) as " according to the law and custom
of burghs " or " of the burgh." There is no allusion to the Burgh Laws.
The much-copied (p. 28) charter of Lorris in France (from Louis VI,
1108-37) has a clause permitting an inhabitant of the town to sell his
property and leave the town without having reason to fear any claim
(A. Luchaire, *Institutions monarchiques de la France*, ii, 148).

[2] Burgage tenure was professedly abolished in 1874 (*Principles of the
Law of Scotland*, Erskine (1881), p. 158).

[3] C. Innes, *Ancient Laws, etc.*, p. xxi.

C. Innes, *Ledger of Haliburton*, p. xlvii.

the Laws, it is held, prove the burghs to have been by then
" ancient institutions." [1] To much the same effect comes
the pronouncement under another honoured name that this
code of laws, as of David's reign, shows the burghs " to have
been, even then, compact, well-organized bodies, and enables
a distinct conception to be formed of the municipal constitution of the little trading communities of that time." [2]
Certainly the Laws as a whole, including the " additions,"
offer a comprehensive syllabus extending at most to 119
articles,[3] making rules as to buying and selling, laying down
the law on problems arising out of such transactions as well
as on burgh life in general, regulating the holding of courts
and the election of magistrates and covering many other
particulars, all which justifies what is said as to their comprehensive and precise character.

What then is the history of these Laws which are relied
upon to establish such forcible conclusions as to burgh
origins ? A legal authority has written of the code that " its
origin is clearly Anglo-Saxon. . . . The kernel of the laws
of the Four Burghs is the Anglo-Saxon law which prevailed
in Northumbria, from Forth to Humber, for the four centuries
prior to the Norman Conquest." [4] Another legal opinion,
not perhaps incompatible with this, describes them as a
compilation by (hypothetical) " commissioners " of King
David, who reported the " burghal customs " which they
" found in existence," and which that King thereafter " recognised and arranged," some " additions," as already noted,
coming later.[5] Since this writer, however, holds that what
he arbitrarily calls burghs before David's time were purely
agricultural communities, which that King and his grandson
first induced to launch out into trade,[6] it is rather difficult
to see how they could straightway contribute a code of urban
commercial usages. A quite different solution is offered in

[1] Murray, *Early Burgh Organisation*, i, 5 ; ii, 321 ; " Several of the laws
seem older than the time of David. Others are more recent." i, 43, ii, 322.
[2] Sir James Marwick in *Scot. Hist. Rev.*, i, 124.
[3] *Ancient Laws and Customs*, etc., ed. C. Innes, pp. 4-58.
[4] Professor Dove Wilson in *Jurid. Review*, viii (1896), 225, 234.
Repeated by Mr MacGillivray, advocate, in *Sources and Literature of Scots
Law*, Stair Society, i (1936), 213.
[5] Murray, as cited, i, 7, 4-5.   [6] See p. 11.

the claim to the Laws as begotten by " deliberations " of the
Four Burghs, the results of which were ratified " in due time "
by " the sanction of the King's Court or Parliament but which,
even independent of that sanction, were received as authoritative by all the burghs of Scotland." [1] Of the proceedings of
the Four Burghs we know almost nothing, apart from their
rare recognition as a court capable of declaring burgh law
and custom in a legal dispute and hearing appeals from burgh
courts.[2] Sanction of the Laws by Parliament is only an
extension of their being " constituted," as their title runs,
by David I. There is no Parliamentary enactment before
an Act of 1474, which refers to a " statute of the Burrow
Lawes " on a question of heirship : " By this Act," comments
Sir George Mackenzie, " the Laws called *Leges Burgorum*,
bound in with *Reg. Maj.* are declard a part of our Law." [3]
The inference would seem to be that the Laws, so curiously
identified, had not been so declared before. It happens
that the earliest record of their application by burghs occurs
only a few years earlier.[4] In 1468 a question had been raised
at Aberdeen as to the shares of property falling to the children
of a man who had been twice married. Advice was sought
from the town council of Edinburgh, who considered the
matter with " men of law " and came to a finding in accordance with the chapter in the Burgh Laws dealing with this

[1] C. Innes, *Ancient Laws and Customs of the Burghs of Scotland*, p. xxxix ;
Exch. Rolls, i, p. lxxxiv ; Hume Brown, *History of Scotland*, i, 92 ; Sir James
Marwick, *Observations on Early Guilds, etc.* (1886), p. 13.

[2] See *The Convention of Royal Burghs*, Th. Pagan (Keith), pp. 2, 10-11.

[3] *Observations on Acts of Parliament*, p. 77. Lord Bankton refers to this
statute only, as, mistakenly, of 1479 (when there was no relevant Act of
Parliament), in support of his statement that the *leges burgorum* are " speci-
ally referred to in our statutes " as " our genuine laws " (*Institute of
the Laws of Scotland* (1751), i, 31).

[4] Other references which have been relied upon (Murray, i, 8) do not
bear such an interpretation. About 1283 we have a legal procedure
justified as " according to law and the custom of burghs " or " as the law
lays down and the custom of burghs " (*quod lex dictat et consuetudo burgorum.
Reg. Monasterii de Passelet*, pp. 382, 385). At Glasgow the same procedure
is declared to be " according to law and the custom of the burgh " (*et
consuetudinem burgi. Reg. Episc. Glas.*, i, No. 236, p. 197, A.D. 1280-90) ;
and, in another case of 1317, as " according to the laws of the burghs of
Scotland " (*Miscellany, Spalding Club*, v, 5). These do not constitute
references to the Burgh Laws proper, like those that follow.

particular issue, which they cite, as also did Dundee, referring
to " The law and consuetude of the four burowyis in the
xxv [xxiv] chapter." [1] If the burghs had in practice observed
the Laws as authoritative, it seems strange that so enlightened
a place as Aberdeen should request guidance from other
burghs, and Edinburgh feel bound to get legal opinion, while
all the time the chapter of the Burgh Laws was so explicit
on the problem. One cannot but note too the impersonal
tone of the reference to the " law and custom of the Four
Burghs " not to a known code binding upon all burghs
alike.[2]

One other authoritative judgment runs that " putting it
at the lowest, the code of laws of the Four Burghs, as we have
it, is not later than the time of the Alexanders, and represents
a body of custom which had been growing up in Scotland
since the days of David I ; much of it having grown
up long before in other countries and brought here by
immigrants." [3] These carriers are introduced to account for
the fact that so much of the burghal code corresponds with
customs familiar in England and the Continent.[4] There is

[1] *Records*, Edinburgh, 20th March 1468 ; *Council Register* (Spalding
Club), p. 29, 27th March 1468.

[2] There seem to be other uncertainties as to the bearing of the Burgh
Laws upon burgh practice. The Laws make provisions (xi, xii, xiii, xxii)
as to trial by combat in the case of burgesses, but a charter by King
William to Inverness expressly exempts the burgesses there and in Moray
generally from such form of trial in respect of anyone in the whole kingdom
(*nunquam inter eos bellum habebunt*, etc., *A.P.S.*, i, 89). Another chapter (lxx)
provides for the election of *prepositi* (" borowgreffis ") in the burgh by
the common advice of the good men there, but this is scarcely consistent
with the position of the *prepositi* in David's time as inferred on p. 97.

[3] J. Maitland Thomson, *The Public Records of Scotland* (1922), p. 147.
The lowest date is that given to the older of the two MSS. judged to have
been " written about 1270 " (Innes, *Scotland in the Middle Ages*, p. 80).
It is at least earlier than 1306, a date which appears in an entry on a blank
space of the original.

[4] " The code was obviously largely based on the pre-existing constitution and laws of English boroughs " (Marwick in *Scot. Hist. Rev.*,
i, 124) ; " imported into Scotland from England and the Continent "
(Marwick, *Introductory* " Lists of Markets and Fairs " (1890), p. 11).
" As a whole they correspond, in many particulars, with similar customs
in English boroughs and their equivalents on the continent " (Murray, as
cited, i, 5). *Cf.* also Innes, *A.P.S.*, i, 39.

another explanation of this phenomenon which will be drawn upon in what follows.

Then from the very characteristics of the Laws so emphasised, exhibiting the burghs as " self-governing corporations " at a time when indisputable records show these to have been of a much more primitive character, a learned investigator refuses to accept them as " genuine productions of the reign of David I " and excludes them from his compilation of documents of that time.[1] It must also be kept in mind that the Laws are derived not from official or record material but from the collections of two nameless lawyers, as to which collections in general we are warned that " their statements as to the authority and date of their contents must be received with caution." [2] In view of all these circumstances it becomes possible to write that " The authenticity and extent of the authority of the codes of burghal law, contained in the *Leges Burgorum* and the *Statuta Gilde* in regulating burgh affairs has never been dealt with con-clusively. It has been disputed how far they were applicable and applied to Scottish burghs." [3] It may be noted, also, how in one of the " Lawyers' collections " King William is credited with a law providing that burgesses in certain legal actions should have the " freedom " to follow the " law " and " custom " of Winchester,[4] a standard reference for English burghs, but here ignoring the national laws supposed to have come from that King's grandfather.

Behind such demurrers lie two general considerations on which there is a large measure of agreement ; one, that the principles of the Laws are to be found in the stock of burghal

---

[1] Sir Archibald Lawrie, *Early Scottish Charters*, p. vii. George Chalmers had earlier come to the same conclusion. The Burgh Laws, as we have them, he says, " bear upon the face of them a much more modern air than the early age of David I could properly exhibit " (*Caledonia*, Bk. IV, p. 726, note " f "). According to Professor Hannay, " it is certain that a portion only of this code can be assigned to the reign of David " (*Edinburgh 1329-1929*, p. xvi). Where and why the line is to be drawn is not said.

[2] *The Public Records of Scotland*, J. Maitland Thomson, p. 28.

[3] David Robertson, LL.B., Town Clerk, and Marguerite Wood, Ph.D., Keeper of Burgh Records, Edinburgh, in *Stair Socy.* publications, i, 101. *Cf.* here p. 77 *n.*

[4] Preface, *A.P.S.*, i, 35.

franchises common both to England and Continental countries, and the other that the Scottish Laws are specifically indebted to those of Newcastle-upon-Tyne. As an example of the former correspondence the significant provision (No. xv) that a serf buying a burgage,[1] and remaining in a burgh for a year and a day without challenge by his lord, becomes a free man, is almost universal where burghs existed. It occurs in the same terms in the charter of Lorris in France of 1155,[2] which was the model for a multitude of French towns. It was summed up for Germany in the saying, *Stadtluft macht frei*,[3] " Town air gives freedom." Kings, lords, churchmen, might have serfs ; only the towns stood out against serfdom.

But the immediate Scottish connection is with the burghal customs of Newcastle-upon-Tyne, which, in turn, " except for one or two references to peculiarly English institutions, might equally well have applied to many a Continental town." [4] These Newcastle customs, it is shyly confessed, " were a principal source of the Burgh Laws " [5] of Scotland,

---

[1] This qualification does not appear in the English version of the Laws (*A.P.S.*, i, 40), nor in the provision regarding serfs in the custumals of Nottingham, London, Waterford, Lincoln (*Borough Customs, Selden Socy.*, ii, 88-9), nor in the foreign equivalents. Thus " Lorris est terre de liberté : tout serf qui y a habité un an et un jour est libre." And this custom of Lorris (*cf.* p. 28 *n*) spread wide in France, including " les provinces anglo-normandes " (Paul Viollet, *Les communes françaises*, etc., p. 18). As all a serf's possessions belonged, at least in theory, to his lord, he could purchase his freedom only by a legal subterfuge (Pollock and Maitland, *Hist. Eng. Law*, i, 410-11). How this would operate in the case of a burgage, which further was open to challenge by the lord, is not explained. The condition would seem to be a later lawyer's interpolation.

[2] " Quiconque sera resté un an et un jour dans la paroisse de Lorris, sans q'aucune réclamation l'y ait poursuivi, y demeurera libre et tranquille " (A. Luchaire, *Histoire des institutions monarchiques de la France*, ii, 148). On this law *cf.* Ein Grundsatz der frühe schon in fast alle Stadtrechte übergegangen ist—" a principle which at an early date had passed into almost all town law " (von Maurer, as cited, i, 395). Professor Wilson thought " it is possible it was an original custom common to all the Aryans. In any case it must have come from Germany to us " (*Jur. Rev.*, viii, 230).

[3] *Das ältere deutsche Städetwesen und Bürgertum*, G. von Below, p. 122.

[4] Carl Stephenson, *Borough and Town*, p. 128.

[5] Murray, as cited, i, 5, note. " Said to have been taken more or less verbatim from the code of Newcastle and other neighbouring towns in Northern England " (Lord Murray in *Stair Socy.* publications, i, 246).

so much so that in part at least they are even verbally the
same.[1] The King of England founded other burghs in that
neighbourhood on the basis of the customs of Newcastle, as
also did the Bishop of Durham, who was responsible for
many burghs.   The foundation charter to Wearmouth
[Sunderland] by Bishop Hugh Pudsey (1153-95), though
" according to the custom of the burgesses of Newcastle,"
reads in its clauses like a transcript, with a few synonyms, from
some of the Scottish Burgh Laws.[2]

It is usual to say that this borrowing from Newcastle is
to be explained by the fact of Northumberland having been
under the rule of David, and " that to this circumstance is
owing the extraordinary coincidence of many of . . . the
burgh laws of Scotland with the privileges and ' customs '
which obtained in the English burghs from the time of
Henry I." [3] Or, as the same writer puts it elsewhere, the
connection between Scotland and Northumberland was such
as " to render it very possible that the framer of a body of
Scotch burgh laws should adopt the customs used at Newcastle." [4] It is perhaps a discordant fact that David did not
possess Newcastle, expressly reserved in the treaty which
gave him Northumberland.[5] Moreover, it must be noted
that the custumal of that town, as we have it, though deriving
from an earlier stage, Newcastle being one of the burghs
with no foundation charter,[6] is actually the work of an inquest

---

[1] See the corresponding extracts in parallel columns in the Preface
to *A.P.S.*, pp. 39-40. Referring to a memorandum of the laws and customs
of Newcastle " written in a hand as old as the reign of Henry II " (not
now discoverable—Ballard, *B.B.C.*, i, p. xxxvii), Cosmo Innes wrote, " It
consists of eighteen chapters, almost consecutively, of the well-known burgh
laws of Scotland " (*Scotland in the Middle Ages*, p. 154). Professor Dove
Wilson wrote that " The first twenty clauses in both are indeed the same "
(*Jur. Review*, viii (1896), 226).

[2] See *Boldon Buke*, Surtees Society, pp. xlii-iii. Some examples are
given in a supplementary Note.

[3] C. Innes, Preface to *A.P.S.*, i, 39.

[4] C. Innes, *Scotland in the Middle Ages*, p. 154. Professor Dove Wilson,
however, thought that " those numerous privileged burghs, which were
known afterwards as ' Royal ' burghs . . . were Anglo-Saxon settlements,
with privileges going back to the pre-Norman period " (*Jur. Rev.*, as cited,
p. 226).   [5] *Chronicles of Stephen* (R.S.), iii, 177.

[6] See p. 17. It later received a charter from King John.

or court of enquiry instituted by Henry II,[1] whose authorisation
it bears. Without that authority it would not be valid in a
court of law. The phrasing of the custumal is therefore the
work of the inquest. If now we accept this account of the
compilation of the Newcastle custumal and find so many of
the Scottish Burgh Laws a literal reproduction, there is no
escaping the conclusion that these cannot be earlier than
their prototypes of the time of Henry II, who only began to
reign after David had been gathered to his fathers.

Nor is any particularly local explanation required for this
relationship. It was an ordinary measure for a new burgh
to have its liberties expressed in the terms of some older
foundation. The practice was universal. On the continent
" The charters of Lorris in Gatinais and of Beaumont in
Argonne have been copied again and again by hundreds of
other communities ; the same happened to Freiburg im
Breisgau in Western Germany and to Magdeburg not only
in Eastern Germany, but in Lithuania and Poland." [2] In
Domesday Book we read how the baronial founders of the
new burgh of Rhuddlan " gave to those burgesses the laws
and customs which are in Hereford and Breteuil," the latter
a place of no particular importance on the confines of
Normandy, these customs being familiar in France and now
found also in England. Cardiff was later to apply to Hereford
for a copy of its customs for its own use ; other towns did the
same and Hereford put on a charge for transmission.[3] The
same conveyance is found in Scotland : Dumbarton in 1222
was to have the liberties and customs of Edinburgh ; Dingwall
in 1227 was granted the liberties and free customs of Inverness,
which itself had been originally granted the liberties and
right customs of the King's other burghs. But we never find
a Scottish burgh founded on the terms of the Burgh Laws,

[1] Stephenson, as cited, pp. 125-6 ; Stubbs, *Select Charters* (8th ed.),
p. 111. A charter to Newcastle by Henry III (1234) confirms all the
liberties which the burgh had enjoyed in the time of Henry II (*Percy
Chartulary*, Surtees Society, p. 334).

[2] Professor Vinogradoff in *Legacy of the Middle Ages*, p. 313. See also
Below in *Das ältere deutsche Städtewesen und Bürgertum*, p. 8. He classifies
them as a " Mutterstadt " and a " Tochterstadt," the latter also being
capable of becoming a " mother-town " in the same way.

[3] *Town Life in the Fifteenth Century*, Mrs J. R. Green, i, 228-9.

as it would be reasonable to expect if these were recognised as a common basis, and as we do find those of Northumberland constituted on the custom of Newcastle, where the charter of Wearmouth offers parallels with the Scottish code. If then the Scottish burghs adopted the Newcastle model to whatever extent, they did so as recent not ancient foundàtions, borrowing, in their uncertainty, as the fashion was, the equipment of an older institution, which was the model for so many others in the north of England. Indeed the Scottish practice then extended to the acceptance of English law generally,[1] just as England had filled in its feudal law from France. And it was as natural in Scotland to attribute ancient laws to David I as in England to King Alfred or Edward the Confessor, each of these rulers becoming " the hero of a legal myth." [2]

There is a set of bare facts about Scottish burgh laws, as to which it is possible merely to state their existence. An inventory of documents returned by Edward I to King John Balliol in 1292 and again appropriated in 1296, includes a roll of " the laws and customs of the burghs of Scotland." [3] That roll was still in the English Exchequer in 1323.[4] It never returned to Scotland and no longer exists. However, in the Register of the Bishopric of Glasgow a few entries are inserted, which are clearly " provisions of burgal policy," but " do not appear in any of the codes of Ancient Burgh Laws of Scotland," though " two of them are almost identical with the special privileges granted to the Burgh of Inverness by a charter of William the Lion," and indeed also to other burghs.

---

[1] E. J. MacGillivray in *Stair Society*, i, 212-3 ; Professor Dove Wilson in *Jurid. Rev.*, viii, 239.

[2] Pollock and Maitland, *History of English Law*, i, 65. " When any legislators of a later age wished to stamp their institutions with a name of authority, they founded them upon the laws and statutes of the good King David " (Cosmo Innes, *Scotland in the Middle Ages*, p. 115).

[3] *A.P.S.*, i, 114.

[4] *Stapleton's Kalendars and Inventories of Exchequer*, ed. Sir Francis Palgrave, i, 132, item 34. In the *Scotichronicon* (v, xlviii), where use is made of the euology of David I by his friend Abbot Ailred of Rievaulx, reference is made for religious foundations to the prologue to that King's laws of the Burghs (*in prologo ejus super statutis burgorum*). But our Laws have no such prologue, and the reference is a fifteenth-century addition to a passage from Ailred.

These provisions are " conjecturally attributed " to the thirteenth century or the reign of William the Lion.[1]

The first of these regulations forbids anyone outside a burgh to have a brew-house (*brascinam*) unless he has power of pit and gallows, which signifies a baron, and he no more than one. The second forbids the making of cloth, dyed or shorn, outside a burgh without the King's permission (*ultra misericordiam*), and appropriate penalties are attached to infraction of this rule. Both these occur in charters to burghs. The next forbids interference with a traveller grazing horse or cattle outside meadows or growing corn (*segetes*). Another lays down that neither a bailie nor a sergeant (*serviens*) in a burgh was to keep a tavern or make bread for sale without royal permission. The last of the set has to do with a legal problem of inheritance.[2] That these jottings are relics of the original roll of burgh laws transferred to England cannot be proved, any more than that the contents of the lost roll have been resurrected in the burgh laws we now have. That the jottings may be chance survivals of what a charter from William the Lion on the fair at Glasgow speaks of as " the assise of my burghs and of my land," [3] can be no more than conjecture, never likely to be verified.

From such loose and conjectural material it were perilous to insist upon definite conclusions, but two at least would seem to have a balance of probability in their favour. One is that the Burgh Laws, as they stand, are not of David's time and that therefore we are not warranted in drawing upon them, as historians do, for an intimate, detailed picture of the burghs at that stage. The other conclusion, with more certainty, is that the Laws can provide no evidence for the existence of burghs before they " emerge " in the charters of King David.

[1] *Reg. Episc. Glasg.*, ed. Cosmo Innes, i, pp. liii-iv ; *A.P.S.* " Preface " by Cosmo Innes, i, 49.

[2] *Reg. E. G.*, ii, 608 ; *A.P.S.*, i, 666.

[3] *secundum assisam burgorum meorum et terre mee. Charters and Documents, Glasgow* (Burgh Records Socy.), Part II, No. iv.

NOTE 1

A few clauses from the Wearmouth charter [A] compared with sections of the Scottish version of Burgh Laws [B].

A

Burgensi cum burgense namare non liceat sine licentia praepositi.

B (iv)

Super burgensem burgensis non potest capere namum sine licentia prepositi.

A

Loquelae quae in burgo moventur ibi tractentur praeter illas quae pertinent ad coronam.

B (vi)

Placita que in burgo surgent teneantur et determinentur praeter ea que sunt corone domini regis.

A

Si placitum fuerit inter burgensem et mercatorem errantem infra tertiam maris influxionem rectum inter se faciant.

B (viii)

Si placitum oriatur inter burgensem et mercatorem terminari debet infra tertiam refluxionem maris.

A

In burgo non debet blodwite nec merchete nec heriot nec stengesduit [? -dint] exigi.

B (xvii)

Si sciendum est quod infra burgum non debet exaudiri blodewit nec styngisdynt nec merchet nec herieth nec aliquid de consimilibus.

A

Cuilibet burgensi liceat vendere terram suam et ire quo voluerit nisi terra sua in calumpnia fuerit.

B (xxi)

Quilibet burgensis potest terram suam de conquestu dare aut vendere et ire quocunque voluerit libere et quiete nisi sit in calumpnia.

ENGLISH RENDERING APPLICABLE TO BOTH LATIN VERSIONS

(1) No Burgess to distrain upon another without leave of the prepositus.

(2) Lawsuits raised in the burgh to be dealt with there, except pleas of the Crown.

(3) A case between a burgess and a travelling merchant to be settled within the third (high or low) tide.

(4) The feudal casualties specified (see Index) not to be exacted in a burgh.

(5) A burgess to be allowed to dispose of his land (*cf.* p. 21) and go where he wished, unless under challenge.

CHAPTER III

BURGH SETTLERS AND FORTIFICATIONS

Foundations by King William and Alexander II. Glasgow, Ayr, Dumbarton. Original burgesses of foreign origin. Were Scottish burghs fortified?

IN the reign of King William direct charters of foundation for burghs became available, though for some burghs there is still only the " word of mouth " or what amounts to circumstantial evidence, while in the case of Inverness the foundation is piecemeal in four separate charters. Dumbarton, too, has four contributory charters between 1222 and 1230.[1] Scottish lawyers had not yet established their styles.[2] In time, often very late, burghs not possessing foundation charters might secure such in a regrant (*de novo damus*), always with the preamble that the original charter had been destroyed or lost. Thus the unimportant little burgh of Cromarty is referred to by Robert the Bruce and James III as *meum burgum*, but its earliest charter is that of 1593, and is given on the presumption that the original one had perished in the course of time or in some of the troubles in that remote quarter. And so in other cases, but no more than a presumption ; there may have been no earlier charter.[3] Any question of standing or precedence would then become a matter of " inquest " or investigation.

As we have already seen in the case of Glasgow and Dumbarton, a question at law might have to be settled on the date of charters. Burgesses of Glasgow going to trade in the Lennox and Argyll were being obstructed by bailies of Dumbarton, who probably sought to levy tolls on other than their own merchants in these districts. King Alexander II forbade any interference on the ground that Glasgow had

---

[1] *R.M.S.*, 1609, No. 190. [2] See p. 16.

[3] " Lawyers choose to presume, that what are now called ' corporations by prescription,' must have had royal charters, now lost or destroyed. But the facts seem to run against that presumption of law " (*Scotland in the Middle Ages*, Cosmo Innes, p. 158).

enjoyed this privilege from of old before he caused any burgh to be founded at Dumbarton.[1]   It was King William who, within the years 1175-8, had granted to Bishop Jocelyn of Glasgow and his successors that they may have a burgh (*ut burgum habeant*) at Glasgow with all the liberties and customs that any one of the King's burgesses had in the whole country, and a market every Thursday.   Further, that all the burgesses who shall be resident (*manentes erunt*) in the burgh should have the King's peace over the whole land both in coming and going.[2]   The peace ensured by royal officials and the royal courts was the highest form of protection.

On the face of it this was the birth of the famous burgh.[3] A corroborative item comes in the fact that the same Bishop conveyed to his old monastery of Melrose the toft which Randolph of Haddington (*Ranulfus de Hadintune*) built " in the first building of the burgh " (*in prima edificatione burgi*).[4] For those who would take the beginning of the burgh back to an ever so remote and conjectural past, the explanation has been offered that " the first building of the burgh may therefore mean the extension of building " to a particular part of the burgh territory,[5] the burgh being already long in existence.[6]   But for anyone not shackled by a contrary theory the facts cited will require no rehandling.

King William, too, is responsible for a charter [1202-7] in which he announces that he has made (*me fecisse*) a burgh at his new castle at Ayr,[7] with a market every Saturday.

---

[1] *Cf.* pp. 17-18.

[2] *Cf.* Tous ceux qui viendront à Bourges pour y rester ou pour y déposer des choses qui appartiennent seront sous le sauvegarde du roi, eux et leurs effets, soit en allant, soit en revenant (Quoted in *Institutions monarchiques*, Luchaire, ii, 147).   " All who come to Bourges to remain or deposit there articles belonging to them will be under safeguard of the King, they and their goods, both going and returning."

[3] " Such was the origin of the burgh of Glasgow " (C. Innes, Preface, *Reg. Episc. Glas.*, p. xxii).

[4] *Lib. de S. Marie de Melros*, pp. 36 and 38.   The same phrasing as for the foundation of Dumbarton, *in prima erectione dicti burgi* (*R.M.S.*, s.a. 1609, No. 190) ;   or for the founding of Lindores Abbey, *de prima fundacione* (*R.M.S.*, s.d. 1364, No. 188).

[5] Murray, as cited, i, 71, note 3.   [6] *Ibid.*, i, 242.

[7] A new castle was made (*factum est novum oppidum*) between Don and Ayr in 1197 (*Chron. of Melrose*).

" I have granted," he goes on, " to all the burgesses who will come there to inhabit my burgh (*qui illuc venient ad burgum meum inhabitandum*) and shall be permanently resident there (*ibi sedentes et manentes erunt*) that they will be free of toll and all other custom throughout the whole land on their personal property." Further, he grants to the burgesses a certain amount of land pertaining to the vill of Ayr, also that all coming with their goods to buy and sell at the foresaid burgh shall have the King's peace in coming and returning.[1] It is a rather awkwardly expressed charter, but it shows the burgh's independence of a pre-existing vill or community, which is to be stripped of part of its lands in favour of the new creation. How this is to be fitted into a scheme merging the burgh and vill in one and so antedating and accounting otherwise for the burgh must be read in the words of its author.[2] A summary would not do justice to the complexity of the argument.

The charter of Dumbarton [1222] issued by Alexander II [3] is on much the same lines. A burgh had been made at the King's new castle there and the burgh and the burgesses settling in it (*in eo manentibus*) were to have all the liberties and free customs possessed by those settled (*manentes*) in Edinburgh, with a market every Wednesday and freedom from toll and custom over the whole land for their own personal goods. Two points in these charters are of categorical importance. One is that the burgesses to enjoy their privileges must be resident and continually so ;[4] the other that though the burgh has been " made," the inhabitants are still to come. The verbs used for the population are in or imply the future. So it is too in the case of Inverness, in one of the charters of King William, " who will inhabit my burgh " (*qui burgum meum de Invernis inhabitabunt*). Also in his charter to Arbroath.[5] The general tone is that of a burgh " to let " for which

---

[1] *Ayr and Wigtown Arch. Assn.*, 1883, pp. 1-2.

[2] Murray, ii, 303-7.

[3] *History of Dumbartonshire*, Joseph Irving, 1920 edition, ii, 287. Ratified 1609, *R.M.S.*, s.d., No. 190.

[4] On continental examples of this residential obligation, see Pirenne, *Rev. Histor*, lvii, 320.

[5] *qui in eodem burgo terram vel domum habuerint et in eo manentes fuerint. Cf.* the same usage by King John for Liverpool (pp. 13-14).

tenants are invited on favourable terms. Freedom from tolls throughout the kingdom was a powerful attraction, rare in Scotland as compared with England.[1] Similar allurements prevailed on the Continent, where the charter of a town " which was to be founded was promulgated throughout the country, just as in our days the press publishes most flamboyant prospectuses about the future resources and amenities of a town which is in process of formation." [2]

We can now grasp the significance of the clause in the Dumbarton charter in which the King concedes to the burgesses " who will come to inhabit the foresaid burgh and be resident there " the immunity of *kersetum*, which in the vernacular was " Kirset(h)," [3] for a term of five full years. " Kirset(h) " meant strictly the period within which a burgess was expected to erect a house upon his toft, implying exemption from any payments till this was done. In France one or, in some cases, two years was the limit : Edward I of England would allow two years for the towns he founded in his French dominions.[4] Five years was quite exceptional, and even more so the ten complete years of *kersetum* allowed in 1226-7 to those coming to and settling and remaining at Dingwall,[5] which can be understood to be, from its remoteness and disturbing neighbourhood, correspondingly less naturally attractive to possible settlers.

This provision of " kirset," which goes unregarded by our writers on the burghs, is surely of the first importance, linking, as we see, the Scottish burghs with the rise of towns on the Continent and so indicating a similarity of origin. It is of concern only to cases of new building, of houses to be erected. It implies a general scheme in novel circumstances. It could have no bearing on the sorts of burgh origins postulated in the current explanations ; therefore it arouses

[1] *B.B.C.*, ii, p. lxvii.

[2] Pirenne, *Economic and Social History of Western Europe*, p. 72.

[3] " Kirseth " or " Kyrset " in the Burgh Laws (No. xxvii) and there limited to one year, and explained in the Glossary as " respite, delay in payment " (*Ancient Laws*, etc.).

[4] Enlart, *Manuel d'archéologie française*, i, Pt. 2, 247-8 ; *Mediæval Town Planning*, T. F. Tout (1917), p. 15.

[5] *illuc venientes et ibi sedentes et manentes.* See charter of ratification 1497-8 in *R.M.S.*, s.d., No. 2387.

no interest in their expounders. What could " kirset " have
to say to towns already existing from antiquity, or to those
which naturally " sprang up " like mushrooms, or were earlier
agricultural communities ? It affected only newcomers to a
chosen site. It was relevant only to houses yet to be built by
burgesses who were yet to come, and so marks definitely the
beginning of a burgh. Speculation as to " burghal constitutions
and usages " at Dumbarton before its charter [1] is therefore vain.

Whence then came the occupants thus attracted to the
burghs ? The answer is provided by the best of the twelfth
century English historians, William of Newburgh, who,
having passed his life in a religious house in Yorkshire, had
full opportunity of knowing what went on in Scotland. He
notes that in the army with which William the Lion made
his unlucky invasion of England in 1174 there was " a great
number of English," because, he explains, the " fortified
places and burghs (*oppida et burgi*) of the Scottish kingdom are
known to be inhabited by English." [2] The section of the
Scottish army which this chronicler describes as " English "
another contemporary, writing in Anglo-Norman verse,
speaks of as " Flemings." [3]

This pronouncement, which reflects so gravely on all
theories of burgh origins as native and spontaneous, is usually
reproduced by historians in a rather softened form. It cannot
escape notice that all the earliest names of individual
burgesses are foreign in character—Mainard " the Fleming " at
St Andrews ; Baldwin, most probably also a Fleming, at Perth ;
Randolph of Haddington, apparently Norman, at Glasgow ; [4]
Geoffrey Blount, a Norman, at Inverness [5] ; one Swain in
Dunfermline and another at Perth, seemingly Anglo-Danes.

---

[1] See p. 18 *n.*

[2] *Hist. Rerum Angl.* (Roy. Hist. Soc.), Lib. II, cap. xxxiv. *Oppida* is
usually translated " towns," but something different from burghs seems
to be in question.

[3] Jordan de Fantosme, *Chronique*, iii, lines 1202, 1486. These racial
distinctions are not to be pressed. Mainard, a " Fleming " at St Andrews
(p. 19) has a Norman name.

[4] Raan Corbeht, Master of the Temple, had at the same time a toft
in the burgh, which " full toft " he transferred to his " man," William
Gley to be held of the house of the Order (*Reg. Ep. Gl.*, i, 37).

[5] *Gaufrido Blundo burgensi nostro de Inuernys.*

Three occupants of tofts in St Andrews under Bishop Robert, founder of the burgh, were Elfgar, Arnald, and William " Cook's-son " (coci), all names of foreign origin.[1] Wherefore it is observed of the burghs by one modern Scottish historian that " English and Flemings were in many cases their leading citizens." [2] Or, more unreservedly by another, " The original founders of our towns are supposed to have been in many cases wanderers from Flanders. . . . When Henry II drove all foreigners out of his dominions, they flocked into Scotland." [3] Another historian had already commented on " the lists of burgesses of Dundee and Aberdeen, of Norman or Saxon names and Teutonic lineage," in contrast with the Gaelic names of " gentlemen of the low country of Angus and Mearns." [4] A learned Inverness historian has pointed out how " for generations after Geoffrey's time the trade of the Burgh was mainly in the hands of merchants of alien origin, whose names have consequently been transmitted to us." [5] More mildly it has been put that " many Englishmen seem to have settled in Scottish towns," [6] or that " the influx of foreigners is responsible to some extent for the rapid growth of the Scottish burgh system." [7] All these are but variations on the theme given out by William of Newburgh more precisely and comprehensively. His affirmation is the easier to appreciate when we learn that much the same process

[1] Early Scot. Charters, Lawrie, No. cclxviii.   [2] Hume Brown, i, 94.
[3] Exch. Rolls, i, p. lxxxi.
[4] Cosmo Innes, Sketches of Early Scotch History, p. 147, note 1.
[5] Dr William Mackay, Records of Inverness, New Spalding Club, i, p. lv. Inverness didn't like clansmen as burgesses. In 1546 there is a ratification under the Great Seal of a statute by the provost, bailies, council and community dealing with the great hurt long suffered " throw indrawing of owtlandis men of grete clannis, nocht habill [able] nor qualifyit to use marchandice nor mak daylie residence nor policie nor na maner of biging within the said burgh, bot alanerlie to bruke [enjoy] and posseid the proffit of the common takkis [leases] and stedingis [buildings] of the said burgh . . . quhilkis outlandis men of grete clannis hes be divers and sinester weyis purchast [procured] thair fredomes throw solistatioun and laubouris of grete clannit men and utheris adjacent to the said burgh, etc. " (R.M.S., s.d., No. 3233. Cf. Commission 1835, Local Reports, Pt. II, p. 97).
[6] Murray, ii, 335.
[7] Maitland Thomson, as cited, p. 147. Cf. also Scotland Under her Early Kings, i, 309.

marked the development of Continental towns, the flocking to these of strangers, *advenae* ; [1] how the Conqueror settled colonies of Frenchmen within or alongside English towns ; [2] and how the Flemings were as prominent and enterprising in the arts of trade as the Normans were in war and administration. But, whatever its beginnings, the town exists by and for the merchants ; [3] the burden of and reason for the charter or its equivalent is the business of buying and selling with privilege and safeguards for those so occupied. The normal holding as the qualification of a burgess was a building plot with garden, not a field. A new class, a " bourgeois " population, was being fitted into the social structure, and in Scotland its first constituents were of alien origin.

It has been argued that in view of the " natural conservatism of mankind, particularly of primitive people, and their dislike of change, it would have been impossible to set up a new institution radically different from what already existed." [4] But Scotland in the twelfth century was being subjected to several new institutions, and there were those who did try to make them impossible. William of Newburgh continues with the information that the Scots restrained their hatred of the newcomers to the towns only by fear of the King, and, when he was taken prisoner, fell upon and slew these English, while the survivors took refuge in the royal fortifications (*munitiones*). It is not imperative that we should confine *munitiones* to castles, also new institutions ; the term may include the burghs as defensive places. Another contemporary English writer records this massacre of " English and French " ; [5] and the same story is told by the later Scottish chroniclers, how the Scots and men of Galloway " ruthlessly slew their French and English neighbours " and there was " a most woeful and exceeding great persecution of the English both in Scotland and Galloway." [6] This was not an

---

[1] Pirenne, *Rev. historique*, t. 57 (1895), pp. 74, 295 ; von Below, as cited, pp. 121-2. " Déjà même les chartes de Louis le Gros [1108-37] et de Louis le Jeune [1137-80] contienne des clauses favorables à l'immigration comme à l'établissement des étrangers " (Luchaire, as cited, ii, 147).

[2] *Cf.* p. 48 and further p. 53.

[3] *Cf.* Pirenne, as cited, p. 71. *Cf.* here p. 163 *n.*

[4] Murray, ii, 321-2.   [5] *Gesta Henrici II* (R.S.), i, 67-8.

[6] Fordun, *Annals*, xi ; *Scotichronicon*, viii, cap. xxii.

attack upon the English as such politically : we are not yet in the age of nations. They were just strangers intruded in strange institutions.

II

Indeed, the very word burgh, as explained earlier,[1] implies defensibility. The term " ' burgher,' " it is claimed, " distinguishes the town-dweller as the inhabitant of a ' burg,' that is a protective, fortified place." [2] Edinburgh was not in the first instance a burgh in the sense of a town but as a burg [3] or defensible residence on the rock, from which the name was extended to the later adjacent settlement of traders within their own defences.   The provision of some defence for trading centres was due to the fact that only in a place so protected could moveable goods be considered safe from pillage.   Not least in Scotland where the traders were, as we have seen, an alien population among a people hostile in feeling and ready, when occasion served, to do their worst to the newcomers.   In such circumstances access to the town and to its market, for which traffickers had to pay toll, would be confined to its " ports " or gates.   This toll we meet in the case of victuals as " ladle dues," a certain proportion collected in this fashion at the town ports.[4]   Under such conditions a town could not be open to enter and leave where one pleased.

Nevertheless, " A Scottish burgh," we are assured, had no walls ; it was not a strength." [5]   This affirmation has passed into general currency, so that it has been fixed upon as a detail of difference from what is found in England : " the Scots burghs were unwalled while the older English burghs were all walled." [6]   A difference, indeed, not only from

[1] See pp. 3-4.

[2] " Er kennzeichnet den Städter als den Bewohner einer Burg, d.h. einer bergenden, befestigen Ortschaft " (Die deutschen Städte und Bürger im Mittelalter (1921), Dr Bernhard Heil, p. 26).

[3] Answering to Celtic dùn or fortification, in Norman times Castrum Puellarum, " Castle of the Maidens," suggesting it as one of the " Maiden Castles " in England and Scotland, a name of unknown signifiance.

[4] See Murray, as cited, i, 270-1.

[5] Ibid., ii, 317. Also in note p. 2.   " A burgh may have had a stronghold, a castle . . . but the burgh itself was not walled or fortified."

[6] Ballard in S.H.R., xiii, 25.

English but also from Continental practice, and, if true, a remarkable tribute to the orderliness and honesty of mediæval Scotland in comparison with other countries, where such precautions had to be taken. A tribute, it must regretfully be confessed, too good to be true. Elsewhere the idea of fortification is so closely bound up with the burgh that it has been fixed upon as the characteristic feature : " the old towns are differentiated from the villages only by " the circuit of wall and ditch.[1]

One source of misunderstanding is to take " walls " in the sense of stone and mortar erections as the only form of " strength." But these, at the earliest stage and even at a much later time, are no more to be expected round burghs than round castles.[2] Yet without such a burgh and castle could both be fortified, as when William the Lion procured from the Bishop of Moray a piece of land in order to " fortify on it the castle and burgh of Invernairn." [3] The nature of the fortification is indicated by the Inverness charter, in which King William undertakes to provide the burgh with a rampart,[4]

---

[1] *Geschichte der Städteverfassung in Deutschland*, Georg L. von Maurer, i, 30 ; p. 44, " Die alten Städte unterschieden sich daher von den Dörfern einzig und allein durch die Stadtmauern und durch die Umgebung mit Wall und mit Graben." Von Maurer explains the terms *urbem aedificare, civitatem aedificare, urbem condere*, etc., as indicating such fortification. *Cf.* here pp. 13, 33. Again, " Die typische Form der älteren deutschen Stadt ist die befestigte Stadt. . . . Die Befestigung war der erste Zweck, für den eine städtische Gemeindesteuer erhoben wurde " (*Das ältere deutsche Städtewesen und Bürgertum*, G. von Below (1925), p. 28, *cf.* p. 4). A mediæval town, he points out, could not establish industry and trade without such protection. Or, as S. Rietschel put it : " Die Stadt ist ein Markt, der zugleich Burg ist " (Cited Stephenson, *Borough and Town*, p. 9). The term *burgensis* came to be applied in principle to all those who " resident dans l'enceinte des murs de la ville " (Pirenne, *Révue historique*, lvii, 320).

[2] See *The Mediæval Castle in Scotland*, W. Mackay Mackenzie, p. 31.

[3] *ad firmandum in ea castellum et burgum de Inuernaren. Reg. Morav.*, No. 25. For sense of firmandum see p. 41.

[4] *fossatum*, usually translated " ditch," but clearly here an earthen rampart, like that of the Peel of Linlithgow in 1304, which had been damaged by a storm and was repaired with sand, *ad . . . fossatum emendandum*. Bain, *Calendar of Docts.*, etc., iv. 459. Du Cange gives the explanation *vallum* as well as *fossa*. A rampart was the natural base for a palisade, as here.

which the burgesses were to crown with a palisade[1] to be kept by them in good condition. Rampart, palisade, and ditch were the normal defensive works of the time, and it is as so equipped that we must understand the " fortified towns " (*villis firmatis*) delivered over to Edward I in 1296 and 1304.[2] Jean le Bel, the Flemish chronicler who accompanied Edward III in his expedition into Scotland in 1333, tells how that King wasted the country as far as Aberdeen " and captured the largest towns, which were enclosed with good ditches and good palisades." [3] A possible alternative was a " mud wall," that is one of clay, such as the English raised round Perth after 1332.[4] Of some such primitive character we must understand the *claustura* at Perth to which King David's favoured burgess had to contribute his share.[5] The word answers to the *negotiatorum claustrum*, " the enclosure or ' cloister ' of the merchants," a defensive erection, known at Verdun and probably many other places.[6] David's son, Earl Henry, gave to Dryburgh a toft " outside the wall of Roxburgh." [7] In the thirteenth century Edinburgh is credited with gates [8] and therefore with a wall in some sense. Excavation in 1833, indeed, disclosed a fragment of a stone wall within and so earlier than that of 1450.[9] Berwick in 1296 would appear to have had rampart and ditch.[10] Such equipment of an early type would certainly make a burgh a

[1] " ' The palissades ' existed as a defence in 1689, but we have not observed any notice of them afterwards " (*Invernessiana*, C. Fraser Macintosh, p. 3).

[2] Fordun, *Annales*, xcvi, cxi ; *Scotich.*, XI, xxvii, XII, iii.

[3] *fermées de bons fossez et de bons palis*. Jean le Bel, *Chronique*, i, ch. xxii ; 1904, p. 110. He notes the same defences for the town of Dinant in 1342, pp. 312, 320.

[4] Wyntoun's *Orygynale Cronykil*, etc., Bk. VIII, lines 3625-6. On clay defences see W. Mackay Mackenzie, *Proc. Soc. Ant. Scot.*, lxviii (1933-4), 117-27.

[5] See p. 20. Most of the towns in England at the time of the Norman Conquest " were distinguished from the villages around only by the earthen walls that surrounded them, or the earthen mounds that kept watch over them " (Ashley, *English Economic History*, i, 68).

[6] Pirenne, *Rev. hist.*, t. 57, p. 73.

[7] *Extra murum.* Lawrie, *Early Scottish Charters*, No. ccxli.

[8] *Reg. de Neubotle* (*c.* 1214), No. 122 ; *Lib. de Calchou* (*c.* 1271) No. 475.

[9] See D. Tait in *Trans. Edin. Geol. Soc.*, xiii (1936), 286-7. See p. 42.

[10] *Scalacronica*, p. 122.

" strength " and repudiates the idea of its being without walls in the sense of a defensive enclosure. But of stone walls also there is evidence for later times.

The idea of unwalled burghs begins with the Spanish ambassador of 1498, who wrote that " there is not more than one fortified town in Scotland, because the Kings do not allow their subjects to fortify them." [1] Probably he would not at that date recognise survivals of early defences, though adequate locally, as fortifications. In any case, Edinburgh also, as the editor points out, as well as Perth, had been surrounded with a wall, King James II having, in 1450, granted leave " to fosse [ditch], bulwark, wall, toure, turrate, and uther wais to strengthen oure foresaid Burgh," and the wall then built has been traced. Yet John Major in his *Historia Majoris Britanniæ* of 1521 wrote that Perth was " the only walled town in Scotland," in which category he includes " even low walls," and goes on to explain that " the Scots do not hold themselves to need walled cities ; and the reason of this may be, that they get them face to face with the enemy with no delay, and build their cities, as it were, of men." Here, too, the qualification as to Edinburgh would apply, but it is further to be noted that in 1503 it was ordained by Parliament [2] that all towns and ports on the sea, such as Leith, Inverkeithing, Kinghorn, Dysart, Crail, and others should expend their common good on the walls of the town towards the sea, with gateways of stone and lime. In 1529 licence was given to Aberdeen " to big wallis with fortalicis about the samyn," [3] but there is no evidence that a wall was ever erected. Inverkeithing is referred to by Defoe in his *Tour* as " an ancient walled town," and a writer of 1763 speaks of " the little town of Inverkeithing once walled round (gates still standing) as all these coast towns have anciently been." [4]

In 1500 we read of the foundation of a chapel " outside the walls of Glasgow city," [5] and nine years later there is a reference apparently to the same chapel " outside the Glasgow

---

[1] *Early Travellers in Scotland*, ed. Hume Brown, p. 47.
[2] Vol. ii, p. 243.
[3] *Reg. Privy Seal*, ii, No. 312.
[4] Cited in *Inveresk and Rosyth*, Rev. Dr Stephen, pp. 5-6.
[5] *Extra muros civitatis Glasguensis : Reg. Epis. Glas.*, ii, 501

walls." [1] These are embarrassing utterances for one committed to the proposition that the burghs were without walls, and the words are not to be explained away by the blunt repetition that " there were no walls. The reference is to land or buildings . . . beyond the burgh boundary." [2] The rest of the escaping explanation, including material down to 1735, overlooks what was said by the traveller Richard Franck in 1656 that " there's rarely a town of any eminency in Scotland, but is, or has been, beleaguered with a strong stone wall," and of Glasgow in particular that it then was " a city girded about with a strong stone wall." [3] Also overlooked is the record by the eighteenth-century historian of Glasgow, who speaks of certain streets as having once been fields " contained within the walls of the city." [4] From Richard Franck, too, we learn how Inverness, when he went there, was " defended with a weather-beaten tottering wall, that's defaced with age and the corruptions of time." One might continue with the case of Peebles, where in 1569, the council and community of the burgh unanimously determined " that the toune and burgh of Peblis be wallit rownd about as thai think maist necessare," to be completed within four years, a wall which only gradually disappeared about the year 1800.[5] Or the case of Stirling where the enemies of the Earl of Arran in 1585 on coming to Stirling " scaled and clam over the walles." [6] In 1691 Dundee makes a return of expenses in " fortifying " the town, repairing ports and guns and purchasing firearms.[7] At Linlithgow a portion of the old town wall still survives. A Scottish writer of 1685 [8] points out that a burgh is distinguished from a " countrey-villege " by trading " rather then be strong Walles or Fortifications as some distinguish," implying that such defensive equipment was familiar.

[1] *Extra muros Glasguenses : Reg. de Passelet*, p. 394.
[2] Murray, as cited, i, 288, note.
[3] *Early Travellers in Scotland*, ed. Hume Brown, p. 191.
[4] *Hist. of Glasgow* (1777), John Gibson, pp. 105-6.
[5] *Burgh Records of Peebles*, pp. 312, lxxiv. *Cf.* map, p. lxx.
[6] *Autobiography of James Melville*, p. 223. On the walls of Stirling see *Extracts, Burgh Records* (1519-1666), pp. 50 (1547), 51, 61.
[7] Visitation of Burghs " in 1691 : see p. 155.
[8] " Philopoliteius " (Alexander Skene) *Memorialls for . . . Royall Burghs*, p. 94.

A sort of intermediate stage occurred when burghs contrived their enclosure by linking up and heightening [1] the " heid dykis " or outside boundary walls of tenements so as to make a continuous encirclement, with entrance only by the ports. But such walls could be climbed or have " passegis " broken through them,[2] and were a constant source of trouble in their proper upkeep. Still, no question of heroic principle was involved ; it was simply that the erection and maintenance of substantial walls was usually beyond the resources of the burgh, or that these were improperly administered.[3] There is no distinction in idea from the case of England or Continental towns. Those of Scotland were enclosed or " walled " as far as circumstances allowed, and the heroics of Major, reproduced by George Buchanan in Latin hexameters, are psychological fancies not historical fact.[4] No doubt they felt they had to explain away the shabby " heid dykis " and, being literary men, could only think up a romantic merit.

[1] *Burgh Records, Peebles* (1555), p. 208.

[2] *Ibid.* (1567), p. 305.

[3] See chap. x.

[4] *Cf.* Hume Brown, *Scotland in the Time of Queen Mary*, p. 40. *Cf.* also p. 112 : " As we read the town records of the time, there is one conclusion we cannot miss—that the prime consideration in the town policy was security and self-defence." John Galt, too, may be quoted : " In ancient times, Gudetown had been fortified with ports and gates at the end of the streets ; and in troublesome occasions the country people, as the traditions relate, were in the practice of driving in their families and cattle for shelter " (*The Provost*, chap. xv).

CHAPTER IV

THE NEW TOWNS

Renaissance of town life in Europe. The "new towns." Towns in France, Wales, Ireland. Policy of the Scoto-Norman Kings. Early town plans in Scotland.

Two basic facts about the Scottish burghs seem to stand clear of debate. One is that their peculiar business from David's time at least, that is, even if they are given anonymous and wholly dubious ancestors, is concentration upon trade ; the other that, in respect of their special franchises and customs, they have many links with similar foreign institutions. An early scholar was thus brought to observe that their collection of laws " is perhaps to be viewed as part of a great Saxon movement, which was taking place simultaneously all over Britain." [1] That this movement, as he continues, was one of opposition " to the oppressive power of the Norman nobles " is a conclusion which is not in keeping with the fact that Norman nobles were themselves founders of towns on such lines.[2] The surmise, however, is echoed by a later historian to the effect that in Scotland " The towns were found to be a counterpoise to the power of the great territorial magnates," [3] to which again the rebutting circumstance is that these magnates had their own burghs of regality and barony. But all such provincial explanations, whether correct or not within their own limits, miss the governing factor of the situation, which, in the words of a modern French scholar, is the " renaissance of town life. From the middle of the tenth to the fourteenth century," he continues, " this movement became extraordinarily widespread, and it was then

[1] C. Innes, Preface, *A.P.S.*, i, 39.
[2] See pp. 47, 49.
[3] Hume Brown, *History of Scotland*, i, 92.

that almost all the towns of Christian Europe were created or reborn." [1]

The revival of town life after the destruction of the barbaric invasions had been undone by the later incursions of Saracens, Hungarians and Norsemen.[2] Commerce and industry had been diverted into different channels, the former engrossed by foreign merchants dealing in luxuries, the latter transferred to workers with no municipal standing but only freemen or serfs on feudal ground. By the middle of the tenth century, however, the new invaders abated their activities, and with reviving trade urban units again came to life.[3] Merchants, as middlemen, and artisans began again to be differentiated from the mass of workers on the land. Men with saleable goods settled for protection in the proximity of a walled town or *burg* to form a fortified *faubourg*, a *foris burgis* or "outside burg." In the south of France powerful abbeys undertook to establish urban settlements in order to develop their lands and add to their revenues by gathering in the floating population on the increase in more settled times.[4] They would erect on unoccupied land a church, a sanctuary and so a protection, let out the land about in lots to settlers, and confer on these certain privileges and liberties.

[1] P. Boissonnade, *Life and Work in Mediæval Europe* (trans.), p. 191. He states that about 420 out of 500 French towns originated in this period, of which also Dr Heil writes : " Then all at once we see towns in the proper sense of the word rise again in Germany " (Da auf einmal sehen wir in Deutschland wieder Städte in rechtlichen Sinne des Wortes erstehen —*Die deutschen Städte*, etc., p. 6). For the same period he gives Germany about 3000 towns, but Boissonnade describes the majority of them as remaining "no more than fortified villages or burgs" (p. 191). *Cf.* also von Below, as cited, p. 3.

[2] " In the course of the ninth and tenth centuries all the towns of France were destroyed " (*The Middle Ages*, Fr. Funck-Brentano (translation) p. 2).

[3] Pirenne, *Economic and Social History of Mediæval Europe*, pp. 67-8 ; Boissonnade, as cited, p. 160. " Dans la seconde période de la féodalité l'histoire des villes sort de l'obscurité où elle était plongée pendant la première période jusque vers le milieu du XIe siècle " (*Histoire des classes ouvrières . . . en France*, E. Levasseur, t. i, p. 237). For a critical survey of literature on the whole subject see *Econ. Hist. Review*, vii (1936-7), 209-16.

[4] Pirenne, as cited, p. 68 : " une quantité considérable de nomades, de serfs et de colons " (A. Luchaire, *Institutions monarchiques de la France*, ii, 133).

Thus arose what came to be known as *bastides* or as " new towns " (*villes neuves*) built " at one go " (*d'un seul jet*) on a definite and generally uniform plan and always fortified. In the north of France such places were named *bastilles* : in character they were *bourgs*.[1]

What would seem to be a foundation somewhat resembling the monastic *bastide* or *ville neuve* appears in a charter of Alexander III (1266), which grants to the abbot and convent of Lindores in Fife and their successors the right to have their vill which was called New Burgh (*Novus Burgus*) near the monastery as a " free burgh," with a market every Tuesday and the liberties of a burgh and market, saving the liberties of the royal burghs. That the vill was already called New-burgh " perhaps presupposes an earlier step on the part either of king or abbey," as " In Scotland, apparently, no new mesne borough could be set up without a royal grant." [2] There may have been an earlier creation by " word of mouth." [3] Coldingham [4] may be another case which never received burghal recognition.

In France the advantages reaped by the early religious foundations of new towns led to imitation by the lords of fiefs and by kings. For the latter there was the political interest, in so far as such places offered a means of extending the royal power over their domain.[5] Thus from the twelfth to the fourteenth century the kings of France and England, bishops, abbots, and lords, vied with each other in the foundation of new towns and attracting population to these.[6] " Every little prince and bishop followed the example of the greatest lords of the south." [7] The same was true of Germany in the twelfth and thirteenth centuries, when in the north-eastern part alone at least 350 towns were founded, and " almost every lord (*Landesherr*) strove to have towns upon

[1] See in general A. Giry on *Bastide* in *La Grande Encyclopédie* and *Bibliothèque de l'école des chartes*, xlii (1881), pp. 451-460 ; A. Luchaire, *Histoire des institutions monarchiques de la France*, ii, 132 ff. ; Enlart, *Manuel d'archéologie française*, i, Pt. 2, 242-4 ; Paul Viollet, *Les communes françaises*, etc., pp. 20-23 ; *Cambridge Mediæval History*, v, 629-30.

[2] See *B.B.C.*, ii, pp. 4, l, lxxvi.   [3] See p. 17.   [4] See p. 20 *n*.

[5] Giry, as cited ; *Camb. Med. Hist.*, v, 630.

[6] Enlart, as cited, p. 243 ; *Camb. Med. Hist.*, v, 630.

[7] *Edward the First*, T. F. Tout, p. 103.

his land." [1]   We shall see William the Conqueror apply the practice in England.   Louis VII (1137-80), a contemporary of David, was the first French sovereign to multiply *villes neuves* systematically.[2]   Louis VIII and Louis IX continued this urban policy.   The English kings, John and Henry III, applied the same system in Guienne and Gascony.   Edward I, however, was the most conspicuous in setting up in Aquitaine " a class of new towns, called bastides, which were at once centres of expanding commerce, bulwarks of the English power, and refuges for the country-folk in times of war and trouble." [3]   As to the last point we may recall the defences in which the English in Scotland found refuge in 1174.[4]

Going forward we find Edward I following the same policy in order to secure the subjugation of Wales.   " A row of ' bastides ' and ' villes Anglaises ' were set up on the Menai and the Conway as on the Garonne and Dordogne, to serve the same purpose of protection and defence, and to further in the same way the spread of commerce and civilisation. . . . But Edward's object was not so much to attract the Welsh to live in his towns, as to settle in them little bands of English soldiers, officials, and traders, who would prove, as in Ireland, the rallying points of an English interest." [5]   Again, " The typical burgus . . . thus appeared in Wales as one of the factors in the policy of the Norman or English conquest—a created importation set up on a foreign model, and that primarily with a view of promoting the political ends of their particular founders." [6]   It was to serve such an end that " In North Wales Edward I would not allow any markets to be held outside his new boroughs." [7]   This restriction of markets to burghs was already a principle of the Scottish system and, in theory, remained so till the end.   In Wales, too, " In view of their political function it was natural enough that the earlier boroughs should take the form of English colonies. . . . 'Adventitious' families, the 'Advenæ' of modern genealogists, made the bulk of the early town population in

---

[1] Von Below, as cited, p. 7.   *Cf.* here p. 45.
[2] A. Luchaire, *Histoire des institutions monarchiques de la France*, ii, 133.
[3] Tout, as cited, p. 101.   [4] P. 38.   [5] Tout, as cited, pp. 115-6.
[6] *The Mediæval Boroughs of Snowdonia*, E. A. Lewis, p. 12.
[7] *Brit. Bor. Ch.*, ii, p. lxvii.

the castle burghs," [1] where again we have an earlier parallel in Scotland.[2]

As alluded to above, the same treatment was applied to Ireland. Of that country in the time of Henry I a contemporary English historian writes that, from poverty and ignorance of agriculture, the soil produced, outside the towns, a wild and squalid population, while English and Frenchmen with a higher mode of life (*cultiori genere vitae*) inhabit the towns with the traffic of markets (*urbes nundinarum commercio inhabitant*).[3] Taking one case from a wider survey, we may note how the Baltic Provinces were in the Middle Ages colonised with German towns in which the burghers were German, most of them from north-western Germany.[4]

We thus see that the new towns were not only an economic but also a political device. Economics and politics were closely intertwined as they always have been and must be. The study of the rise and significance of towns has possibly been too much guided by economic considerations. Possibly, again, the mediæval founders sometimes thought more of their political effect than of their economic possibilities. Because they had no real economic basis nineteen out of twenty-three baronial foundations in Lancashire were failures.[5] Scotland provides several examples of the same defect. Fyvie ceased to be a royal burgh at a comparatively early stage.[6] Auchterarder was an ancient royal burgh which fell into decay.[7] Earlsferry and Newburgh, which was ultimately made royal, and the much later Falkland and Auchtermuchty, never flourished enough to reach the tax-roll of the Convention of Royal Burghs or afford the expense of being represented in Parliament.[8] Only their fairs showed activity.

---

[1] Lewis, as cited, p. 41. " Edward I also attempted to confine the trade of North Wales to fixed centres, but the object here was to benefit English burgesses settled in these boroughs by giving them the monopoly of trade " (E. Lipson, *Economic History of England*, i, 200).   [2] P. 36.

[3] William of Malmesbury, *Gesta Reg. Angl.* (R.S.), lib. v, p. 409.

[4] *The Towns of Mediæval Livonia*, John Leighly, p. 287. I owe my knowledge of this publication to Dr Simpson, Aberdeen.

[5] *Encyc. Brit.*, 14th edition, art. " Borough."

[6] *Exch. Rolls*, i, pp. 21, lxxxviii.   [7] *Exch. Rolls*, i, 51 ; *A.P.S.*, iii, 240.

[8] See *Local Reports* 1835, under names ; *Estate of the Burgesses*, etc., J. D. Mackie and G. S. Pryde, p. 5.

There were others for which economically not much is to be said and which led a precarious existence. Economic reasons would certainly have justified the erection of the port of Leith into a royal burgh, but it was not to be. There were no such reasons for the early burghs of Edinburgh and Canongate, apart from their proximity to Leith, but the castle of the one and the religious house of the other were good enough reasons from the point of view of policy.

II

The twofold task of establishing together intermunicipal foreign trade and political control, which rulers were handling on the lines just described, was a cardinal one for twelfth-century Scotland with no tradition of Roman municipalities or, there is the slightest reason to suppose, with anything like a professional merchant class. Towns in the proper sense would there have to be in the " created " category. Such foreign trade as existed was apparently with individual customers in luxury articles, as we may judge from Turgot's *Life of St Margaret*, that lady having " caused merchants to come by land and sea from various regions and to bring very many precious wares," such as cloth of different colours, dress ornaments, and precious metals. Political organisation was loose, ineffective, and unreliable. Even the Church was represented only by incoherent groups of baffling " Culdees." The ruling dynasty was not securely seated. Succession to the throne was ill-defined and inevitably bred civil war. Two kings had perished in this way at the end of the tenth and early in the eleventh century respectively. The second half of the eleventh century had seen the king who could claim, but only on the female side, to represent the MacAlpin line supplanted by a capable, dissident mormaer in Macbeth. The death of the restored Malcolm Canmore had been followed by the transitory accession of three different rulers, with competing claims, in the short space of four years, and for a hundred and fifty years the province of Moray was to give birth to a succession of " pretenders " to the Crown. The first task that lay before the members of the Canmore family was that of establishing their line on the throne, a matter of primary importance in the political conditions of the time, and then on this basis building up a kingdom comparable to other kingdoms of which they had knowledge. For an example of how this could be done there was the case of England, with which they were personally familiar, a backward, divisive realm, transmuted by the conquering Normans into an organised, enterprising unity. The Normans, whatever less admirable qualities they displayed, were not only efficient soldiers but also the most capable colonisers and administrators of the age. They had a financial system, and " This familiarity with hard cash, this knowledge of book-keeping, is found as soon as Norman records become reliable, and stamps a character on Norman administration from the first." [1] All this was in marked contrast to the loose, personal contrivances of contemporary Scotland.[2]

It was with Anglo-Norman help that the family of Malcolm Canmore established itself after the four troubled years of conflicting substitutes. But the links with the new rulers of England were even more intimate. Henry I had married a daughter of Canmore, and her brother David, probably also his predecessor Alexander, had been brought up at the royal uncle's court. David, as Earl of Northampton in right of his wife, passed part of his early life as an English baron. Norman culture and ways, which were those of the most advanced people of western Europe, found a ready reception in the minds of these royal pupils, whom their record shows to have been of exceptional intelligence. " The more recent (*moderniores*) kings of Scots," wrote an English chronicler of the early thirteenth century, " profess themselves to be rather Frenchmen, both in race and in manners, language and culture." [3] One who was David's contemporary speaks of him in particular as " polished (*limatus*) from his boyhood through intercourse and friendship with us." [4]

---

[1] *The Loss of Normandy*, F. W. Powicke, p. 65.

[2] Exchequer was adopted from England (*Exch. Rolls*, i, p. xxxiii), where it had been constituted by Henry I, brother-in-law of David, who probably copied the institution.

[3] Walter of Coventry, *Memoriale* (R.S.), ii, 206, A.D. 1212.

[4] William of Malmesbury, *Gesta Regum Anglorum* (R.S.), ii, 476.

With all this, too, came observation and instruction on affairs of state, the strengthening of royal authority and the manner of administrating a kingdom. In the time of his son the Conqueror's policy would be familiar and justified. The conquest of England had been much more than a military affair. The national spirit of the Church in England had to be nullified and its power and the ability and training of its hierarchy brought into the service of the new ruler.[1] Native bishops and abbots were supplanted or succeeded by Norman nominees of the Conqueror ; that these men were not always worthy of their office did not bear upon the system, which had another end in view : " he stood ready to increase the power and independence of the Church, but always as an organ of the State, as a part of the machine through which the government was carried on." [2] Or as the historian of the Conquest puts it, " The Prelacy of England was to be used as a means of rivetting the fetters of England." [3] The great monastic houses on the Welsh marches and in East Anglia were fostered as bulwarks against opposition. " The new Benedictine foundations were made wealthy and powerful as buttresses of the Norman power. They were established as frontier garrisons." [4] The Church as a whole, with its organisation and prestige, could provide a backing for the royal power and be a source of experienced and dependent administrators.

Other institutions in the country which the Conqueror could direct to serve his purpose were the shire with its sheriff and the borough, the latter already familiar on the Continent. He and his barons [5] established a good number

[1] The question of ecclesiastical reforms does not come within the present survey. " But honest as they were, the King's reforms tended directly to the increase of the royal power " (*History of the English People*, J. R. Green (ed. 1894), p. 86).

[2] *Polit. History of England*, ii, G. B. Adams, 49.

[3] E. A. Freeman, iv, 131.

[4] *English Mediæval Art*, E. S. Prior, p. 20. On William's " work of securing the monasteries of England for the new régime," see *The Monastic Order in England*, Dom. David Knowles, pp. 106, 111.

[5] " The baronage of the Conquest founded new towns along the unsettled borders of Wales. . . . They have been credited in fact with a definite scheme of town colonisation " (E. Lipson, *Economic History of England*, p. 174).

of new boroughs, while in many of the larger of the old ones from London to York he planted colonies of French or, more probably, mainly Flemish burgesses. Towns, like castles, dioceses, and monasteries, were politically to be part of a garrison policy.

It was with such an example and such ideas in their minds, that these Scottish kings faced the problem of their own position and the state of their country. After the successful placing of Edgar on the throne military operations were unnecessary ; there need be no conquest. But reliable support and men capable of filling new administrative positions were a necessity, and these were only to be found by the introduction of Norman friends and dependants among the native population. And so came the lengthening procession of Norman gentlemen who found place and office in Scotland during the twelfth and thirteenth centuries and whose names are conspicuous in the annals of the time. And with them, as before, English proper and Flemings. It was a time when Dr Johnson's gibe was reversed and the fairest prospect in England was the high road to Scotland.[1] Normans supplied the officers of the royal household, who formed the first ministers of state, and the sheriffs who occupied the royal castles as centres of local administration. They were the power and strength behind the throne, for their interests were bound up with those of the kings who were their patrons.

No less significant and effective was the organisation of the Church on what was virtually a new model. No administrative value could be found in the unorderly groupings of Céili Dé (Culdees) who made up the ecclesiastical body as David found it and which he broke up. No special ties bound them to the throne. They were outside the general structure of Christendom. To David I is almost wholly due the diocesan organisation of the Scottish Church, while he

---

[1] " Both Normans and English came to Scotland in crowds in the days of Margaret, Edgar, and David " (Professor Freeman and Professor Stenton in *Ency. Brit.*, 14th ed., art. " Normans "). " The original founders of our towns are supposed to have been in many cases " Flemings who had " flocked into Scotland " from England (*Exchequer Rolls*, i, p. lxxxi).

and some of his baronial friends, by their many foundations, gave monasticism a firm footing.[1]

The scale of David's ecclesiastical endowments, imitated by his immediate successors, has provoked surprise in historians, one of whom remarks on his " almost reckless bounty to the Church," [2] while an earlier writer must have felt that in this there was something more than a " pious orgy," when he wrote, " That it was not merely as a priest-ridden king that David augmented the power and possessions of the Church, we may judge from the equal attention which he bestowed upon the law." [3] Or, as a later writer has it, " His liberality to the Church was the outcome no less of wisdom than of piety." [4] Political " wisdom " it must be. And it is an orthodox historian of the early sixteenth century who, under the heading of " Profuse (*prodiga*) construction of monasteries," affirms that there was something wonderful (*mirum*) about this family in that it was always intent (*semper intenta*) upon the foundation of monasteries.[5] All which, however, becomes more understandable when we realise that David was building up not only a Church but also an orderly kingdom, just as " during the eleventh and twelfth centuries strong dynasties laid the foundations of English, French, and German nations." [6] Pious instincts would be, of course, the full clerical explanation ; it is not to be expected that a writer of this class or even the grantor himself would stain a religious foundation with a secular purpose.

---

[1] See p. 9. *Cf.* " he definitively made the Church of Rome the national Church of Scotland " (Hume Brown, *History of Scotland*, i, 94). Thirteen dioceses were Scotland's mediæval complement. St Andrews of old was now reconstituted on a monastic basis—an English fashion. Three were as yet foreign. Two have been claimed for Alexander I, but with " no good evidence " (Lawrie, *Early Sc. Charters*, pp. 262, 282-3). One was founded under King William. Thus of the eight in David's kingdom he was responsible for at least five, more probably seven, and in a sense for all the dioceses. [2] Hume Brown, as cited, i, 86.

[3] C. Innes, *Scotland in the Middle Ages*, p. 11 [4] *Exch. Rolls*, i, p. xl.
[5] John Major, *Historia Majoris Britanniæ*, liv. IV, cap. v.
[6] Alfred Cobban in *History*, March 1944, p. 47. " We owe to him all the civil institutions and structure of our present society " (C. Innes, *Scotland in the Middle Ages*, p. 115). " Of the familiar Scotland of Bruce and the Stewarts David was unquestionably the creator " (E. W. Robertson, *Scotland under her Early Kings*, i, 320).

Nonetheless, what the historian of French institutions says, with regard to the liberal grants to the Church by the Capetian kings, holds good here : " This generosity has not only the effect of attaching the clergy to the dynasty by ties of gratitude and affection ; it is without question of political service (*utilité*) . . . since, in return for services rendered by them to the ecclesiastical body, they assure the co-operation and resources necessary (*indispensable*) for the very existence of the monarchy." [1] A devout enthusiasm may play its part, if only in the sense in which the statesman may rejoice in a concurrence of pious and political ends. It must also be kept in mind that bishops and abbots and the whole clerkly class were not only a Church, but beyond that, the prime source of supply for the civil service of the kingdom. The mediæval bishops of Scotland, like those of England, are prominent in virtue of their State duties. It could be said of William the Lion that he would allow no elections of bishops to be made except at his own bidding, " in this," it is significantly added, " following the grievous abuses of Norman tyranny throughout England." [2] Incidentally it may be noticed how " we are justified in believing that the parochial system . . . is an outcome of Anglo-Norman influence in the early part of the twelfth century." [3]

It is this revolutionary policy that we find exemplified also in the burghs, by which Scotland is brought into line with the other kingdoms, where, as we have seen, the establishment of " new towns " (*villes neuves*) was a flourishing practice. The basis of these institutions was laid in the reviving and spreading occupations of trade and industry, so that we can find " foundations of the same type from Wales to Languedoc and from Scotland to Saxony." [4] No doubt this commercial purpose was a characteristic of " the early Scottish burgh," [5] but in combination with an element also important at the time, the strengthening and working of the power of the

---

[1] M. Achille Luchaire, *Histoire des institutions monarchiques de la France*, ii, 106-7.

[2] Giraldus Cambrensis, *De Instructione Principum*, p. 202.

[3] Dowden, *The Mediæval Church in Scotland*, p. 112.

[4] Stephenson, *Borough and Town*, p. 128.

[5] Ballard, *S.H.R.*, xiii, 23, 26.

Crown.[1] It offered scope for the application of a political policy of establishing groups of loyal, peaceable subjects without local prejudices and local kindred, and, like the Norman lords and the foreign colonisers of monasteries, bearers of a cosmopolitan culture. This was the policy which David's grandson, Malcom IV, was to exemplify on a big scale when he cleared part of the restless province of Moray, " as Nebuchadnezzar had dealt with the Jews," scattering the native inhabitants in other districts and planting in their place " a personally devoted and peaceful people." [2] In effect every burgh, like every castle, bishopric, and monastery, was to be, at least in one intention, a royal garrison. The consciousness of this fact may have been part of the impulse that prompted the massacres of 1174.

These kings of the Canmore dynasty were thus adopting the methods by which Norman kings had made good their hold on England, and anticipating the practice of later English kings in confirming their dominion in Aquitaine, Wales, and Ireland.

Indeed the idea of planting a foreign colony for at least an industrial purpose could recur at a long subsequent time, when for example in the reign of Charles I the burghs had to resist a proposal to erect Stornoway into a free burgh " to be planted by the Earl of Seaforth with Hollanders who were to prosecute the fishing there." The patent was granted to the Earl but afterwards cancelled, the burghs having offered to do the planting and peopling of Stornoway themselves.[3]

One avenue of evidence has not been adequately explored in England in comparison with the Continent [4] and has been scarcely touched in Scotland, namely, the original topography of early burghs. Yet much debate could be dispensed with were such an enquiry carefully carried out. Old houses disappear, but the street lines remain, and it is to preserve and

---

[1] Cf. " la fondation de villes nouvelles fut l'un des principaux moyens de gouvernement employé par Alphonse de Poitiers dan ses états (Giry, Bibliothèque de l'école des chartes, xlii (1881), 456).

[2] populum in ea peculiarem et pacificum collocando (Fordun, Annals, iv). Henry I had shown the way when in 1106 he planted Flemings from England in Wales (William of Malmesbury (R.S.), ii, 477).

[3] See Theodora Keith (Pagan) in S.H.R., x, 257-8.

[4] Stephenson, as cited, p. 186.

guide these, to secure the bounds of individual properties, that we find in later times, and may infer from the beginning, such burgh officers as *lineatores* or *limitatores*, that is "liners." Moreover, Scottish towns in general expanded slowly, and it is possible, by fixing the positions of the "ports" or gates and following the archaic names of streets, to arrive in a number of cases at a diagram of the original lay-out. It

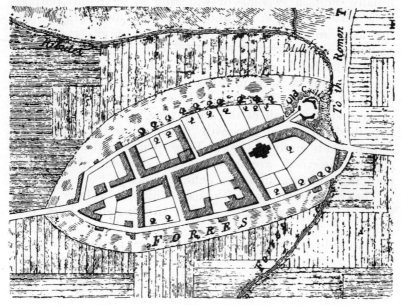

Fig. 1—Forres in 1798. Chalmer's *Caledonia*, vol. I, p. 131

must be realised, too, that town-planning is no new idea. Actual "new towns" were regularly laid out. In 1296 Edward I was requiring the citizens of London to select four skilful men "such as best knew how to plan, order, and lay out a new town." [1] The site of the prospective new town is understood to be Berwick-on-Tweed,[2] which Edward had just captured and burnt and now proposed to rebuild as an English base.

[1] *qui mieux sachent diviser, ordonner, et arrayer une novele vile.* Cited in *Towns and Town-planning*, etc., T. Harold Hughes and E. A. G. Lamborn, p. 22. See *Calendar of Letter Books of the City of London*, ed. R. R. Sharpe, p. 25.   [2] Stubbs, *Select Charters* (1913), p. 483.

Where the burgh is articulated with a castle or an ecclesiastical building the result in plan is relatively simple. Like a backbone the axial main street, usually dignified as the High Street, stretches from the castle at one pole to the burgh enclosure at the other, as we see it still existent even in the late eighteenth-century plan of Forres (Fig. 1). The burgh street, too, being a sort of elongated market-place usually shows a swelling or widening to serve this purpose, as is very obvious at Edinburgh in the Lawnmarket.[1] But the axial market street is common in burghs everywhere and is a characteristic form of lay-out. To it the flanking rectangular blocks of building can easily be adapted. Other examples can be seen in Elgin (Fig. 2), Inverness (Fig. 3),[2] and Old Peebles (Fig. 4), all obviously the outcome of one general idea and all of the early type.[3] The result for the hypothesis of casual " growth " or pre-burghal agricultural settlements is surely obvious. These places, and others which can be discerned, are in origin the outcome of deliberate planning and execution at a definite time.

The rectangular market-place, which is a later feature than the street market.[4] Perth, showing this later plan (Fig. 5), has there lost its market-place, which has probably been built upon. It follows in its rectangular blocks a normal *bastide* or " new town " plan, and the absence of wall on the water front is to be explained by its use as wharfage, just as at Hull (Fig. 6) where the wall

[1] " Sometimes the market-place was contrived by a simple widening (*eine einfache Verbreiterung*) of the middle high street " (Von Below, as cited, p. 32).

[2] " It appears certain, however, that the original boundary of the Burgh was the ' auld fosse ' of the reign of King William the Lion, the position of which on both sides of the River is beyond doubt " (*Records of Inverness* (New Spalding Club), i, p. ix). The plan shown has been derived from that given there as frontispiece.

[3] The later Peebles has been claimed as the position of the thirteenth century town at which there was a castle, on the grounds that " In the old Town there is not a vestige of any castellated or defensible edifice. . . . There is no appearance of an environing wall " (*Charters, Docts., and Records* 1165-1710, Introd., p. lvi). They obviously looked for traces of stone constructions.

[4] *The Towns of Mediæval Livonia*, John Leighly, pp. 268-9, citing Franz Maurer, *Der Mittelälterische Stadtgrundriss*, etc.

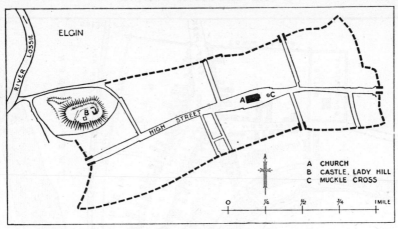

FIG. 2.—ELGIN. Based on details in Wood's *Town Atlas of Scotland,* 1822, and *Elgin, Past and Present,* by H. B. Mackintosh, 1914.

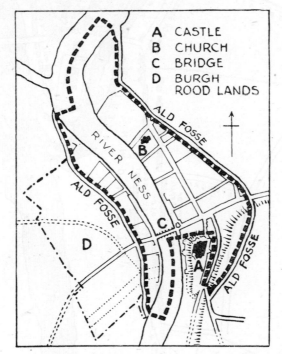

FIG. 3.—INVERNESS From a plan of the burgh in the 16th century prefixed to vol. I, of *The Records of Inverness,* New Spalding Club.

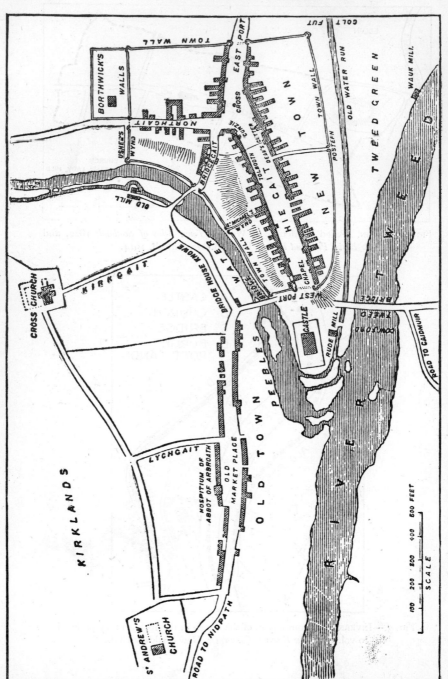

FIG. 4.—PEEBLES. From *Burgh Records*, ed. Wm. Chambers, LL.D., p. lxx.

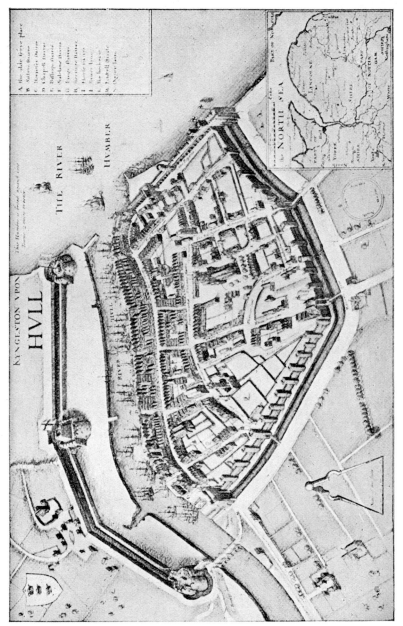

Fig. 6.—Hull. From Engraving *c.* 1665.

appears on the opposite side of the river, and at Inverness which continues there the line of the ditch. An additional street was laid out parallel to the main one, giving us a North Street and a South Street, as at St Andrews, where they radiate from the Cathedral, it being a Bishop's burgh, and at Perth where of old were the same names, as is noted by

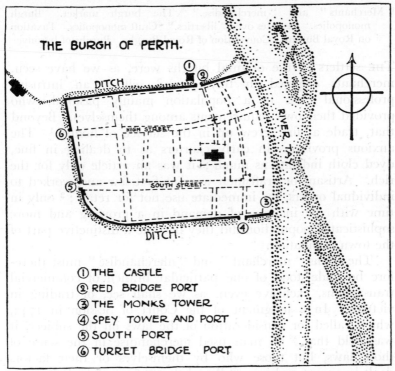

THE BURGH OF PERTH.

DITCH

HIGH STREET

SOUTH STREET

DITCH.

RIVER TAY

① THE CASTLE
② RED BRIDGE PORT
③ THE MONKS TOWER
④ SPEY TOWER AND PORT
⑤ SOUTH PORT
⑥ TURRET BRIDGE PORT

Fig. 5.—Perth. Plan in *Auld Perth* 1906, by Thomas Maclaren, Assistant Burgh Surveyor.

Sir Walter Scott in his novel dealing with the town. But in all cases we see planning towards a definite object. "Leave men alone in their cities," writes Mr Belloc, "and they will build you Crooked Streets of their very nature," and he has a liking for crooked streets. But the original builders of a town like Perth were not left alone, and their streets were regular, because over them was a guiding hand, that of the founder or founders of an artificial institution.

CHAPTER V

BURGH PRIVILEGES. BURGHS OF BARONY

" Merchants " and " merchandise." The burgh market. Burgh monopolies. Disputes over " liberties." Craft monopolies. Taxation on Royal Burghs. Convention of Royal Burghs. Burghs of barony.

THE settlers in the original burghs were, as we have seen, merchants engaged in buying and selling, an intrusive professional class in a population mainly pastoral, who provided their own requirements among themselves. Beyond that, trade at first grew up in the service of luxury.[1] The anxious provisions in early charters as to dealing in fine, dyed cloth indicate as much ; it was an article only for the rich. Artisans or craftsmen were at first few and worked to individual orders, for immediate use not for retail ; [2] only in time with the increase of demand in a growing and more sophisticated population did they become a distinctive part of the town population.

The terms " merchant " and " merchandise " must therefore be understood of one particular branch of commercial transactions, exclusive even, as we shall see, of trading in victuals. In a judgment of the Court of Session in 1743, which called for consideration of the laws on the subject, it was held that " no man used merchandise in the sense of those laws, but those who by themselves or their factors dealt in export and import," and that " from the whole tenor of our law it is plain, that nothing passed under the name of merchandise as far down as 1597 but foreign trade." [3] It was this traffic which was to constitute the sphere of burgh monopoly—the purchase for export of wool, hides, skins (including furs), etc., which foreign merchants were to buy only from burgesses, and the venting of foreign products in

---

[1] Ashley, *Economic History*, i, Pt. i, 115, 130 ; *cf.* Fordun, v, cap. xliii.

[2] N. S. B. Gras in *Legacy of the Middle Ages*, p. 487.

[3] Morison's *Decisions of the Court of Session*, p. 1927. The date specified is that of the first imposition of duties on imports.

cloth, wine, wax, spices and other specialised articles, which could be sold for retail only to burgesses. Apart from burgesses none could share in such trade save by permission of the burgesses or a higher authority.[1] The rank of burgess at this stage was confined to a resident occupying a burgage tenement ; those who might receive favoured treatment would be without such a qualification and have to pay for their privilege.[2]

Merchants, however, were townsfolk and round them were the people of the countryside able to supply provisions from their surplus of meal, cheese, butter, eggs, etc. Victuals, therefore, anyone could sell anywhere by bringing them to the market and paying toll. The occasion for such sale in necessaries was even extended to apply to any day in the week as well as the market day proper.[3] There was therefore no monopoly of traffic in foods, which had to be sold at a price fixed by authority ; but there were repeated Acts against any attempt to evade toll or corner supplies by purchasing victuals before they reached the burgh for sale on the street market or at a stall (" forestalling," " engrossing ") ; or hoarding in expectation of a scarcity and a higher price ; or buying to sell elsewhere at a profit (" regrating ").[4] Business was expected to conform to ideas of religion, ethics, and the public good.

As the mediæval merchant travelled with his wares, whether buying or selling, then, apart from food supplies, there was at first no call for a fixed market day, and such is

[1] *E.g.* by King William's charter no one could buy or sell over the shire of Inverness but a burgess or a stall-holder (*stalagarius*) of the burgh or by favour (*per gratum*) of the burgesses (*A.P.S.*, i, 88). By a charter of 1358-9 no inhabitant of the shire of Forfar should buy wool, hides or skins except a burgess of Dundee or by royal permission (Ratification in 1641, *R.M.S.*, s.d., No. 986). By charter of 1285 to Lanark no foreign merchant was suffered to buy any merchandise in the burgh or shire save from burgesses (Confirmation, 1540-41, *R.M.S.*, No. 2308).

[2] See p. 136.

[3] *A.P.S.*, 1449-50, 1493. At Edinburgh (1478-9) victuals were to be sold on Monday, Wednesday and Friday (*Records*, s.d., p. 36).

[4] " On the stock exchange every jobber is a regrater and engrosser, and every broker is a forestaller ; and the more they succeed in these mediæval crimes and sins the more they are honoured " (*Principles of Political Economy*, Nicholson, ii, 27).

therefore in the beginning not necessarily implied in the notion of a burgh here any more than apparently in England.[1] Stirling, a burgh of David's time, was not granted a weekly market till 1226 ; Elgin of the same time not till 1234. Dumbarton, granted a weekly market on its foundation, had no fair given till four years later. A yearly fair of two weeks at Aberdeen dates from 1273.[2] That all this was no matter of oversight or loose drafting is shown in the case of Kinghorn, which was given a weekly market in 1285 for the " service " (utilitate) and " betterment " (melioracione) of our burgh," [3] which obviously was already in existence. The Abbey of Dunfermline petitioned Edward I in 1304 to allow them a weekly market and a yearly fair at Kirkcaldy, which they described as " one of the most ancient burghs of Scotland " and as having been gifted to the Abbey by King David, but which was ten leagues or more from any market town. The wish of the Abbey was granted.[4] In time, however, both market and fair seem to have become bound up in the general idea of a burgh, so that a charter of novodamus, proceeding upon the assumption of the loss of an original charter, will include as a matter of course the right to a weekly market and at least one annual fair, probably in acceptance of established custom.[5] On the other hand we shall find at a later stage how market towns were established which were not burghs.

The value of the weekly market was in the circumstance

[1] Cf. Ballard : " is it not possible that the markets were so essential to the existence of a borough that it was deemed unnecessary to mention them ? " (Domesday Boroughs, p. 90) ; " a market was possibly an appurtenance of a borough " (Ib., p. 98). Ashley : " The possession of a market could be claimed only on the ground of a royal grant, or of immemorial usage " (Econ. Hist., i, Pt. i, 98).

[2] B.B.C., ii, 251.

[3] Ibid., p. 248. German scholars have derived the town from the market. Cf. Dr Heil, as cited, p. 18 : " Dadurch wurde aus dem Markte eine Stadt." It is not, we see, the case in Scotland.

[4] Bain's Calendar of Docts., etc., ii, Nos. 1624, 1653.

[5] Such a charter in 1593 to Cromarty as a royal burgh " from of old " (ab antiquo) besides a weekly market specifies one of two annual fairs as called " St Norman's market." But no calendar of saints includes this name, which would seem to preserve the fact that marketing began under the Norman sheriff.

that it provided a regular occasion for local trade. As we have seen in the dispute between Dumbarton and Glasgow the burghal merchant was peripatetic, going far afield with and for his wares. Some privileged communities, indeed, could take the whole land for their province, free of tolls and under the king's peace in going and coming. The fixed market gave the opportunity for those who had home produce to sell and could purchase things not to be procured elsewhere, such as the work of skilled craftsmen. We shall see how in the case of Kelso the servants of the Abbey were allowed, as a special privilege, to trade from their windows with passing traffickers, except on the day of the market at Roxburgh,[1] when everything for sale had to go there and stalls for the display of goods could be set up.

The local market, however, provided a greatly less opportunity for profitable transactions than did dealings in goods imported by sea or land. The bulk of these might be relatively small, but the profit was in large measure. And Scotland badly needed goods only to be procured abroad, even apart from the demand for articles of luxury for its new nobility. As late as the fourteenth century Froissart records of Scotland that " There is neither iron to shoe horses, nor leather to make harness, saddles, or bridles : all these things come ready made from Flanders by sea ; and, should these fail, there is none to be had in the country." [2] For the building up of a business on this line in the twelfth century we have the career of Godric, the Lincolnshire trader, who from a capitalist became a saint. He took cargoes to and from England, Flanders, and Denmark, and frequently (*multototies*) visited Scotland, always buying native products cheap and selling them dear where they were in demand, so acquiring very great riches.[3] International trade was in revival and Scotland was sharing in such activity. About thirty years after the charter founding Ayr we have record of a trade by that burgh with Ireland,[4] and in 1264 it was a

[1] See p. 91. [2] *Cf.* further *Exch. Rolls*, i, pp. cxv-xvi.
[3] *Libellus de vita et miraculis S. Godrici*, Surtees Society (1847), pp. 29-30. He often visited St Andrews as the sort of place where he could combine profit with piety (*mercator simul et peregrinus*), p. 31.
[4] *Cal. of Docts.*, Bain, i, 249.

E

place where ships could be built for the king in alarm at the prospect of Norse invasion.[1] And if some twenty years earlier a French nobleman had provided an " admirable ship " at Inverness,[2] we can be sure it was not the first or only vessel dispatched from that port.

It has been noted how just a few early burghs were given the privilege of trading free of toll over the whole land.[3] The more general practice, however, was or became that of attaching to a burgh a certain area within which it possessed a monopoly of trade. None except a burgess, a stallholder, or by favour of the burgesses of Inverness was, by a charter of King William, to do any trade within the extensive sheriffdom of that name. Only a burgess of Lanark could exercise merchandise within that shire (1285). As late as 1621 Peebles was confirmed in its monopoly of trade over that sheriffdom.[4] To other burghs a more restricted area might be allotted. Rutherglen had from King William the privilege that within certain boundaries nothing was to be offered for sale unless this had first been done at the burgh,[5] there of course paying toll. Inverkeithing, since the same reign, controlled the district between the rivers Leven and Devon, over which its burgesses should have " toll and custom and all rights (*rectitudines*) pertaining to a burgh." Renfrew by its charter of 1397 was to have all tolls and customs and the sole market within the barony.[6] Inverary, erected from a baronial into a royal burgh as late as 1648, was to have the only market and fair within the sheriffdom of Argyll, except Kintyre where it was intended to have a separate burgh.[7] The particular area thus for trading purposes annexed to a burgh was known as its "liberty," that is, its

[1] *Exch. Rolls*, i, 6.

[2] *mirabilem navem.* Matthew Paris, *Chron. Majora* (R.S.), v, 93.

[3] See pp. 33, 34, 68.

[4] Peebles had the right to so much oats for every cultivated unit in the sheriffdom, payable by laird or tenant to cover the tolls due from them on corn, wool, skins and hides they would bring to market. When some refused, the King in 1623 instructed the Sheriff to enforce payment and recover arrears (*Records*, 1165-1710, pp. 362-3).

[5] *B.B.C.*, i, 170.

[6] Ratification in *R.M.S.*, 1513-46, No. 2705.

[7] *nisi in burgo de Kintyre erigi ordinato* (*R.M.S.*, s.d., No. 1901).

sphere of monopoly.[1] It has even been suggested as possible
to draw a map of the country on the lines of these exclusive
areas, but the creation of additional royal burghs within the
liberties of those already existing, as Dingwall (1227) and
Tain within the sheriffdom of Inverness, makes the under-
taking more difficult than it seems. Such areas of monopoly
had been once constituted in England, but rarely " and cannot
be found after the thirteenth century," while no parallel
provision occurs in Irish burgh charters.[2] They have been
offered as one example of " the Scottish habit of pushing
English rules to extremities," another being, as in the Inverness
and Perth charters, that of forbidding a tavern anywhere in
the shire except in a burgh or in a vill with a resident knight,
while all that answers to this in England was that there
were towns in which the keeping of inns was confined to
burgesses.[3] But in such matters England can scarcely be
accepted as marking the limits of propriety.

The foreign merchant was correspondingly restricted in
his dealings. He was not to buy or sell anything in the
sheriffdom of Perth outside the burgh, a ban extended also
to Aberdeen (1214), Stirling (1226), and Lanark (1285).[4]
For Berwick we learn that no foreign merchant was to sell
anything in the burgh except in wholesale (1302),[5] the idea
being to confine the retail trade to burgesses, a limitation
also to be observed in regulations for Perth, here, however,
leaving a period during which the foreign merchant could
" cut " his cloth for sale in the market (*in foro*).[6] By the
chronicler, too, we are informed that it was provided (*provisum
fuit*) by Alexander III that trade with foreign merchants
should be confined to burgesses.[7] He seems to regard this
restriction as an expedient to reduce the export of natural
home products, of which there was a deficiency ; but his
meaning is not clear.

[1] Its " royalty " was its range of jurisdiction, comprehending in early
times not only the strictly urban district " but, in many instances, considerable portions of land which belonged to the inhabitants either in
their private or corporate capacities " (*Gen. Report* 1835, p. 90).

[2] Ballard, *S.H.R.*, xiii, 25.

[3] *B.B.C.*, i, pp. lxvii, lxxi.

[4] *B.B.C.*, i, 169-70, 213 ; ii, 242.

[5] *B.B.C.*, ii, 288. [6] *B.B.C.*, i, 213. [7] *Scotichronicon*, x, cap. xlii.

From these conditions came the two general characteristics of royal burghs, that they should each possess a monopoly of merchandise within a given area, and should be the only centres of foreign trade. Both were to give rise to friction. Indeed there seems reason to suppose that originally there was no mercantile distinction between royal burghs and burghs in barony, the latter as yet few. In pronouncing upon the dispute between Glasgow and Dumbarton over trade in Lennox and Argyll Alexander II made no account of the fact that the latter, in contrast with the other, was a royal burgh. Nor did he do so in the case of Rutherglen claiming Glasgow as within its liberty, where it could levy toll upon merchants, but fixed the limits of Rutherglen by ancient custom.[1] In both cases antiquity is the deciding consideration, not the category of the burgh. Indeed the same king interpreted the original charter of Glasgow to cover the right of buying and selling throughout the whole kingdom.[2] In 1304 the question as to Rutherglen came up from the other side, the Bishop of Glasgow seeking from Edward I a renewal of the right to levy toll on the burgesses of Rutherglen for all goods sold or bought in Glasgow, a right in which his town had been " seised from time beyond memory." [3] The Abbey of Arbroath was granted the right to have a port at the same time as a burgh, and a port implies shipping, which in turn implies trade overseas. Further, the burgesses were to enjoy freedom from toll and custom through the whole land and all its ports.[4] The grant to St Andrews is extended later (1153-7) to convey to the burgesses of the bishop all the liberties and customs which the King's burgesses had in common throughout the whole land and in whatever ports they should put to land ; [5] and still later (1363) the right of buying and selling within the burgh of Cupar and all lands pertaining to the diocese.[6] In all this there is nothing short of what a royal burgh could have. When, in the reign of David II, Berwick and Roxburgh

---

[1] *antiquitus capi solebant. Reg. Epis. Glas.*, i, 114, No. 135 ; *Local Reports*, 1835, Pt. ii, p. 371.

[2] *Reg. Epis. Glas.*, i, No. 183. [3] *Cal. of Docts.*, Bain, ii, No. 1627.

[4] *Liber S. Thome de Aberbrothoc*, No. 1, p. 3.

[5] *B.B.C.*, ii, 381. [6] *R.M.S.*, s.d., No. 134.

were still in English hands, whereby the royal tolls on exported
goods were lost, the Earl of March was commissioned to have
at Dunbar a free burgh, with burgesses and full burghal rights
and a free port where the customs could be duly levied,
Dunbar to have for its " bounds," or area of exclusive trade,
the whole earldom of March and share privileges with the
royal burgh of Haddington within the same earldom.[1]   In
this case, too, a royal and a baronial burgh were on precisely
the same footing. We shall find indeed an Act of 1672 laying
down that the Act of 1633, which summed up and ratified
previous legislation, had erred in " applying the priviledges
granted to burrowes generally to royall burrowes onlie, to
the prejudice of the burghs of regallities and barony." That
was certainly possible. It should be kept in mind that in
mediæval times there was not the stringency of definition to
which we are accustomed, nor the same weight given to
technical discrimination. Special circumstances and local
custom, as we shall find, could bypass statutory law, and a
question be provided with an improvised solution on its
merits. It was practical convenience and not constitutional
theory, though that can be supplied, that brought burgh
commissioners into Parliament, and later was, in defiance of
theoretical principle, to introduce representatives from certain
burghs of barony, which, not being, like the royal burghs,
in the position of tenants-in-chief, were not technically entitled
to representation. The strict differentiation between the two
classes of burghs may have been imposed by the multiplication
of burghs in barony.

II

In a charter by David II of 1364 we get a summing up of
burgh rights in general. There is granted to the burgesses
of Scotland a free faculty of buying and selling everywhere
within the " liberty " of their burghs, none to buy or sell
within the bounds of the liberty of another except by permission
(*nisi licentiatus*). No bishop, prior, or ecclesiastical person,
no earl, baron or secular person, is to buy or sell under any
pretext (*sub quocunque colore*) or whatever his standing, wool,

---

[1] *R.M.S.*, i, No. 340.

skins, hides or other merchandise save from or to the merchants
of the burghs within whose liberty they reside, presenting
the articles for sale at the market and market-cross of the
burghs and paying the king's custom. Foreign (*extranei*)
merchants coming with their ships and merchandise must
sell to the merchants of the burgh and make purchases from
them, or be penalised by the king.[1] The determining
principles of this charter were repeated in legislation under
later kings, as by James III (1466-7) that none but freemen
burgesses or their agents should take part in foreign trade,
but that prelates, lords, or barons could export goods by
their servants and buy abroad things for their own use, thus
saving the middlemen's profits ; by James IV (1503) that
none dwelling outside burghs should practise any merchandise ;
by James VI (1592) confirming previous Acts on burgh
privileges and that none but free burgesses should deal in
merchandise, but that noblemen, barons, or other landed
men could buy merchandise for their own use but not to sell
again, or thereby be liable to the penalties for unfree traffickers,
proper machinery for the exaction of all such penalties being
now provided ; again by the same King in Acts of 1607
ratifying all ancient liberties and privileges of the free burghs,
apparently in response to an instruction by the Convention
of Royal Burghs in 1602 to the burgh commissioners in
Parliament that they should " lament " to the king the decay
of the estate of burghs by " the new purchest [= procured]
erectiouns of brughis of barronyis with the haill liberteis of
fre burrowis " ; [2] and lastly by Charles I (1633) when all
the preceding Acts from the time of James III, as expressing
the privileges of the free burghs are ratified and approved,
these liberties and privileges being further competent only
to royal burghs that had a vote in Parliament and bore the
burden of burghal taxation.

This comprehensive body of legislation would seem to
make the case for the royal burghs watertight, but that its
restrictions on their behalf were not strictly observed is
confessed in the Act of James VI. At all times, however,
and in all countries, laws are being broken or there would be

[1] *Records, Convent. of Royal Burghs*, i, 540.
[2] *Ibid.*, ii, 130.

no need for courts of law.[1] In particular disputes were apt
to occur over the precise range of a burgh's " liberty " or
area of monopoly.[2] This might be subject to exceptions.
Thus Dundee with a " liberty " extending over the sheriffdom
of Forfar was limited by the rights of other royal burghs
within the sheriffdom ; and Cupar-Fife similarly by the
" liberties " of St Andrews and Dunfermline. A clash of
interests was almost bound to come. Dundee and Montrose
had their quarrels over their respective boundaries ; [3] so had
Ayr and Irvine over their respective shares of the sheriffdom,
till it was settled that Irvine's liberty covered the baronies
of Cunningham and Largs, as the original charter of 1372
expressed.[4] The shire of Inverness, which was the monopoly
area of that burgh, covered originally the whole country
north of it, and Inverness was thus brought into conflict
with the later foundations at Dingwall, Tain, Dornoch, and
Wick,[5] while Sir Thomas Urquhart discharged some of his
characteristic invective against Inverness for its efforts to
destroy the liberties of the little burgh of Cromarty.[6] In
1501 the magistrates, council, and community of Inverness
raised an action against the " indwellaris and inhabitantis "
of Dingwall before the Lords of Council, summoning them to
produce the infeftments, evidence, etc., for the privilege they
exercised of buying skins, hides, salmon, iron, and other
merchandise " that suld cum til the mercat of Invernes "
and selling the same to strangers or exporting them without
paying custom. The defence on the part of Dingwall was to
produce its charter from Alexander II and plead that they
had possessed this privilege in peace " past prescriptions." [7]

---

[1] So, too, in France the kings repeated some trading prohibitions
but so often that one must believe they were little observed (peu suivis)
(Levasseur, i, 666-7).

[2] Cf. throughout Theodora Keith on The Trading Privileges of the Royal
Burghs of Scotland, Eng. Hist. Rev., xxviii (1913).

[3] Hist. MSS. Comm. Rep., ii, 205-6.

[4] Muniments of Irvine, i, 12-13, 42-3 ; R.M.S., s.d., No. 398.

[5] Records of Inverness, New Spalding Club, i, p. lxxiii ; Invernessiana,
C. Fraser Macintosh, p. 174.

[6] Introduction to the Universal Language. Cromarty at least was a separate
sheriffdom.

[7] Acta Dominorum Concilii, p. 27. See also Invernessiana, pp. 176-8, 184-5.

Dingwall by its charter had been granted the liberties and customs of Inverness, but was still within that extensive shire, over which the monopoly of trade had been conferred by William the Lion on the burgh of Inverness. Judgment was postponed but none is entered. A royal pronouncement of 1455 is that the grants to these burghs were made without prejudice to the rights of Inverness.[1]

Dumbarton from the earliest times,[2] with Rutherglen and Renfrew, ran a secular feud over privileges with Glasgow as long as it remained a mere burgh of barony or regality. Renfrew also claimed customs from Paisley and on that score sued the baillies of the abbey for non-compliance, but the Lords Auditors in 1493 decided against Renfrew's claim on the ground that the town of Paisley had been created a free barony and regality before the date of the charter to Renfrew.[3] Edinburgh was always much engaged in keeping her port at Leith in its subordinate position, and, to a less extent, in limiting the activities of Canongate, buying up the superiority of the latter in 1636. Her constant dread was the opening up of a new port on the Firth of Forth, which would drain away some of the foreign trade through Leith upon which she throve.[4] All these conflicts, however, were but cross-currents in the sea of monopoly.

One industry which might have been expected to escape the net of the royal burghs was that of the rich fisheries round the coast. But that too was enmeshed. An Act of 1573, proceeding upon the disregard of earlier Acts, lays down that

[1] *Invernessiana*, p. 127.   [2] See pp. 17-18.

[3] *Comm.*, 1835, *Local Reports*, Pt. ii, p. 355.

[4] In 1506 King James IV had docks and houses constructed at a new port called Newhaven, but in 1510, for certain reasonable considerations, by charter under the Great Seal, conveyed the port in fee and heritage to the burgh of Edinburgh (*R.M.S.*, s.d., No. 3551). After the Restoration the Earl of Lauderdale had the gift of Cromwell's citadel at Leith " with the privilege of erecting it in a burgh of regality ; which he did, to force the magistrates to buy it from him ; for he boasted to settle a trade there which would break theirs." To stop this cost Edinburgh £5000 sterling. This happy but costly ending was contrived by the Provost, Sir Andrew Ramsay, and was the foundation of a close friendship between the two eminent public men, the Earl previously hating the Provost as a supporter of a rival statesman (Sir George Mackenzie, *Memoirs of the Affairs of Scotland*, pp. 24-5).

all " slayers " of white fish and herring on the coast, round the isles, or within the firths, must bring their catches to " free " ports, there to be sold to all, and what was over to be disposed of to free burgesses to be salted and " transported." A later Act (1581) prohibited foreign merchants from carrying on any such business at the lochs of the west and north isles, or buying any fish except what was salted and barrelled by the freemen of free burghs. Reasons given for such legislation are that only in this way could it be assured that the king would receive the custom due to him from what was exported, and the royal burghs not be deprived of part of the traffic proper to them. It was no doubt difficult to impose these regulations upon the remoter regions, but it is due in part to the fishing industry and the shipping business which grew out of it that Andrew Fairservice in *Rob Roy* could acclaim the row of little royal burghs " yoked on end to end " along the southern coast of Fife.

In the burghal endowment of monopoly craftsmen as well as merchants had a share in respect of their own occupations. Just as it was illegal for unfreemen to buy and sell, so it was for such to make things for sale. So much would follow, in the first place, from the fact that originally no distinction was recognised between the different classes of privileged burgesses, between merchants proper and artisans who were engaged in the manual trades.[1] An exclusive right in craft work was thus implied and would be taken for granted. The position is succinctly expressed in the words of a decree by the town council of Edinburgh in a dispute over craftsmen with Leith in 1570 : " it be of veritie that the cheif libertie and fredome of ane fre burgh of ryaltie consistes in twa thingis, the ane in using of merchandice, the uther in using of craftes." [2] Crafts, however, were apt to find a footing outside burghs, wherefore came in 1592 an Act to suppress " the exerceise of craftismen in the suburbis of the frie-burrowis." It was

---

[1] *Cf. Report*, 1835, pp. 73, 78 ; Gross, *The Gild Merchant*, i, 107. The commissioners of 1835 thought the distinction was made " more palpable and complete " by the formation of a merchant guild (p. 78).

[2] *Extracts, Burgh of Edinburgh*, Sc. Burgh Recs. Socy., iii, 273. For a similar pronouncement in 1729 see *Edinburgh Guilds and Crafts*, Marwick, p. 201.

claimed that their work was of poor quality, and so " hurtfull " to the lieges. Further, that such a practice gave occasion to apprentices and servants to leave their masters and take up residence in the suburbs, thereby withdrawing (" substracting ") themselves from the jurisdiction of the provost and bailies of the burgh. Thus, too, the free craftsmen, resident in the burghs, not only lost business but had to shoulder their whole part of the charges of the burgh, from which the suburban craftsmen, who should share in the burden, went free. It is accordingly enacted that hereafter there should be no " exercise of craftes " in suburbs [1] adjacent to free burghs, the magistrates of which were empowered to seize and confiscate all work done or being done there, whether the material belonged to the craftsman himself or had been supplied by another for manufacture.[2]

But the trouble went beyond suburbs. Three years after the passing of the Act a fee is paid by Stirling to an agent of the Convention of Burghs for action to be taken against " werkmen in clachannis " (villages).[3] In 1659 the burgess tailors of Inverness were petitioning the magistrates and town council to take action against " outlandish men " who were filching their trade.[4] No one could be prevented from making things at home for personal use, but to do so for retail was quite another pair of shoes.

The craftsmen just as much as the merchants were wedded to the principle of monopoly.[5] There was a proposal in 1669 " that all tradesmen should be declar'd free in all the Burghs Royal of Scotland, for payment of a very small acknowledgment," which was the case in Holland. This, it was

---

[1] 1671 : " Found not to be suburbs at the distance of a mile from the royal burgh " (St Ninian's v. Stirling in Morison's *Decisions, etc.*, p. 1907.)

[2] But see note on p. 83. The Act would not apply to a suburb which was in a barony.

[3] Keith, as cited, p. 268.

[4] *Domestic Annals of Scotland*, R. Chambers, ii, 254.

[5] In 1725 the incorporation of girdle-smiths of Culross in a test case claimed, by royal grants, the " Exclusive privilege of making girdles in Culross for the service of all Scotland," this art having been " first invented in Culross and carried to the utmost perfection there." The Court of Session decided " That no such perpetual monopoly could have been granted in prejudice of this or any other burgh " (Morison, *Decisions, etc.*, pp. 1924-5.)

believed, would encourage foreign artisans to come and
settle in Scotland, giving the country the benefit of their
skill and experience. As it was, people were " forc'd to buy
all things abroad, because our Deacons and Trades here
will allow no expert tradesman to live among them ; nor
are any admitted to be artificers, except such as either married
the daughters of tradesmen, or have serv'd as prentices ;
whereby the ignorance and unskilfulness of workmen is
transmitted to posterity, without any possibility of reformation." [1] The proposal, however, which would open the doors
of crafts to strangers, met with opposition and was abandoned
for political reasons. The King desired the support of the
burgh commissioners in Parliament, and the craftsmen might
be able to influence the election of these, as certainly was the
case in Edinburgh, which usually gave a lead to the burghs.
" And thus," our author sums up, " the public good is made
subservient to the meanest interests, and is over rul'd by the
most inconsiderable and unworthy persons." [2] The craftsmen,
too, had other ways of expressing their resentment at measures
they considered as being to their disadvantage.[3]

The argument buttressing the privileged position of the
royal burghs was always that they had to provide a share in
any grant of money to the king. Primarily as tenants of the
king they were liable to contribute to " aids " or occasional
payments. Thus in 1210 when King William paid a large
sum to King John of England, as part of an amicable agreement, the barons promised ten thousand merks and the
burghs six thousand,[4] a proportion for the burghs which is
considered to be excessively stated. It is the principle,
however, which matters here. And so in the Stirling Charter
of 1226 it is laid down that those, other than burgesses,
dwelling in that burgh who wished to share in the market
must contribute with the burgesses to the royal aids.[5] The
same obligation has place in the Aberdeen charter, and in

---

[1] *Memoirs of the Affairs of Scotland*, etc., Sir George Mackenzie, p. 176.
Because he had not served the usual term as an apprentice, James Watt
was prevented by the guilds from setting up as an instrument maker in
Glasgow. In 1757 he was established by the University within their
precincts as their mathematical instrument maker.

[2] *Ibid.*, pp. 176-7.   [3] See p. 120.
[4] *Scotich.*, VIII, lxxiii.   [5] *communicent cum illis ad auxilia nostra.*

that by Alexander II to Lanark ;[1] and when Alloa, which was a burgh of barony, received the privilege of sharing in foreign trade, this was in return for its shouldering its share in payment of the " cess " or taxation laid upon the royal burghs.[2] Incidentally, the Stirling charter gives a glimpse of other residents than burgesses in the burgh, who, for a charge from which burgesses were free, could erect their stalls—a stall being a board on trestles in the market-place, a class of temporary *stalagarii* (" stallangers "), or have more permanent booths.[3] One of the Inverness charters from King William prohibits anyone exercising merchandise in the sheriffdom unless a burgess or a stall-holder (*stalagarius*). Others not burgesses would be sons living with their fathers, menial servants, apprentices, etc.

The proportion of public supply which fell upon the royal burghs had been in the fourteenth and fifteenth centuries usually one-fifth,[4] but later settled down to one-sixth of the total. The distribution of this amount among the individual burghs was the work of the Convention of Royal Burghs. This venerable body, still surviving in the sense in which the Papacy represented the Roman Empire " sitting upon the grave thereof," comes into notice in the latter part of the sixteenth century,[5] but how or from what it originated cannot be said with any assurance. There are notices of activities in common among burghs from earlier dates but, writes the historian of the Convention, " It is difficult from these records to assign a definite origin to the convention, to decide whether it was a development of the court of the four burghs,[6] which had powers as a law court which the convention never possessed, whether it originated in the meetings of burgesses summoned to parliament, whether it was an institution devised by the estate of merchants, independent of any legal

---

[1] *R.M.S.*, 1540-1, No. 2308. The charter is there attributed to Alexander III, but this is an error (*Records*, pp. xiv, xxvii).

[2] *Report*, 1835, *Local Reports, Burghs of Barony*, p. 7.

[3] *Cf. Records of Inverness*, New Spalding Club, p. lxix-lxx. At Stirling the corporation of fleshers, eight in all, had " the choice of the 12 best stalls in the market rent free " (*Report*, 1835, p. 87).

[4] *Exch. Rolls*, i, p. cvii ; ii, p. lxx ; iv, p. cxxx. See p. 147.

[5] *The Convention of the Royal Burghs of Scotland*, Theodora Pagan, p. 15.

[6] *Cf. Ibid.*, pp. 13-15 ; Rait, *Parliaments of Scotland*, p. 12.

or parliamentary origin and connection. Perhaps a blend of the three may be the solution."[1] These alternatives, however, do not seem to favour blending.

The Convention was composed of representatives of the royal burghs with the addition of the early ecclesiastical burghs of barony and such others as, though not royal, had been endowed with royal privileges and paid their share of burghal taxation. Certain small royal burghs, however, which were handicapped by poverty never exercised the privilege of representation,[2] being unable or unwilling to meet the expense, or in some cases did so only for a time.

It was a point with the Convention that representatives should be of the merchant class.[3] In its palmy days this body exercised a far-reaching control over matters affecting the royal burghs, carefully safeguarding to the extent of its power their privileged position, assessing from its tax-roll the proportion of taxation to be paid by each, striving to impose uniformity upon their administration, imposing regulations as to merchandise, and making compacts in foreign countries to further the interests of Scottish traders abroad, whose activities it also superintended. In time,

---

[1] *Ibid.*, p. 25. A section on " The Court of the Four Burghs," the work of Sir John Skene, is given in *Ancient Laws and Customs of the Burghs of Scotland, 1214-1424*, pp. 156-8. It tells how in 1405 it was decreed that two or three burgesses from each royal burgh south of the Spey should meet yearly in the Convention of the Four Burghs " to determe upon all things concerning the utilitie of the common weil of all the King's burghs &c." But the MS. from which the six chapters of the collection are taken " does not ascribe their enactment to the Convention of Burghs " (*Ancient Laws*, pp. iv, 156), and No. IV deals with transactions by the Templars, who had ceased to exist as an order in 1312. Sir John, it has been written, " was satisfied with transferring to his work whole pages of the rambling note-books of nameless lawyers, and to attribute them to the legislation of fabulous monarchs " (Cosmo Innes, *Scotch Legal Antiquities*, p. 3). Of Skene's collection Stair writes : " The remaining tracts . . . were either written by private hands, as *Quoniam Attachiementa, Iber Camerarii*, etc., or by magistrates of boroughs, as *Statuta Gildae*, and therefore have had at no time any proper authority " (*Institute of the Law of Scotland*, ed. 1838, p. 15). A good deal of early burgh material appears to derive from such " rambling note-books."

[2] See Pagan, as cited, pp. 27-8 ; *The Estate of the Burgesses in the Scots Parliament*, J. D. Mackie and G. S. Pryde, pp. 4-5.

[3] Pagan, p. 32 ; *Cf. R.C.B.*, i, 25, " merchantes and trafficquaris."

however, the revolutionary changes in trade and industry sapped the old burghal system, and the Convention became an anachronism, on which a representative from Glasgow in 1834 pronounced to the Royal Commission in these terms : " The Convention of burghs has no proper legislative or judicial powers ; and the debates of its members are little better than idle discussions which lead to nothing." [1] The Commissioners, in their Report, were of opinion that " its continuance is no longer necessary or expedient." But it still continues, not without expediency.

III

Besides royal burghs there were from the early times burghs " in "—later expressed as " of "—barony and regality according to the status of the domain in which each was constituted, " a classification unknown to England." [2] A lord of regality had a jurisdiction over his lands equal to that of a king,[3] but this relation did not of itself bring a corresponding extension of the commercial powers of the burgh.[4] That, however, might be done by special arrangement. Thus Glasgow was made a free burgh of regality in 1450 with a confirmation in 1476.[5] In 1490 it was given the right to have a tron or public weighing machine, the customs of which, that is of exported goods, were to go to the archbishop,[6] and in the same year it is bracketed with Ayr, Irvine and Renfrew, all royal, as one of the " free burghs " to which vessels should come.[7] It would thus seem to have attained to the privileges of a royal burgh before being actually invested with that dignity in 1611. But then Alloa, only a

[1] *Report*, 1835, Appendix, p. 14.

[2] Gross, i, 200.

[3] That is, including the four crimes normally reserved to the royal courts of justice.

[4] See case of Stirling *v.* Falkirk, p. 146, and *Records of Convention*, etc. Under the 1587 Act of Revocation burghs of regality and barony formerly holding of Prelates were now to hold of the King with the same freedom and liberty as they had before annexation.

[5] *Reg. Glasg.*, ii, Nos. 356, 410 ; *A.P.S.*, ii, 190-1.

[6] *R.M.S.*, s.d., No. 1915 ; *Reg. Glasg.*, ii, 458.

[7] *Descriptions of the Sheriffdoms of Lanark and Renfrew*, Wm. Hamilton, p. 188.

burgh of barony and regality, could receive the privilege of
export on terms. [1]

Burghs of barony in the general sense, such as Canongate
and St Andrews, are found as early as royal burghs, and it
has already been suggested that in early times, so far as
commercial privileges were concerned, no hard distinction
was drawn between these classes. The baronial burghs at
this early stage are few and, seemingly for the most part,
ecclesiastical. Always they are erected by a subject-superior
under licence from the King, a requisite not observed in
England.[2]

An early lay creation of this class is claimed for Kirkintilloch as due to William Cumyn by license of King William,
who confers the liberties and privileges belonging to a burgh,
" as freely . . . as any of my barons have a burgh from my
gift within my realm." [3] The language is unexpected, but
we have a reference to " the burgh of Kirkintilloch " in
1399,[4] and the " ancient evidents," including that as to King
William, were good enough for the Earl of Wigtown, when
he issued an elaborate charter of novodamus or renewal in
1670.[5] Prestwick was apparently an early foundation of this
type,[6] in favour of Walter, the first Steward.

It was not, however, till the middle of the fifteenth century
that this type of burgh was virtually revived and entered
upon a flourishing phase. Trading had developed and was

---

[1] See p. 76.

[2] Ballard in *Scot. Hist. Rev.*, xiii, 24. There would seem to be an
exceptional case at Kelso, since in 1323 we have an abject submission of
the " burgesses of Wester Kelso " or the " burgh of Kelso " (*burgum de
Calko*) to the Abbot, confessing his sole right to all the liberties of the
burgh in making burgesses, stall-holders, etc. (*Reg. Cart. de Kelso*, ii, No.
459). Yet in 1614 we have Kelso erected into a free burgh of barony
by royal charter with a confirmation twenty years later (*R.M.S.*, s.d.,
Nos. 1055, 237). Nothing is said of an earlier standing as such, though in
1607 Kelso had been made a lordship in favour of Robert, Lord Roxburgh
(*R.M.S.*, s.d., No. 2003).

[3] *Kirkintilloch*, Thomas Watson, p. 146. Purporting to be a notarial
transcript from the register of the Metropolitan Church of Glasgow.

[4] *Reg. Epis. Glasg.*, i, No. 319, p. 296.

[5] *Kirkintilloch*, pp. 147-157. The Commission of 1835 as to William's
charter says " is stated " (*Local Reports*, App., p. 109).

[6] See p. 110 n.

continuing to do so and new channels for its exercise would seem to have claimed attention. More royal burghs were of course possible, but those already existing would not view addition to their number with complacency. Between 1450 and 1516 four new ones were created, but in the same period fifty-one burghs of barony came into existence.[1]

The earliest of this new series was Strathaven erected by charter to the Earl of Douglas in 1450.[2] After it " a troop cometh," one hundred and ninety-one between the birth of Strathaven and the Union of the Parliaments.[3] A few date from towards the end of the eighteenth century and at least four from the early part of the century following, the list ending with Kilsyth in 1826, but for several places claimed as of this class no evidence of date is available.[4] Down to the seventeenth century at least representative charters show leading features in common, the most distinctive of which is the confining of trade to the burgh itself,[5] or " power of buying and selling therein " as for Abernethy in 1628, repeating a charter of 1476, or for Kelso in 1634 dealing in all merchandise " allowed to be sold in any other burgh of barony." [6] This particular limitation does not appear in the late charters ; the gulf between royal and baronial burghs was closing, but it still was there.

The baronial burghs as such were also given the right to have craftsmen, a weekly market, and one or more annual fairs. The number credited with incorporations (e.g. Hawick, Kelso, Girvan) or with exclusive privileges for burgesses is in each category so very small as to be negligible. Apart from market tolls, trade and manufacture were virtually free.[7] In just a few cases, e.g. Paisley, Galashiels, the erection is accompanied by a grant of land. The revenues accruing from the burgh, in market dues, petty customs, etc., go to

---

[1] Ballard, *S.H.R.*, xiii, 22.

[2] *R.M.S.*, s.d., No. 340.

[3] Ballard, as cited, p. 22.

[4] *Comm.*, 1835, *Local Reports, Burghs of Barony* (1836).

[5] *in ipso burgo* (Spynie, 1451 ; Paisley, 1488 ; Dunse, 1489-90), *in eodem burgo* (Fraserburgh, 1546), *infra dictum burgum* (Melrose, 1621).

[6] *R.M.S.*, s.d. ; *Local Reports*, as cited ; Ballard, *S.H.R.*, as cited.

[7] *Local Reports, Burghs of Regality and Barony*, 1836, and *Appendix to Gen. Report*, pp. 90-1, 94-5.

the superior,[1] very rarely as common good to the burgh ; Maybole in 1589, Prestwick in 1600, and Kelso in 1634 are in the latter category.[2] The petty customs of Fraserburgh (Faithlie) were to go to nourishing (*pro intertenemento*) the burgh and the upkeep (*sustentatione*) of the port.[3] At Abernethy any surplus over a certain figure for the customs went to the superior.[4] Bo'ness in 1669 was erected into a burgh of regality for the Duchess of Hamilton and her heirs, they to appoint "baillies and keepers" of the markets and fairs, and all customs, tolls, anchorages, shore dues and others to be applied "to the use of the said Dutches and her forsaids." [5] This personal superiority is that expressed in a complaint by Aberdeen in 1590 on a monopoly of its provostship by one family as to its being "thrallit to serve ane raice of pepill, as it war ane burch of baronaye." [6]

Similarly the administration of this type of burgh was a matter of dependence on or individual arrangement with the superior, and, as in analogous cases in England, varied accordingly.[7] Here, too, each town is an individual case. At Hawick, by the charter of Douglas of Drumlanrig in 1534, the burgesses were given the right to elect yearly bailies and officers for the government of the burgh. At Kelso the charters of James VI committed to the superior, the Earl of Roxburgh and his heirs, the power of appointing the burgh bailies, clerks, and officers. What was "popularly called the town council" [8] consisted of fifteen members, of whom

---

[1] "There seems no ground for doubting that such grants were mainly intended to defray the necessary expenses of a police, or other municipal establishments, in such burghs ; but it is equally certain that in many cases those taxations have been diverted from their public purposes, and employed by the superiors as a source of private emolument and income" (*Report*, 1835, p. 47).

[2] For cases see tabulated information in Appendix to the *General Report* of 1835 ; Kelso in *Local Reports, Burghs of Barony* (1836). The Earl of Wigtown in 1670 sold the feu-farm of the lands of Kirkintilloch to the burgesses and heritors and to the burgh the right of electing officials and holding courts (*Loc. Rep.*, p. 109).

[3] Charter *de novo* of 1588 in *R.M.S.*, s.d., No. 1526.

[4] *Local Reports*, as cited, p. 4.   [5] *A.P.S.*, vii, 580.

[6] *Rec. Conv. of Burghs*, i, 32. *Cf.* here p. 124.

[7] For special cases see p. 130.

[8] *Local Reports, Burghs of Barony*, p. 101.

F

the baron-bailie appointed eight for life and the trades elected other seven annually. It was not properly a town council, only assessors of taxation. At Fraserburgh the superior was perpetual provost and nominated the bailies and council yearly, the new council, however, to be chosen with consent of the old one. The Kirkintilloch transaction is noted above. Melrose supplies a limiting case. It is described as of old a burgh of regality on its re-erection in 1621,[1] but, according to the local report from the royal commissioners in 1836, " The powers of regality and of creating a magistracy conferred by the charter have never been exercised. No treasurer, councillor, deacons, burgesses or corporations have ever been created. . . . There is neither property, revenue, expenditure, nor debt. There are no taxes of any kind levied within the burgh, except the customs of Melrose fair, which belong to the superior." [2] These are only some typical possibilities and on the whole, just as happens with the royal burghs, there is no common system or prevailing pattern. In general terms, then, the characteristics of this class of burghs were these : (1) They possessed no outside area of monopoly, and within the burgh trade was virtually open to all ; (2) their government was at the discretion of the noble superior and usually under his control ; (3) they had no property as common good ; (4) they had no part in export and import trade, and this was to be the main ground of their conflict with the royal burghs ; (5) they had no inherent claim to representation in Parliament or the Convention of Burghs ; (6) they were not directly liable for cess like the royal burghs, but contributed to national taxation only as included in the shire. Exceptions to any of these features are so few as to be negligible, except for their individual significance.

It was possible for a burgh of barony to be raised to the status of a royal burgh and thereby acquire a fuller privilege with the corresponding liability in public taxation. Pittenweem is one instance. It existed as a burgh of barony in 1526, its creation as such going back to the time of James III. Fifteen years later it is translated into a royal burgh, the

---

[1] *R.M.S.*, s.d., No. 127.

[2] For details see *Local Reports, Burghs of Regality and Barony*, 1836, and Appendix to *General Report*, 1835. On some special cases see here, p. 137 *n*.

specific difference being that it is thereby entitled to participate in export and import trade.[1] Stranraer, created a burgh of barony in 1595, and even as such a trouble to Wigtown, was made royal in 1611.[2] Alloa, without a change of status, received royal trading rights by paying " cess " like a royal burgh.[3]

It is to be noted in the matter of raising a burgh of barony or of regality to royal rank that, should the superior not consent to the erection, his rights of superiority remained, " and consequently the borough thus erected, and all the tenants of it, held not of the crown, but of a subject superior, contrary to the general rule of burghal tenements. But even where the lands erected into a royal borough are holden of a subject, the borough holds of the crown all the liberties and privileges contained in their charter." [4]

A particular case of a burgh of barony occurs in Portsburgh, which lay immediately south of the " ports " of Edinburgh on that side. The lands there extending from Bristo on the east to Bruntsfield and Tollcross on the west belonged to the family of Touris of Inverleith, by whom they were conveyed in 1648 to Sir Adam Hepburn of Humbie. On these lands, however, groups of craftsmen had long established themselves, so that by this date there were no fewer than eight such in existence—hammermen, bakers, weavers, wrights and masons, shoemakers of the easter and wester parts, and tailors similarly differentiated ; all which had actually been made incorporated bodies by charters from Touris of Inverleith as superior, six of them in the year 1582. Ten years later the Act was passed banning craftsmen in the suburbs of royal burghs.[5] What

---

[1] *R.M.S.*, s.d., Nos. 388, 2294.

[2] *R.M.S.*, s.d., No. 366 ; No. 1665.

[3] P. 76.

[4] *An Institute of the Law of Scotland*, John Erskine of Carnock, ed. 1871, i, 344-5. *Cf.* here cases on p. 168. A baron had proprietorial powers within his barony not possessed by a royal burgh as such within its liberty (Morison, *Decisions, etc.*, pp. 1936-7). He could refuse new settlers within his bounds, which a royal burgh could not.

[5] The Court of Session decided in a case of 1669 that " the said Act of Parliament did not reach the inhabitants of any barony," and was to be interpreted only " of suburbs belonging to burghs royal, either in property or superiority " (Morison, *Decisions, etc.*, pp. 1905-6).

happened in the present case is that in 1648 Hepburn sold his rights in these lands to the magistrates and council of Edinburgh, and that in the year following the King erected them into the free burgh of barony of Portsburgh. The lands were to be part of the common good of Edinburgh, and the magistrates of that city were to have the right of choosing the bailies and other officers of the burgh of barony, in which there were no burgesses and no guild brethren.[1] But it was the fate of baronial burghs in the immediate neighbourhood of Edinburgh to be absorbed, sooner or later, in the royal burgh.

Canongate, the adjoining burgh of regality, had a constitution from its superiors, the Abbots of Holyrood, who, however, retained no right of appointment to office. But in 1639 Edinburgh was confirmed in the superiority acquired three years before and forthwith appointed a baron-bailie to act with the two resident and elected bailies, an arrangement which subsisted till 1856, when the administration of Canongate was merged in that of the city as a whole.[2] The port of Leith was granted to Edinburgh by the charter of 1329, but neither charter nor Act of Parliament could supersede baronial rights without consent,[3] and Edinburgh therefore had to come to an accommodation with the superiors of lands in Leith and in the long run acquire these superiorities by purchase. In 1636 Leith was erected a burgh of barony with Edinburgh as superior, the latter having the right to choose bailies and other officers and make regulations (*statuta*) for Leith.[4]

[1] *Report*, 1835, *Local Reports*, p. 330 ; *R.M.S.*, s.d., 1649, No. 2021.
[2] *R.M.S.*, s.d., 1639, No. 929 ; *History of the Canongate*, John Mackay, pp. 15, 17, 21-22.
[3] See p. 83.
[4] *R.M.S.*, s.d., No. 605.

CHAPTER VI

MONOPOLY DIFFICULTIES. MARKET TOWNS

Trade as national not merely a burghal interest. Monopolies for new enterprises. Difficulties and inconvenience of burghal rights and monopoly areas. Sir Robert Bruce and the Perth demand (1592). Parallel case of Linlithgow *versus* Edinburgh and Glasgow Railway (1859). Hardships of outlying districts. Case of the Hebrides. Establishment of market towns and fairs.

EVEN new royal burghs were received with disfavour as reducing the value of those already in existence. In 1584 the Convention ordained that, in the event of a new one being erected within the liberty of another, all the burghs were to use their power in opposition.[1] In the last resort the neighbouring royal burghs thereby affected would oppose the admission of the new candidates to membership of the Convention, an exclusion which might weaken their standing, but such opposition was ineffective.[2] Royal burghs, however, would at least take a share of taxation. Burghs of barony on the other hand appropriated part of the home trade with no corresponding financial liability. Opposition to these therefore was a matter of course, " as we see in many instances and particularly in Lews [Lewis] and Borrowstounness, to keep which from being burghs, the [Convention of] Burghs have spent a great deal of money." [3] On the whole opposition was of little avail. But in baronial erections there was no departure from the governing principle that trade should be confined to burghs. Not till almost the last quarter of the sixteenth century was a breach made in this principle, and subsequently widened to a subversive extent. By this time, too, and on through the seventeenth century, economic ideas were suffering change, trade appearing no longer as a concern

---

[1] *R.C.B.*, i, 197.

[2] Pagan, as cited, pp. 29-31.

[3] Sir George Mackenzie, *Pleadings before the Supreme Courts of Scotland* in *Works* (1716), i, 63. *Cf.* Pagan, as cited, pp. 121-2, 126-7, 137, etc.

of individual burghs, but, as in other countries, a national interest. A national economy intruded upon a burghal economy, and the town was to be held subordinate to the greater economic unit of the country as a whole. " Merchandise," sums up our Aberdeen author of 1685, is " an imployment whereby not onely Burghs, but Kingdoms and Commonwealths doeth mostly prosper and flowrish, if well and rightly improven," so that " the advancement and improvement of Trade " was not a matter concerning the merchants of the burghs alone, but also for " the Powers and Rulers of the Kingdom . . . seeing it mostly advances the good of the whole nation, and the decay thereof tends so much to the Publick prejudice." [1] Scotland, in fact, was being affected by the current " mercantile " doctrine : the exalting of production over consumption ; the consequent superiority of manufactures over the supply of natural products —the author just cited advocating leather and shoes to take the place of the native hides and skins, plaiding or other cloths to use up the wool—and action by the state to secure these and analogous ends.[2] The Stewart kings of the time, therefore, had been personally interesting themselves in business for the national interest. It became a political ambition to rival the English in the making of cloth and the Dutch in fishing, these being the outstanding commercial successes in the respective countries. Thus before and after he came to the throne of England James VI was favouring the introduction of foreign workers to improve the Scottish product of cloth.[3] In *Basilicon Doron* he had written, " take example of England, how it hath flourished both in wealth and policie since the strangers craftes-men came in among them. Therefore not only permit, but allure strangers to come here also ; taking as straite order for repressing the mutining of ours at them, as was done in England." At the second attempt such foreign workmen were settled in the Canongate, whereupon the magistrates of that burgh sought to force them to become burgesses and freemen, an obligation

---

[1] " Philopoliteius," *Memorialls for . . . the Royall Burghs*, pp. 98-6. *Cf.* here p. 7 *n.*

[2] *Ibid.*, chap. xv. *Cf.* here pp. 144-5.

[3] Keith, *Commercial Relations of England and Scotland*, 1603-1707, pp. 21-2.

from which they had been exempted by the King and which was not on that account reimposed by the Privy Council.[1]

Other undertakings during the first half of the century, for the expansion of cloth and fishing industries, did not have much success. For one thing, the new cloth manufacturers were handicapped by not being able to sell in retail,[2] a privilege reserved by law to the burgesses of royal burghs. A novel method of promoting new industries was extended from England in the grant to individuals of a patent or monopoly in the manufacture or improvement of such things as glass, soap, leather, paper, etc., which involved the stoppage of exports of necessary raw material at home as well as the exclusion of competitive products from abroad. This could be justified as of assistance to " the first interprysaris, practizearis, and inbringaris of new proffitable trade never hard of nor knowen afore." [3] Such measures, however, by reducing imports were opposed to the vested interests of the burghs, and in 1623 the Convention, through an imposing deputation, protested to Royal commissioners that " Quheras the monopolies and restraints of importation of forraine wair [ware] are prejudiciall to the subject and to the mercheand estait in speciall, in thair fre tred and negotiatioun, both in exportatioun of native commodities and importatioun of forraine, it is maist humblie craved that all monopolies and restraints may be recalled and publicatioun of the same maid at the mercat croces of the frie borrowis of this realme." [4]

---

[1] *R.P.C.*, viii, s.d., 1609, 366-7.

[2] See *Joint-Stock Companies*, W. R. Scott, iii, 126.

[3] *R.P.C.*, x, s.a., 1616, 641 ; *Melrose Papers* (Abbotsford Club), p. 262. An inventor of an " engine " for transporting coal from the pits to the sea was to be the only person allowed to use it for twenty-one years, provided it was " ane ingyne nocht knawin in the kingdome at no time of before " (*R.P.C.*, vii, 279). On the other hand the Privy Council refused in 1615 to sustain a monopoly in the preparation of red herring, as the process had been practised since about 1609, and declared the industry of making red herring to be " in all tyme comeing frie to all his Majesteis lauchfull subjectis, tradismen and trafficquairis, to be usit be thame at thair pleasoure " (*R.P.C.*, x, 641)—a revolutionary note in Scottish business. *Cf.* the case of Culross girdles in note, p. 74.

[4] *R.C.B.*, s.a., p. 147. " The burghs were more concerned in opposing patents obtained for individuals for the introduction of new processes than in trying to introduce or promote industries themselves " (Pagan, *Convention of Royal Burghs*, p. 213).

This comprehensive crave by the burghs was not likely to be granted.

The attitude of the craftsmen was the same as that of the merchants. Their vested interests, too, were being threatened by the introduction of more highly skilled "strangers" in other industries besides cloth. Scottish leather was very bad. Accordingly Lord Erskine procured a patent for a better process of tanning and brought seventeen English tanners to go through Scotland as instructors, any other leather than that stamped as his to be prohibited for thirty-one years.[1] But most of the Scottish shoemakers ("cordiners") were also tanners and these combined to "cross" the new project, stirring up popular feeling by greatly raising the prices of boots and shoes, for which they blamed the new manufactures.[2] The Council retorted by putting a limit upon prices. A bitter struggle went on for some years, implicating cordiners and tanners all over the country, but by 1625 it was recognised that, owing to the new method, the Scottish leather business had developed considerably.[3]

On these lines, then, the burghs, with their own monopolies to guard, had not proved co-operative.[4] And besides their inadequacy to a programme of national economic organisation, instances of the local irksomeness of burgh privileges were coming into prominence. In 1592 Sir Robert Bruce of Clackmannan sent out a servant with some goods, which had to pass through Perth. Because the "carrier" of the goods would not pay custom these were seized. Thereupon Bruce, denouncing this claim as a novelty ("novatioun"),

[1] *R.P.C.*, xii, s.a., 1620, pp. ix-x.

[2] *Ibid.*, p. 424.

[3] *R.P.C.*, 2nd series, i, p. lxxxvii.

[4] "No attempts were made to develop manufactures or fisheries through the agency of the convention, nor did it, as after the union, take much interest in the general industrial development of the country" (Pagan, as cited, p. 208). In 1616 the Convention, after prolonged debate, assented to the King's proposal to restrain the export of wool in order to benefit the new cloth manufacturers, "but to undertak ony burdyne on that mater, outher [either] anent the home-bringing of strangearis, or geving of assurance to his Majestie and the saidis Lordis that the haill cuntrey woll wald be wrocht within the cuntrey, the Conventioun planelie and flatlie refusit " (*R.P.C.*, x, 572).

took their weapons from some Perth merchants passing his house of Gastonhall on their way to Dundee. As already observed, merchants travelled with their goods, and it was an obligation on a burgess to have an outfit of arms.[1] Bruce offered to return the weapons if his goods were released without payment of any custom, otherwise he would repeat his treatment of Perth merchants passing by. The sequel was a resort to violence, in the course of which the baillies, council and community besieged Gastonhall, released two of their townsfolk who had been imprisoned there, plundered the house and carried off Bruce himself. The Perth version was that they had from time immemorial the right to levy the custom, that after the seizure of weapons they had returned the goods, and had besieged the house only to free their neighbours and bring Bruce to answer to law. Both parties were adjudged by the Privy Council to be at fault and the case was committed to an assize,[2] the outcome of which is not recorded. Perth may have based its claim on its position as a " thoroughfare," a designation at times associated with that of " burgh." [3]

A parallel case occurs as late as 1859, when, petty customs being still in force, the Court of Session decided that the burgh of Linlithgow was entitled, by its charters and Acts of Parliament, to levy the usual customs and tolls on goods carried through the burgh by the Edinburgh and Glasgow Railway.[4]

A broader and more deeply rooted aspect of burghal monopoly appears in a case of 1628 when the " gentlemen " and " otheris inhabitants " of the parish of Logie Durno in Aberdeenshire approached the Privy Council with the complaint that they were " distant from anie burgh and fra all publict mercats and faires saxtein myles or thairby, and that they can nocht be provydit with flesh, fish nor no otheris necessars for furnishing of thair housholds without extraordinar great charges and expenssis," which indeed had ruined many of them. They accordingly ask for liberty to hold a public

[1] See p. 136. [2] *R.P.C.*, v, 6-8, 80-1.
[3] *Cf.* Act, 1425-6, specifying " induellaris in burgh or throuchfaris," and Acts of 1426-7, 1496, etc. (*A.P.S.*, ii, 10, 12, 238).
[4] *Cases in the Court of Session*, Dunlop, xxi, 1215-6.

market weekly at the Chapel of the Garioch, as the most suitable place in the parish, but only until the Martinmas term. Should the burghs or other persons concerned find themselves affected (" interessed ") by such a market and appeal to the Council, the lords are desired to deal with the whole case on its merits.[1] The weekly market was granted on the terms proposed.

One is curious to know how restriction to markets in burghs affected such distant quarters as the Outer Isles, where the royal burghs had blocked the proposal to establish a burgh in Lewis.[2] " Formerly," we are told by an eighteenth century government agent, " the People of these Islands and the Isle of Skye with the little Islands in the neighbourhood of Skye landed their commodities at Glenelg and on the Western Coast of Ross and from those places Carried them on Horseback to Inverness, from whence they Carried back Merchant Goods of several kinds sufficient to serve them for a year ; but about 40 years ago they began to trade by Sea to Glasgow, and for some time past have had no commerce at all with Inverness which has given a Severe Blow to the Trade of that Town." [3]

This sort of hardship for country places remote from any burgh must have been widespread and of long standing. In 1538 the burgh of Irvine had represented to the king how " in the trublus tyme sen the feild of Flowdoun " merchant chapmen had held open (" plane ") markets on Sundays at various parish kirks within Cunningham, part of the burghal area of monopoly,[4] selling wool, skins, and cloth, which were staple goods, as well as meal, malt, fish, and flesh, while there were also booths for the sale of all kinds of small ware. Parish churches were, of course, a convenient centre for such traffic contrary to law, when necessity was the mother of contravention. The king's decision shows a weakening of the absolute attitude towards such a practice : no one was to sell anything at the kirks in question but meat and drink except, it is conceded, " pure (poor) chapmen that beris thair pakkis upoun thair bakkis." [5]

[1] *Spalding Club Miscellany*, ii, 267-8 ; *R.P.C.*, 2nd series, ii, 409.
[2] See p. 56.   [3] *The Highlands in 1750*, ed. A. Lang, p. 45.
[4] See p. 17.   [5] *Muniments of Irvine*, p. 41.

This judgment amounted to a grant to the places mentioned of a market with certain limitations, even so, a privilege that was exceptional as affecting burgh interests. To the great abbey of Kelso King William had given permission for their men in Kelso to buy fuel, timber, and corn from visiting merchants on any day except that of the market at Roxburgh, and sell bread, ale, and flesh at their windows, as well as fish brought on their own horses or waggons. Goods brought in waggons from elsewhere must be disposed of at the Roxburgh market, and on that day no buying or selling was allowable in Kelso, but only at Roxburgh, where the proper customs could be collected.[1] This may be regarded as a big concession to Kelso Abbey. There was contrary treatment for a fair at Newbattle, no doubt originating in the proximity of that Abbey, which David II ordered the sheriff of Edinburgh to suppress as "contrary to the custom of the kingdom and prejudicial to the Burgh of Edinburgh."[2] Markets and fairs outside burghs were equally prejudicial to these and generally not to be suffered. Brechin appears to be the only example of a non-burghal market from the time of David I, when the grant was made,[3] down to 1570, and that Montrose and Dundee, being royal, tried in the fourteenth century to suppress.[4] The particular grievance of these, the nearest ports, no doubt was the "concession" by David II in 1369 to the "merchants" of Brechin to have free entry and exit for their ships and boats on the rivers Tay and South Esk.[5] A fresh charter was secured by the bishop in 1451 granting a free market and market-cross for all kinds of merchandise with the same rights of navigation as above and also a regular visit by the Chamberlain's "Ayre" or circuit court.[6] Brechin, indeed,

---

[1] *Lib. S. Marie de Calchou*, No. 13, p. 15 ; *Local Reports*, 1836, App. p. 167. There is a curious difference in one place between the transcripts of the charter in these sources. In the former it is "selling" (*vendendi*) fuel, etc., in the latter "buying" (*emendi*) ; in both, "selling" the fuel, etc., is allowed to visiting merchants.

[2] *Charters &c. of Edinburgh*, No. 8.

[3] *Reg. Epise. Brechin*, No. 1, p. 3.   [4] *Hist. MSS. Comm.*, ii, 206.

[5] *R.M.S.*, s.d., 1370, No. 308. Date from regnal year.

[6] *R.M.S.*, s.d., No. 493. *Cf. Report of Commission on Markets and Tolls*, vii (1891), 583 ; Ballard, *S.H.R.*, xiii, 18 ; *Cf. Reg. Ep. Brechin*, i, pp. xix-xx.

would seem to have lacked little of being a free burgh,[1] but actually it remained no more than, in several ways, an exceptional market town.

These are obviously exceptional cases of infringement upon burgh monopoly, and could do little to mitigate the local difficulties and hardships which that monopoly imposed. " The pedlar," says Andrew Fairservice in *Rob Roy*, " ca him what ye wull they're a great convenience in a countryside that's scant o' borough-towns." Some advantage could be secured by fairs not attached to burghs, and of such we hear at Crieff,[2] Foulis (Perthshire),[2] and authoritatively at Ruthven [3] (" Erlisruthane ") in Forfarshire. Clackmannan had the privilege of one annual fair lasting for eight days before it was erected into a free burgh of barony in 1551, when it received two fairs on specific days, on which open trade was permissible,[4] and the right of a market cross. The erection was made in favour of Sir Robert Bruce of Rait because of the very great number of the lieges who resorted to the town.[5] Pressure on the rigid burgh system was clearly increasing, and so by 1571 we have the first combination of market and fair at a place which was not a burgh, when Bowden in Roxburghshire was equipped with a weekly market " for selling and buying " with two annual fairs, each of a day, the superior, Walter Ker of Cessford, to depute the " necessary guardians " of the market and fair days.[6]

The market town, illustrated by these precedents, was the simplest expedient for increasing the opportunities of shopping so much desired by outlying districts. But it departed from the legal maxim that all trade must be confined to burghs, and, possibly for that as one reason, preference was shown at first for the older institutions. In the ninety years following the novel example of Bowden eleven sites of markets or fairs were legalised in places that were not burghs, of which five

[1] Actually so styled in a charter of 1488, but apparently in error (*Reg. Episc. Brech.*, i, pp. xix-xx note). Still, as contributing to taxation, it was represented in Parliament in 1478 (Rait's *Parliaments*, p. 255). It was made a royal burgh in 1695.

[2] *Reg. P.C.*, iii, 690. Crieff is said to have been a burgh of regality (*List of Markets*, etc., Marwick, p. 34).

[3] *R.M.S.*, A.D. 1504, No. 2802.   [4] *licitum est publice mercari*.

[5] *R.M.S.*, s.d., Feb. 1550-1, No. 572.   [6] *R.M.S.*, s.d., No. 1988.

were for a combination of both, but over the same period appeared as many new royal burghs and no fewer than seventy-four burghs of regality or barony. Then between the Restoration and the Union of 1707 the ratio between the two main groups undergoes a marked change. As against 52 regular burghs comes the establishment of 136 places, not burghs, with markets (5) or fairs (131) and 110 with both, in all 246.[1]

By 1669, indeed, these minor foundations had taken on the aspect of a general policy which evoked criticism. " In this session of Parliament," writes a prominent contemporary, " very many fairs were granted to noblemen, gentlemen, and towns : [2] whereupon a most judicious merchant observ'd, that though it was commonly belief'd, that these were advantageous to the country, and tended much to the ease and service of the people, yet they would prove very prejudicial to trade and commerce ; for when there were few fairs in Scotland, they were much frequented by strangers, who thought them worthy of their monies, from England, Ireland, and sometimes from Holland, France, and Flanders ; but now the commodities of the country were vented in so many places, at so many different occasions, that not any one fair would be so considerable as to deserve any concourse of strangers, or even of country merchants who liv's remote ; and all these fairs were so many new occasions, given to the peasants, to intermit their ordinary employments, and to debauch at such meetings." [3]

That this prodigal provision of non-burghal markets and fairs was intended to facilitate and develop local trade at the expense of the burghs is clear from the terms of the grants. The hardships arising out of burgh monopoly have become a reason for outflanking law and custom in the public interest. Thus one of the many Acts of 1669 gives power to the Earl of Nithsdale to establish a weekly market and two yearly

[1] For these figures see Ballard in *S.H.R.*, xiii, 21-2, basing on the list in *Report of Commission on Markets and Tolls*, vii (1891). The " List " is also published separately (1890) as by Sir James Marwick, Town Clerk of Glasgow.

[2] *E.g.* to Perth an additional fair in 1669 (*A.P.S.*, vii, 569). It already rejoiced in at least four.

[3] Sir George Mackenzie, *Memoirs of the Affairs of Scotland*, etc., p. 177.

fairs at "the Milntoun of Ore "[1] as "a place tuelff myles distant from any mercat toun or burgh Royall, and most convenient for the ease of his Majesties leidges in the adjacent parts of that Cuntrie for buying and selling of all sorts of commodities." An explanation of this type runs like a refrain through the grants. Another Act of the same year empowers the Earl of Dundonald to have at two places a weekly market and two fairs, at another, a fair and a weekly market, all for buying and selling of horses, cattle, sheep, fish, flesh, malt, and all sorts of grains, cloth, linen, and wool, and all sorts of merchant commodities—a full bill of sale for a mere market town. It was the Earl·and his successors who were to uplift the tolls on all this merchandise, and this advantage, too, was to be characteristic of such grants.[2] Market towns were not incorporated but formally were in the class of baronial burghs directly contributory to their superiors. Even where the destination of the tolls is not so expressed, it may be assumed that they took this road. The parliament of 1681 produced many more erections of this class than even that of ·1669 or 1672. Another warrant went to Bethouns (Beatons) of Balfour to have a weekly market and two yearly fairs at their village of Kennoway, Fife, which they point out in their petition to the King and Estates was "well peopled and of considerable resort, being seated upon the King's highway that leads to the north and to the south of the Kingdoms. And that it lyes midway betuixt the Burghs of Kirkaldy and Coupar in Fife six miles distant from either of the saids Burghs. And so is a very convenient and necessary place to have a weekly mercat to sell bread, flesh, fish, and other provisions and commodities needfull for the accomodation of the inhabitants and strangers repairing thereto and the countrie about the same." The tolls and customs were to go to the petitioners.[3] Convenience would certainly be a justification of the grant in 1693 to Sir Donald McDonald of Sleat of two yearly fairs at Portree "in the Isle of Sky."[4] Fifteen new or additional grants of markets or fairs or both marked this year.

[1] Probably Urr in the Stewartry of Kirkcudbright (*Report on Markets &c.*, as cited).

[2] *A.P.S.*, vii, 569 ; pp. 561-2.   [3] *A.P.S.*, viii, 439-40.   [4] *A.P.S.*, ix, 93.

There was not the same equipment for every place, since local conditions would differ. Ballegarmo (Ballerno) in Perthshire, though six miles distant from Perth or Dundee or any other burgh, had to do with two annual fairs.[1] On the other hand " Middlethrid of Gartmore " (Perthshire) received no fewer than four fairs with a market as well.[2] Dalry, however, in the Cunningham district of Ayrshire, belonged to the very small class which had a market only with no fair. The grant was to the Laird of Blair for the familiar reason that his village lay " at some distance from any Royall Burrow or mercat Towne," but also, and this implies a general principle, " for the incress of policy at the said Villadge." Again, as in most cases, the market tolls went to the laird.[3] Among the similar grants of 1696 is one to the Marquis of Athole of two weekly markets at two different places, one being Blair of Athole, for horses, cattle, and other merchandise, the tolls to go to the Marquis and his successors. Here, too, no fair was included.[4]

This steady extension of trading facilities, not only in new burghs but more drastically in markets and fairs, plainly meant an extending erosion on the exclusive privileges of the royal burghs. The alarm thus occasioned in these quarters is reflected in a charter of confirmation of their rights and privileges to the burgh of Stirling in 1678, in which the King binds himself and his successors " on the word of a prince " not to erect any town or village into a burgh of barony or regality, or grant the power to have a market or fair, within two miles of Stirling.[5]

[1] *A.P.S.*, ix., p. 442.　　　　　　　　　[2] *Ibid.*, p. 441.
[3] *Ibid.*, p. 445. Two fairs were added in 1695.　　[4] *Ibid.*, x, 107.
[5] *Charters &c. Stirling*, No. lviii.

CHAPTER VII

BURGH ADMINISTRATION. THE MERCHANT GUILD

Burgh administration. *Prepositi*. The Provost. The Merchant Guild.
Other ruling bodies. The Town Council. Burghs in feu-farm.

As a great historian has pointed out, " there was no room for the government of towns in the feudal machinery." [1] That had to take shape on other lines to meet the very different conditions of a commercial and urban instead of an agrarian community. On how these were originally determined our information is practically non-existent. Even of France it can be said that, except for clauses applying to royal officers, early charters of privileges leave us in an ignorance nearly complete as to the administration of towns.[2] So far, indeed, as Scotland is concerned, no clause of election of burgh officials is known before 1469.[3] Yet self-government in the royal burghs had been in operation long before that time, and had become in fact an outstanding characteristic of such a burgh. As to the stages in the growth of so novel a practice in feudal life, we can only grope in the dark. Nor can what may hold good of one case be simply transferred to others. Even early burghs differed in size and complexity, and there never was in administration that uniformity or sharp differentiation of functions on which we count to-day. That was not the mediæval manner. If a system worked, however illogical or unlegalised, it stood. As is said of England so here, " every town has its own history, and the conditions of its development varied with the exigencies of local circumstances." [4] All this applies only to royal burghs ; the degree of self-government possessed by a burgh of barony was generally at the will of the superior.

[1] Lord Acton, *History of Freedom and other Essays*, p. 38.
[2] *villes de bourgeoisie.* Luchaire, *Institutions &c.*, i, 140.
[3] *Report*, 1793, p. 4.
[4] *Econ. Hist. of England*, E. Lipson, i, 190.

In a royal burgh, however, the burgesses were the King's tenants, and the rents of their burgages, the customs on trade, and the issues of courts held in the burgh went to the royal revenue. At first then we seem to have the application of a feudal device to its administration. The official on a royal manor in Domesday Book who accounted for its revenues was a *prepositus*.[1] William the Lion had a *prepositus* on his manor of Gorgie.[2] This official, apparently on the same terms, was introduced into the burghs, and at first, it would seem, by royal appointment or at least subject to royal approval. King David, in a mandate respecting the rights of the church of Dunfermline, refers to " my prepositus Suein " as one who would see his order obeyed.[3] Many of his charters are addressed to *prepositi* in company with earls, barons, sheriffs, etc. There is, too, a suggestion of royal control when David exempts Baldwin of Perth from all but two of his obligations as a burgess.[4] We have the plural form, *prepositi*, in the case of Stirling 1130,[5] and in the reign of King William there is a grant of land to the *prepositi* and the rest of the burgesses of Inverkeithing.[6] The pronouncement by the Royal Commission of 1835, the wording of which one may safely attribute to its distinguished members Cosmo Innes and Thomas Thomson, is to the effect that if we could rely on the capitulary known as the Burgh Laws " as of uniform authenticity, and of the date usually assigned to it " the question of appointment " might be easily solved," as it is provided there (No. lxx) that the *prepositi* should be elected at a specified date by the common council of the good men of the town. The qualification, however, is too serious for a firm conclusion. King William and Alexander II speak of " my bailies " of Inverness and Aberdeen respectively, who were to assist the burgesses in maintaining their right customs.[7] In the reign of Robert I (1318) we have a mandate

[1] Ballard, *B.B.C.*, i, p. lxxxv, *The Domesday Boroughs*, pp. 45-7.
[2] *Liber Cartarum S. Crucis*, p. 29.
[3] Lawrie, *Early Scottish Charters*, No. lxxxv. For a similar commission to the *prepositus* at Elgin see No. cx.
[4] See p. 20.
[5] Lawrie, as cited, No. lxxxvi.
[6] *prepositis et ceteris burgensibus. B.B.C.*, ii, 378.
[7] *A.P.S.*, i, 89, 288 ; *Charters &c. Aberdeen*, p. 8.

G

involving references to the courts and bailies of the *prepositi*.[1]
It may be, therefore, that, to begin with, the bailies were
those of the *prepositus*, his agents, before we get them later
in the same century as " bailies of the said burgh." Still,
under whatever description, they were ultimately " the
King's bailies " just as " every individual is the King's vassal
in his burgage tenements."[2]

That the *prepositus* was the link between the burgh and the
Crown is clearly indicated by English cases. King Richard in
his charter of privileges to Lincoln gave power to the citizens
to choose yearly as *prepositus* one of themselves who should also
be suitable for the King.[3] Later, Lincoln has two *prepositi*,
as also have other towns, with in each example some provision
for approval.[4] In the case of Nottingham, Richard laid down
that the burgesses may elect a *prepositus* from themselves, but
that the King, if he considered their choice unsatisfactory,
should remove him and the citizens elect another acceptable
to the King.[5]

It is in their primary function as collectors of the royal
revenue from the burghs, except the customs, which were
separately accounted for by " custumars," that we find
prepositi figuring in the Scottish financial records of the
fourteenth century. This goes on till 1359 when *prepositi*
suddenly cease to be the accountants and their place is taken
by bailies, who previously had made but a very rare appearance in this capacity.[6] When, further, we find among these
later *prepositi* a musician, a dyer, a weaver, a shoemaker, a
porter and often a cleric or clerk, we may boldly infer that
this officer is not quite on the same footing as his original

---

[1] *A.P.S.*, i, 466.   [2] See Morison, *Decisions*, etc., p. 1936.
[3] *Foedera*, i, 52. There was the same provision for Norwich in King
Richard's charter of 1194.   [4] *Rotuli Cartarum*, p. 56 ; *B.B.C.*, i, 244-5.
[5] *Rot. Cartarum*, p. 39 ; *B.B.C.*, i, 244.
[6] In June 1330 the account for Peebles is rendered by two *prepositi*,
who are named ; in February 1330-1 the account of the *prepositi* is rendered
by two bailies, also named, one of whom is a tailor ; in December 1331
by a *prepositus*, the aforesaid tailor (*Exch. Rolls*, i, 274, 299, 353 ; *cf.* also
pp. 411, 517). In every case, however, the account is that of the *prepositi*.
It seems unlikely that we have to do with officers " Generally rendered
ballivi, but sometimes *prepositi* " (G. H. Pryde, Ph.D., *Ayr Burgh Accounts*,
p. xxii, note 4, *q.v.*). *Cf. coram prepositis et ballivis de Glasgu* (*Reg. Epis. Gl.*,
i, No. 236, A.D. 1280-90). Any superior might have *prepositi*.

namesake and is the nominee of the community. So, too, the bailies are now definitely those of the burgh. The chief business of the *prepositus* was that of conveying the annual payments to Exchequer. To do this the burghs now chose bailies, as Ipswich did in appointing two bailies for this purpose in place of a *prepositus*.[1] The title was revived in Scotland with an only municipal significance like the English mayor. Such a change of status can be accounted for by the fact that the royal interest in the burghs had been committed to the care of the Chamberlain, who himself or his deputies held a yearly court (" eyre ") in each to ensure their proper administration. This supervision had been exercised from at least the late thirteenth century and the nature of the record would suggest that it reproduces the conditions of a still earlier time. In it the Chamberlain is defined as one " having the knowledge and power to guide and govern the burghs." [2]

It is perhaps not wise to translate *prepositi* as provosts, as, though etymologically they are the same word, there is danger of confusion from the associations of provost in its later and modern meaning as presiding or chief magistrate, while the earlier *prepositi* usually occur in pairs. And in their days of full self-government burghs could get along without a provost. Even Linlithgow had none till 1540 ; [3] Lanark none till it was given power to choose a provost annually in March 1540-1.[4] As late as 1708-11 there was no provost in at least nine royal burghs, while Selkirk had " alwayis forborn to chose a provost " for the reason that " they were brought into a grate dale of debt by their former provost Hayning." [5]

---

[1] Townsend Warner, *Landmarks in English Industrial History*, p. 49.

[2] *tiel qi sciet & poet gyer et gouerner les Burgs.* Cambridge MS. in S.H.S. Miscellany, ii, 32. " The treatise called *iter camerarii*, or the Chamberlain ayre, seems not to be authentick " (Bankton, *Institute &c.*, i, 32). See further on the Chamberlain, pp. 165-6.

[3] *R.M.S.*, s.d., No. 2196.

[4] *R.M.S.*, No. 2310. The first mention of a provost is in 1542 (*Records &c.*, p. xxviii).

[5] " Setts of the Royal Burghs of Scotland " in *Miscellany of the Scot. Burghs Socy.*, p. 203. " The provost is from courtesy and custom stiled lord provost " (Gibson's *Glasgow*, p. 127).

If the evolution of the provost is thus somewhat confused, it is no less so with the town council. The case is pretty much the same in England.[1] What we do get in our early thirteenth century charters—at Perth, Aberdeen, Stirling, Elgin—is the institution of a Merchant Guild.[2] This, too, was in imitation of England, to which the institution was introduced from the Continent and where its first positive mention is not earlier than 1093.[3] But even in England information as to its precise character and functions is meagre.[4] The same is true for Scotland in an even greater degree. In respect of trade and commercial interests, it has been written, "The merchant guild of Scottish burghs was a shadow."[5] To give the institution some substantial detail recourse is had to the *Statuta Gilde* of Berwick, the earlier part of which is attributed to 1249, while the closing clauses are expressly dated 1281 and 1294. These statutes, it is claimed, though originally enacted for Berwick, were "subsequently accepted by the other burghs of Scotland."[6] It is true that in a charter of 1327-8 Dundee was granted and confirmed in a merchant guild "as freely as ever our burgesses of Berwick have and enjoy theirs."[7] The difficulty about this arises from the fact that the *Statuta Gilde* profess to be for a general guild embracing all "particular gilds" (No. 1) and so "are not the rules of a merchant guild,"[8] presenting us in fact

---

[1] "There is no charter of our period [1042-1216] which speaks of a body that might afterwards develop into a Town Council" (Ballard *B.B.C.*, i, p. lxxxviii).

[2] "It is doubtful, however, whether guilds actually took shape at these dates or for long after" (Murray, i, p. 464).

[3] Ashley, *English Economic History*, i, Pt. i, 71 ; Gross, *Gild Merchant*, i, 5.

[4] Cunningham, *Western Civilisation* ii, 64, *Growth of English Industry and Commerce*, 3rd ed., p. 220 ; Ashley, pp. 72-3. A number of English towns, including London, Norwich, Colchester, etc. (Tait, p. 232), had no Merchant Guild.

[5] Murray, i, p. 470. "The obscurity surrounding the subject is great" (*Scot. Hist. Rev.*, xxxii, 80).

[6] *Miscellany Scot. Burgh Rec. Socy.*, p. lxiv ; Warden, *The Burgh Laws*, p. 88.

[7] *Charters &c. Relating to Dundee*, 1292-1880, p. 10.

[8] Murray, i, 462. Gross, however, considers, from a particular item that "the general gild . . . was a Gild Merchant" (i, 211).

with a unique phenomenon in this field.[1] Whatever the
precise bearing of the words in the Dundee charter, it seems
out of the question that these Berwick statutes could be baldly
accepted and applied in other burghs as the normal elements
of a merchant guild.[2] There is no parallel to the reference
in the Dundee charter.

Nor did the formation of a merchant guild occur as a
matter of course. It followed a grant or licence, and the
issue of such to different burghs goes on down to at least the
close of the seventeenth century.[3] More than half the guilds,
indeed, apart from speculation, are of a date later than the
Reformation.[4] Certain burghs were not very keen about
being saddled with this privilege, and in some cases it was
actively opposed by the trades.[5]

It will be found, however, that in course of time the part
played by the Merchant Guild is reduced in scope, until its
alderman or dean and his court become merely a department
of municipal administration, and the body of the Guild
continues as a more exclusive section of the merchants proper.
Originally membership was not confined to that class. Thus
when the charters of Alexander II to Aberdeen, Stirling, and

[1] " How the mayor of Berwick and the other good men of that town
should have abrogated the several guilds which previously existed in the
burgh, should have created a new guild, and should have transferred to
it all the property of the others, is not explained. . . . It seems strange,
also, that a code enacted for the regulation of the merchant-guild should
have dealt, as this code does, with the election of the magistrates and
governing body of the entire community " (Marwick, *Edinburgh Guilds and
Crafts*, p. 27).

[2] *Cf.* Robertson and Wood, *Stair Socy*, i, 101. " The statutes of the
guild . . . are only the acts of the town council of Berwick . . . and
how they could ever be reputed as extensive over the whole kingdom is
what I cannot apprehend " (Bankton, *Institute of the Laws of Scotland* i, 31-2).
See Stair on p. 77 *n.*

[3] See lists in *Scottish Review*, xxxii, 69-70. These are in correction of
the list by Gross.

[4] *Ibid.* All this puts in a questionable light the statute attributed to
William the Lion extending to all merchants of the kingdom the right to
have a Guild.

[5] *Ibid.*, pp. 78-9. " The Gildry or Gild Merchant is not to be confused
with the Company of Merchants or Merchant Company of Edinburgh,
which was established in 1681, and is still in existence " (Gross, as cited,
i, 219, note 2).

Perth specifically exclude weavers and fullers from the Guild as was done also in English cases [1] with so far no satisfactory explanation, it may lawfully be inferred that this exclusion did not apply to the other crafts and that these were represented in the membership.[2] Such in fact was the case in England, which apparently is the model here as elsewhere. The membership of one English guild (Shrewsbury) has been minutely investigated and shows that it "must have had nearly every householder, poor or rich, as a member . . . the gild did not exclude dyers, butchers, fishermen, etc.," [3] thus emphasising what had already been shown "that, generally speaking, craftsmen were freely admitted to the Gild Merchant in the twelfth, thirteenth, and fourteenth centuries." [4] It is most unlikely that Scotland would have a different practice, and what evidence there is points to identity.[5]

Covering thus the whole burgess population, the Guild would appear to be the first official recognition of that as a self-regulated unity, a big step towards full burghal autonomy, as against control by a superior.[6] The Guild can profess to speak and act for the community as a whole, a new voice and combination in a feudal state which in itself allowed no place for such popular activities. For this earlier time it has been claimed that "The merchant guild assumed the

[1] Gross, i, 108.

[2] The Burgh Laws exclude dyers and butchers from the Merchant Guild, unless they give up the personal practice of their craft (xciv), but has no ban upon those excluded by the charters.

[3] Archdeacon Cunningham in *Transactions of the Royal Historical Society*, New Series, ix, 102.

[4] Gross, i, 107. At this stage " It would be safer to translate the words into ' Market Gild ' " (R. H. Gretton, *The English Middle Class*, p. 20).

[5] In an Aberdeen case of 1793 before the Court of Session it was pleaded that " Originally all burgesses of royal burghs were equally entitled to carry on trade, whether foreign or inland, and craftsmen might even have been members of the Guild or Merchant Company " (Morison, *Decisions &c.*, p. 1979).

[6] *Cf.* Tait, pp. 232-3 : " The one important privilege that was peculiar to boroughs, though not universal, was the merchant gild. Though granted only for the regulation and advancement of their trade, it was utilised in practice to give a kind of semi-corporateness to the borough community " (p. 263). *Cf.* Stephenson, as cited, pp. 150, 151.

government of the burgh." [1] Thus in 1372 the Guild at
Montrose could enter into an agreement with that of Dundee,
whereby each burgh received reciprocal trading rights within
the district of the other.[2] In 1403 [3] an election of the " officers
of the Guild " at Edinburgh is the same thing as that of the
town administration. At the First Head Guild (*Prima Gilda
Capitalis*) are chosen, as " officers of the Guild " a *prepositus*
(provost), dean of guild, treasurer, sergeants of the guild,
pricers (*appreciatores*) of flesh and wine, and the " duodene "
or " lie dusane " (dozen) of the burgh, who, despite the name,
number forty-eight.[5] Under date 1416 [4] we get a similar
election with a similar list, the provost now styled " alderman,"
a title taken over from the Guild as provost was from the
royal *prepositus*. In 1463 the procedure and officers are the
same, while the thirty-two of the " dusane " are " everie ane
stylit be his craft." [6] It has been noted how in 1450-1 the
skinners required certain statutes to be recorded in " the
common book of the guild of the said burgh," [7] which was
approved by the magistrates and council, this, with other
things, seeming " to imply that the guild was then regarded
as one and the same with the community of the burgh." [8]
Of Aberdeen it is reported that before 1590 while the provost,
bailies and sergeants were elected in the Head Court of the
Burgh, the Common Council appeared " to have been in
general chosen in " the Court of the Guild, otherwise the

[1] Marwick, *Observations on Early Guilds of Merchants and Craftsmen* (1886),
p. 16, and *Edinburgh Guilds and Crafts*, p. 29.

[2] *Hist. MSS. Com.*, ii, 206.

[3] But according to Sir James Marwick, " There can scarcely be a
doubt, however, that the date 1403 has been erroneously transcribed for
1453 " (*Edinburgh Guilds &c.*, p. 29).

[4] *Extracts from Records*, i, 1.

[5] *Ibid.*, p. 2.

[6] *Ibid.*, p. 20.

[7] *Ibid.*, p. 9.

[8] Marwick, *Edinburgh Guilds &c.*, p. 30. " But at what point and by
what means the general jurisdiction of the Merchant Guild of Edinburgh
became merged in or superseded by the Town Council there is no means
of ascertaining. In Edinburgh the two were practically synonymous,
although, in a somewhat perplexing manner, the Guild Court seems to
have retained a separate identity " (*Castle and Town*, Robertson and
Wood, p. 213).

Court of the Baillies of the Guild, which all Guild brethren were bound to attend and where their names were entered in the rolls regularly called.[1]

So far, then, the burghal community had been able to secure self-expression in the Merchant Guild. This phase passed when in time the Guild was reduced to being but one member in the municipal organism. In England by the fourteenth century it had been in decline, after which it either completely disappeared or was merged in the general scheme of burghal administration.[2] In Scotland from the late fifteenth century it was to take the latter course.

The break-up of its earlier identification with the community as a whole followed on the emergence of the crafts as individual groups with their own common interests. These had been drawing together as voluntary societies or fraternities engaged, among other benefits, in making provision for the maintenance of religious services in private chantries for the immortal welfare of their members,[3] a devotion characteristic of the time in nobler quarters. The charitable side may be illustrated by the obligation undertaken by the whole crafts of Edinburgh in March 1579-80 " to tak and sufficientlie sustene and uphald from begging thair awin puir, sic as ar faillit craftismen, with thair wyffes, bairnis, and servandis." [4] A beginning for a craft guild as a religious fraternity is suggested by the designation of its head as " deacon," apparently borrowed from ecclesiastical usage, also by the possession of an officer known as the " kirkmaster," [5] who may be the same as the deacon. In supplications to the provost and council of Edinburgh the leading place is sometimes taken by the " kirkmaster," and in one case (barbers and surgeons) he is designated " ane kirkmaister and ourisman

[1] *Report, Select Committee*, House of Commons, 1793, p. 5. See further here on Aberdeen, p. 106.

[2] Gross, i, 159-60 ; Mrs Green, ii, 194-5.

[3] See further p. 117. *Cf. The English Middle Class*, R. H. Gretton, pp. 65-6 ; Ashley, *Econ. Hist.*, i, Pt. ii, 136-7, 140.

[4] *Records*, iv (1573-89), 154. *Cf.* also for 1564-5, iii (1557-71), 193.

[5] A " kirkmaster " (*Magister Ecclesie*) is one of the officers appointed with " liners," " wine-tasters," etc., at the Aberdeen election of 1398. See p. 106.

to quhome the haill brether of the craftis foirsaid sall obey." [1] On such lines the crafts attained organisation as individual bodies in imitation of the older Merchant Guild, which from being comprehensive became but one of many guilds.[2]

We thus reach a new determinative departure in town life, the results of which will have to be followed out on their own account. Meanwhile by an Act of 1469 the election of a Dean of Guild is transferred to the town council, and in 1496 the council of Edinburgh accordingly exercised this power and in addition appropriated the funds and limited the privileges of the Guild, its head becoming only one of the magistrates. Not till 1833 was the right to appoint its own head restored to the Guild.[3] In 1518 the Town Council in answer to a " supplicatioun " from the Guild issues to the fraternity an authoritative Seal of Cause as it had already been doing for craft guilds.[4] This warrant prescribes the duties of the " courts of Gildry," and the Guild is to have power to make rules " for the common weill of the haill merchandis of this realme," [5] Edinburgh being usually regarded as a model for the other burghs. Accordingly an Act of Parliament in 1593 approves the power and jurisdiction of the Dean of Guild and his council in burghs in general, as these are exercised in Edinburgh, being empowered to deal with actions between merchants or between merchant and mariner ; Dean and council to be appointed yearly by the council of the burgh, and their judgments to have the

---

[1] *Records*, etc., i, 102. *Cf.* also pp. 80, 82, 127. *Cf.* " And divers of the Crafts of Edinburgh . . . having had altars in St Giles's Church . . . the chief officer of the several Fraternities of Crafts, was indifferently stiled Kirkmaster, Godsman, or Deacon . . . the title of Kirkmaster or Godsman was obliged to make way for the more general one of Deacon " (Maitland, *Hist. of Edinburgh*, p. 318). *Cf.* here pp. 106, 117.

[2] " The supposed descent in this country of the Trade Unions from the mediæval Craft Gilds rests, as far as we have been able to discover, upon no evidence whatsoever. The historical proof is all the other way " (*Origins of Trade Unionism*, Sidney and Beatrice Webb, p. 13. *Cf.* pp. 14, 18-9).

[3] *Castle and Town*, Robertson and Wood, p. 176 ; *The Dean of Guild Court of Edinburgh*, Robert Millar, p. 21.

[4] See p. 117.

[5] *Records, Edinburgh*, i, 181-3.

same force as in the good towns of France and Flanders.
All which shows the Guild functioning as a municipal department,[1] and does something to explain the late appearance of
so many Merchant Guilds and the opposition they sometimes
met : a new municipal magistrate and court might not seem
necessary or desirable. Cases occur in which there was only
a Dean who was no more than a municipal officer with no
court.[2] A wider survey is that presented by Mackenzie,
who, pleading in a case of 1672,[3] submits that " Guildries
were appointed in burghs to supervise the conduct of
merchants and restrain abuses, which burghs of regality and
barony wanted [i.e. lacked]. . . . And without debating
what was the design of our legislators in erecting Guildries,
yet we now find by experience . . . that Guildries have
conduc'd so little to advance trade that they tend rather to
secure the monopoly which they at first procured, and to
establish by mutual compacts those exorbitant prices for
commodities which are now exacted." On this account he
could see no reason why " guildries, which are but deaconries
amongst merchants, should not be discharg'd " as certain
other deaconries had been.[4]

As we have seen, however, all early towns did not possess
a Guild Merchant, and in these municipal organisation would
have a different basis. It is impossible, however, to offer
a pattern applicable to either class of burghs. The sweet
simplicity of magistrates and town council may be present
in Acts of Parliament of the early fifteenth century, but is
not discernible in such records of local government as we
possess. At Aberdeen, which had a Merchant Guild, about
Michaelmas 1398 an alderman, bailies and other officers
were elected with the assent of the whole community, and

[1] On the duties of the Dean of Guild and his council at Aberdeen in
1685 see *Memorialls for . . . the Royall Burghs* by " Philopoliteius," pp. 140-5.
He was " the Town's Fiscall " for the prosecution of offences against
trade regulations, decided in the differences between merchants as in the
Act of Parliament, and had control of the funds in the " Geld-Box " for the
relief of the poor brethren of the Guild.

[2] *Scottish Review*, xxxii, 80 : " whose duties were sometimes no more
onerous than that of adjusting weights and measures."

[3] See p. 146.

[4] *Pleadings &c.*, Works (1716), ii, 65.

on the same day twenty persons as common councillors (*in communes consiliarios*). At Edinburgh, another Guild town, we have seen elections in a different form with a body of men styled " the dusane " or the " duodene " but composed of three or four times that number, whose business is the " common profeitt " and the hearing of complaints and who have a " dusane day " with a fine for absence.[1] In one entry they are the " twelve councillors " (*duodecim consules*),[2] but, we may gather, only nominally that mystic figure. We must not, however, attach technical precision to the terms used by mediæval writers.

Apart, however, from the Guild any burgh, from its very nature, would, in accord with mediæval practice, develop a court to enforce its regulations and settle disputes, a body which in the exercise of these functions would assume powers of administration.[3] In the opinion of the Royal Commission of 1835, " It is a matter of notoriety, that Head Courts were an integral part of the constitution of the royal burghs of Scotland." [4] Even at their time Banff afforded " a singular exhibition of a head court in its utmost purity," composed strictly " of all the heritors and burgesses within burgh," and occupied with allotting the land tax and reviewing the transactions of the magistrates and council.[5] This was an abbreviated survival from earlier conditions, the process of which may be traced, for illustration only, not as a routine, in the case of Peebles, which had no Merchant Guild till 1621. The head court sitting in October 1456 (Michaelmas term), in January (Yule) and April (Pasch or Easter) of the following year, appointed bailies, flesh and ale pricers, and sergeants or officers, admitted burgesses, and did legal business. But as head courts normally met only thrice in the year—at Edinburgh

---

[1] *Records*, i, 64-5.

[2] *Ibid.*, i, 2.

[3] The classic case being The High Court of Parliament.

[4] *Local Reports*, i, 105. In the General Report the phrasing is " probably once existed " (p. 46).

[5] *Report*, as cited ; *Local Reports*, i, 106. But see the criticism in *Annals of Banff* (New Spalding Club), i, 272-3 : " The present Head Court of Banff, which is not infrequently referred to as an almost unique relic of antiquity, bears very little resemblance to the ancient Head Court of the burgh, except in name."

four times,[1] at Banff twice [2]—some executive body was necessary to supplement the work of the bailies. Such a body appears in the " Inquest " of twenty members in January 1457-8. Two years later we meet the " Doussan " (dozen), who subsequently in February 1463-4 are specified as " for the reformatioun of the town," meaning apparently for its good or improvement, and number seventeen ; half their names appear in the " Inquest " chosen at the April head court thereafter. Then come tentative steps towards a more general body : six men to give the bailies counsel (1468) ; twenty-four of the best neighbours of the town to act for its utility and common profit (1503) ; finally a " counsale " of twenty-five " for commoun actiones setting forward," who issue various ordinances (1555) ; while on the same occasion we have the first mention of a " lord provost," who is chosen by the bailies, council and community.[3] After which the " dozen " drop out of sight, but the " Inquest " is active down to at least 1573. The administration now is by provost, bailies and council, with or without direct co-operation by the community. A few years later the Act of 1469 begins to be followed.

This record need not answer for any other burgh,[4] though we do find the " dozen " and the " inquest " elsewhere. That the name of the first does not at any time correspond with its number suggests that the idea of the institution was borrowed from England where so many towns, particularly after 1300, have a council amounting to just so many or double that figure.[5] The " dusane " existed at

---

[1] *Records*, iv, 140 (1579-80).

[2] *Annals of Banff*, i, 273.

[3] *Records*, p. 217.

[4] At Elgin on 4th October 1540 the " heid burrow court " held by the provost and bailies admits burgesses, decides legal cases, and chooses an " alderman," three bailies and four sergeants for a year. Next day it names the common council as the magistrates already elected and thirteen others, and appoints pricers of flesh, ale, bread, etc., and " lynaris of land." On the 19th there is an assignment of land by the provost with the consent of the council and community (*Burgh Records of Elgin*, New Spalding Club, i, 47-8).

[5] Tait, *Eng. Hist. Rev.*, xliv (1929), 189-90 ; *Eng. Mediæval Borough*, p. 264 ; Pollock and Maitland, *Hist. of Eng. Law*, i, 659.

Perth,[1] but is not on record at Stirling, Aberdeen, or Dundee, which had their own manner in self-government.

So far as one can gather, the dozen was mainly a consultative or advisory body ; the " inquest," where it is found, seems more of an executive. The name "inquest" too betrays an outside origin, however much the idea was extended in practice. It is surely the " Frankish Inquest," a legal expedient accepted by England from Normandy [2] and the forerunner of trial by jury. The Norman kings used it also for fiscal and administrative purposes,[3] and it was made to serve these ends in Scotland. As a legal body its special function was in determining heirship, but this might be done also by a special inquest embodied for the particular case or by the burgh court.[4] Similarly the standing body could perform other functions. In a dispute at Peebles about the setting of the burgh customs it was pleaded that the " inquest " had no power to do this, their proper business being the " serving of brevis " where necessary,[5] that is, determining upon questions of property. But we find them also issuing ordinances on the head dikes of the town, on the setting of the police watch, at other times done by the bailies and community, and fixing market prices.[6] At Stirling the provost and bailies elected an " inquest " to determine prices.[7] This body is noticeable also at Lanark where, besides its legal activities, the bailies joined with it in administrative acts proper in later times to the town council.[8] The " inquest " is prominent at Prestwick, where it is concerned with fiscal and legal business,[9] and in the sixteenth and into

---

[1] *The Perth Hammermen Book*, 1518-68, Colin A. Hunt, p. ii.

[2] *Hist. of English Law*, i, 93.

[3] Vinogradoff, *English Socy. in the Eleventh Century*, p. 4.

[4] *Records, Peebles*, pp. 112-3.

[5] *Ibid.*, p. 332.

[6] *Records, Peebles*, passim.

[7] *Records* (1519-1666), p. 89, A.D. 1598 ; *Cf.* p. 5. The same was done by the Burgh Court at Banff in 1628 (*Annals of Banff*, i, 61).

[8] Renwick, *Preface to Records of Lanark*, p. xxviii. For the appointment of an " Inquisicio " at the head court see pp. 9, 11, 22, 28. " There is no record of an election of magistrates earlier than 1563 " (*Preface*, p. xxvii).

[9] *Burgh Records* (Maitland Club, pp. 1, 27, 28, etc., 55, etc., 76, 78, 85, etc.).

the seventeenth century chooses the "overman" ("ouris-man") or "provest" and the two bailies, acting with the assent of "the haill communitie." [1]

The difficulty about these bodies is that, though differing in name and constitution, they appear to have the same powers as to both justice and administration. At Banff "Head Courts formerly resembled ordinary burgh courts in many respects, much of the business being precisely similar," and "Prior to 1737 the record of business transacted at Head Courts was entered along with the proceedings of the Town Council and ordinary Burgh Court." [2] Since 1677 at least the "town's Court" and the Council met weekly, yet their activities are substantially the same, the Court appearing frequently to impose decisions of the Council. What is called a "lawless exercise of power in Banff, may be proved both by witnesses and by the acts of the town-council abusively called acts of head court." [3] How is one to differentiate? These bodies cannot reasonably have started together on a common footing. The burgh court or standing "inquest" may, to begin with, have dealt with cases arising out of the "watch and ward" or police duties of citizens which date from the beginning ; the Head Court with major matters affecting the burgh as a whole, for example elections and the admission of burgesses ; while the Town Council substituted for the "common counsellors" or the "dozen." But each was a court in the public interest and as such tended to act in that interest wherever it came in question. The result was overlapping. All which is no more than the suggestion

[1] *Burgh Records*, pp. 72, 79, 81, etc. After 1616 there is a gap in the records till 1726, when and subsequently the magistrates are chosen by the burgesses and freemen. Prestwick was a Stewart foundation as head burgh of the bailiary of Kyle-Stewart which after 1404 was part of the principality and was held of the heir-apparent as Prince and High Steward. James VI in his charter to the burgh of 1600 (*R.M.S.*, No. 1042) acts as the administrator of Prince Henry, to whom goes the "reddendo" of the burgh. It was only a burgh of barony, but, as defined in 1446, all within the barony of Kyle-Stewart had to bring their goods for sale to the market of Prestwick and were to accept the weights and measures of Prestwick, which, in its turn, used those of the royal burgh of Ayr (*Records, Prestwick*, p. 114).

[2] *Annals of Banff*, i, footnote, 272, 274.

[3] *Reports of Grievances* (see p. 178), p. 116.

of a trail across a tangled terrain, till a better way is found.[1]

It was not till the fifteenth century that the administration of burghs attracted the notice of Parliament, possibly as a result of the now accepted presence of representatives from the burghs. Parliament, however, recognised only the existence of magistrates and council, and the election of these alone was the purport of the Act of 1469, at first so imperfectly obeyed. This concentration by Parliament probably led the burghs in time, reluctantly, it would seem, in some cases, towards the simplified form of administration, in which other elected bodies ultimately ceased to function, and which itself was to be individualised as a corporation.[2]

The apparent confusion in the earlier stage, with the sometimes naïve ways [3] of securing the general approval of

[1] It should be added that certain royal burghs were in time constituted as sheriffdoms within their own liberty and territory, the provost to be sheriff and the bailies sheriffs-depute, thus relieving burgesses from attendance as royal vassals at sheriff-courts elsewhere (Dundee) and the burghs from the particular jurisdiction of the territorial sheriffs, while the profits of the burghal sheriffship went to the burgh (Perth). Examples are these, with date of commission, from *R.M.S.* except where otherwise indicated : Dundee (1359), Perth (1394), Edinburgh (1482), Forres (1496), Selkirk (1540, *Loc. Rep.*, ii, 395), Lanark (1540-41), Haddington (1542), Irvine (1601), Dumbarton (1641, *A.P.S.*, v, 453).

Bathgate was a special case. Originally it was a barony attached to the shire of Renfrew, from which, however, it was disjoined in 1530-1 (*R.M.S.*, s.d., No. 983), and so was described in 1594 as having been of old " ane shirefdome within the selff " (*A.P.S.*, iv, 80). In 1663 Thomas Hamilton was made sheriff " with the new gift of erection of ane burgh of Barronie " (*A.P.S.*, vii, 512).

[2] Dr Pryde sums up that " in most burghs a standing council seems to have evolved during the fourteenth and fifteenth centuries from variously named *ad hoc* committees and from special officials like liners, ale-tasters and flesh-pricers—all of whom would be, in effect, named by the bailies, perhaps with the approval and acclaim of the *haill toun* " (*Ayr Burgh Accounts*, S.H.S., p. xxv). But as we see, the committees overlap in their activities, are not strictly *ad hoc*. At Dunfermline " the first reference to a ' consall ' of the burgh was in 1515 " (*Burgh Records*, Beveridge, pp. xvi, xvii).

[3] *E.g.* at Peebles on a day in January 1459-60, " The balyais . . . with the doussan and with thaim of the eldest of the town, present in John Smayllis hous gaderyt " (*Records*, p. 134) ; at Edinburgh in February 1478-9 " the provest, the greitt dusane of the towne and dyvers uther nicht-bouris . . . thinks it speidfull, etc." (*Records*, i, 36). A meeting had to be held in a private house until a town-hall (*pretorium*) or tolbooth was erected.

public measures, has analogy in England where many towns were equipped with two councils.[1]

Another possible avenue to autonomy was opened in the fourteenth century. A practice was then in operation whereby burgh revenues were, in certain instances, farmed out, that is leased, to individuals for the payment of a definite yearly sum, the speculator, it may be assumed, making some profit out of the transaction. Thus in 1290 the Earl of Strathearn was, in this sense, the farmer of the revenues of Auchterarder.[2] In 1327 the revenues of Berwick were leased by two co-farmers (*confirmariorum*) and in 1330 by one of the partners.[3] There was an advantage to the exchequer in being assured a definite payment without the trouble and expense involved in direct collection. It was a simple step to allow the burgh itself to farm its revenues, it might be on a lease for a period of years, as in the case of Linlithgow, which paid the usual gressum or feudal charge on the renewal of the lease.[4] But already a permanent arrangement on this line had been reached in making the lease one of feu-farm, that is in perpetuity, for the payment of a yearly return (*reddendo*) covering all contributions. The earliest example is Aberdeen in 1319, the burgh showing the largest annual payment after Berwick and six times that of Edinburgh [5] which followed ten years later. For Aberdeen the grant in feu-farm (*ad feodofirmam*) is to the burgesses and community ; [6] for Edinburgh to the burgesses and their successors.[7] The idea of a burgh as a

---

[1] Tait, as cited, p. 321 ff. ; Mrs Green, *Town Life*, ii, p. 278, note 2, and p. 277. " In short every conceivable experiment in government was tried in one town [English] or another, or in the same town at different times, to the great confusion of systematic order. In one the original council of twelve or twenty-four might be maintained in its early representative character ; in another its constitution was gradually transformed."

[2] *Exch. Rolls*, i, 51.

[3] *Ibid.*, i, 63, 311. For other cases see p. lxxxvii. The fermes of Banff were in 1367 " let to Queen Margaret, in 1370 to John of Kylvynton, and for some years prior to 1500 to Alexander, Earl of Buchan " (*Annals of Banff*, New Spalding Club, i, 7).

[4] *Ibid.*, i, 273, 301.

[5] *Ibid.*, i, pp. lxxxvii-viii. That of Edinburgh was subsequently increased, but was still just under that of Inverness in 1375. Inference is dangerous.

[6] *A.P.S.*, i, 478.   [7] *Charters &c.*, Edinburgh (B. R. Socy.), No. iv.

corporate body, a *persona ficta* or legal entity, had not yet been formulated. Dundee comes into the feu-farm list by 1365, Inverness and Montrose ten years afterwards, and Perth in 1376.[1] In time the composition was extended to all royal burghs, which thus paid a lump sum as " firma " and issues of their courts,[2] the *reddendo* or money return in the cases above mentioned " exceeding that paid under the immediately preceding lease of the Chamberlain," where that is known.[3] Only the most valuable source of income, the " great customs " on staple goods, such as wool, hides, furs, etc., which furnished the exports, was retained in the hands of the king,[4] who of course ·could transfer this item to a third party.[5]

This arrangement was revolutionary for the burghs. It has been argued as not unreasonable that a grant of feu-farm carried with it by implication the right to choose magistrates, but this, unless expressly stated, has been questioned.[6] It would seem that the burgesses having to provide the " firma " should have some control over the management of their finances. No clauses of election, however, appear in burgh charters before 1469, when also an election Act was passed which was to be the parent of fresh complexity and prolonged municipal conflict.

[1] *Exch. Rolls*, ii, p. lxxxv.　[2] *Ibid.*, pp. 493, 540.　[3] *Ibid.*, p. lxxxv.
[4] *Exch. Rolls*, i, p. xcv.　*Cf.* pp. 594, 615, etc.　[5] See p. 18.
[6] *B.B.C.*, i, p. lxxxvi ; Stephenson, *Borough and Town*, p. 167.

H

CHAPTER VIII

MUNICIPAL CONSTITUTIONS. CRAFT GUILDS

The craftsmen and craft guilds. "Seals of Cause." Municipal representation. Election Act of 1469. "Setts" of burghs. Merchants *versus* craftsmen. Complexity in forms of election. "Outland" men as magistrates. Breaches in burghal qualifications. The Freedom of the Burgh.

It has been observed how in course of time a cleavage had appeared in the ranks of the burgesses. On the one side now were the merchants, who simply bought and sold, wholesale and retail, and were alone entitled to handle the export and import trade, which was the most profitable part of business. On the other were the craftsmen, small masters, who, with their journeymen and apprentices, made things or did handiwork of any sort—a household organisation, the master supplying workshop and tools [1]—in their early days making to order, but in time accumulating stocks of their products, which they offered for sale on their stalls in the market-place or their booths on the street.[2] They had to be their own salesmen, apparently so as to ensure individual responsibility for their work : an ordinance of the Convention of Burghs in 1529 laid down that " na marchand man within this realme be marchand till ony craftisman " under pain of forfeiting the goods.[3]

It has been already noted how practitioners in a craft, once they were of any number, would tend to draw together in common interests, such as the maintenance of a chaplainry

---

[1] *Records, Edinburgh*, i, 33.

[2] *Cf.* of a later date in England : " The essence of the new economic situation lay in the separation of the distributive from the productive function. The business faculty which was needed to keep the larger industries in touch with a distant market had been increasingly specialised by a distinct class of traders, whilst the master-craftsman had been left to confine his attention to the management of production " (*Industrial Organisation in the Sixteenth and Seventeenth Centuries*, George Unwin, p. 103).

[3] *R.C.B.*, s.d., p. 510. In Scotland a craftsman was a " tradesman " and the crafts were the " trades," whereas in England a tradesman was and is a retail dealer—baker, butcher, etc.—who in Scotland was and is a merchant.

in the church and charitable benefits for their fellow-members, and so form voluntary associations after the example of the merchant guilds. It happened that in England, during the latter half of the fourteenth century, legislation was found necessary to ensure the sound character of craft products, the elimination of " knavery " and " false workmanship," for which purpose persons of each craft were to be chosen to carry on a " search " for such lapses. We get " precisely similar Scotch legislation " [1] in 1424-5, probably, like other cases, an imitation due to James I, when, in prevention against fraud by " untrew men of the craftis," each craft was to have a wise man as deacon or " maister man " over the rest, who was to be elected by the members of the craft, with the advice of the officials of the town, and was to supervise and test all work. This measure provided a formal constitution for a craft guild, and proper authority to enforce regulations upon its members. It did not have a long run. The reason for this is obviously dissension over prices. Just over eighteen months later it is enacted that, while the deacons were to remain till next Parliament, their part was to be only that of ensuring that the workmen were skilled and their work satisfactory. The business of fixing cost of material, the wages of the workman, and the price of the article, hitherto, it is implied, done by the deacons, was now committed to the aldermen and council of each town, as was also the wages due to such artisans as masons and wrights, who did not produce articles for sale. This was an extension of the power which the municipalities already exercised in fixing the prices of food and liquors. Finally, in 1427, the original Act was annulled on the grounds that it had tended only to harm and cause general expense.[2] It was forbidden for the future to elect such deacons in any burgh. Those otherwise elected were not to exercise the functions of deacons beyond that,[3]

----

[1] Ashley, i, Pt. ii, 72.   [2] *commune dispendium.*

[3] Mr Renwick, however, takes *nec alias electi ulterius exerceant officia decanorum* to signify " that those already elected shall no longer exercise the functions of deacons." But the Act of the previous year suspended existing deacons at the meeting of the present Parliament. The intention would seem to be to provide for the future ; crafts would continue to appoint deacons, but these were not to have the powers conferred by the Act of 1425.

and were not to hold their accustomed assemblies, which were considered to savour of conspiracies.[1] Early in the year following this drastic enactment, came one ordaining that the council of every burgh was to choose a warden (the term used in English legislation) from each craft, who, with the assistance of impartial advisers, was to examine workmanship and fix a price on the finished article, with a penalty for those offending against the price set.

This problem of prices and wages was to be a battleground down the centuries, and was to surround the craft guilds with an atmosphere of hostility. There was no thought of leaving either to be settled by free bargaining between the parties concerned, except, by the Act of 1487, in the case of merchants from abroad, on whose goods no price was to be set " bot be bying and selling with thair auin consent." There was a tenderness for foreign merchants, since Scotland particularly needed imports. Apart from such necessity, it was the mediæval idea that trade and manufacture were a public service, carried on for the good of the community, and therefore should be subject to public control.[2] The buyer was entitled to a sound article ; the seller to a price which should maintain him in his station in life, the " just price." Economics was treated as a part of conduct. How far could one go in business without incurring the deadly sin of avarice ? Could one take advantage of another's necessity without being open to a charge of usury, a term which covered all forms of extortion ? Economic conditions generally were directed by ethical-religious conceptions. In conformity with such conceptions prices and wages ought to be fixed by a competent authority, whether the State, the municipality, or in landward sheriffdoms the barons, as specified in the Act of 1427.

[1] *que conspiraciones sapere presumuntur* (*A.P.S.*, ii, 14). Probably for the reason thus given in a different context : " People of the same trade seldom meet together even for merriment and diversion, but the conversation ends in a conspiracy against the public or some contrivance to raise prices " (*Wealth of Nations*, Adam Smith, ch. x, part ii).

[2] *Cf. Town Life in the Fifteenth Century*, Mrs Green, ii, 135. " John II of France, in his famous ordinance of 1335, proclaimed in 227 articles a maximum tariff for merchants' goods and the wages of the workmen. The Statute of Labourers in England in 1349 had similar objects " (*Guilds in the Middle Ages*, Georges Renard, translation, p. 49).

On these lines conflict continued between the crafts and the legislature as representing the rest of the community, but particularly the hostile merchant class. It must be kept in mind that the crafts were monopolist [1] and that their vested interests did not necessarily coincide with general ideas about a "just price" and adequate wages. On the other hand recurrent debasement of the coinage was bound to raise prices, as it did in England,[2] where, too, the novel idea of a competitive price was coming into conflict with that of a price established by custom.[3]

The crafts, having failed to retain their brief patronage by Parliament, turned to another authority in the ruling body in the burghs, from which each could secure a "seal of cause" (sigillum ad causas), which was treated as a charter of incorporation. This was also an English practice.[4] Thus the eighteenth-century historian of Edinburgh records that "The Corporation of Cordiners or Cordwainers [shoemakers] . . . were at first erected into a Fraternity by a Charter from the Town Council of Edinburgh . . . in the year 1449 on a religious account," each member contributing to the support of an altar in St Giles,[5] "And by a second Seal of Cause . . . anno 1479, was granted to certain Masters and Headsmen of the trade, a right to search and inspect the several sorts of work brought to the market by shoemakers,"[6] So, too, the Skinners provided an altar in St Giles in January 1450-1, but had no seal of cause till 1474.[7] It is commonly claimed

---

[1] Les hommes du moyen âge ne connaissaient le travail industriel que sous le forme d'un privilège collectif, constituant un monopole en faveur du corps qui en était investi. "The men of the Middle Age knew manufacturing only in the form of a collective privilege, constituting a monopoly in favour of the body so invested." (Cited in The Mediæval Mind, H. O. Taylor, i, 340, from A. Luchaire, Manuel des institutions françaises, p. 360).

[2] Cunningham, English Industry and Commerce, i, 536, 542-3.

[3] Ibid., i, 467.

[4] Ashley, as cited, i, Pt. ii, 159. So called because usually authenticated by the burgh seal.

[5] "A saint and a chapel were the requisite grounds (le fonds nécessaire) of every fraternity" (Levasseur, as cited, i, 577. Cf. ii, 132).

[6] Maitland, Hist. of Edinburgh (1753), p. 305.

[7] Records, i, 9, 28-30. For a similar sequence in France see Levasseur, ii, 573.

that the merit of the guilds was in securing good workmanship. But, as we see, whatever credit there is on this score, must be at least shared with the authorities, national and municipal. Left to themselves guilds could generate " untrew men," deception and fraud. The business morality of the early time, contrary to a popular superstition, was not superior to that of to-day.[1] In January 1475-6 the Edinburgh weavers " petitioned the Common Council to erect them into a Society, which request was readily granted," [2] the Council confirming the rules for the craft submitted to them, providing, among other things, that each master craftsman should be a burgess and possess proper tools, and fixing the term of apprenticeship as not less than five years. These were precautions against inferior workmanship.[3] The other crafts followed suit, and the same procedure was adopted in the other burghs. The Hammermen of Aberdeen had their first seal of cause in 1519, the Bakers one in 1534.[4] In some cases however, incorporation by seal of cause might be late. At Renfrew, for example, the only incorporated trade was the tailors, and its seal of cause was granted by magistrates and council in 1687, being partly renewed in 1783.[5] In this way the crafts were properly organised with their deacons, rules of admission, and regulations in practice, but subject to municipal authority. They were then incorporations, and the practice of crafts could be confined to the members of such. The equivalent in the case of burghs of barony or regality was a " letter of license " from the superior or the

---

[1] See Ashley, i, Pt. ii, 73. *Cf. Piers Plowman* (text, 1377), *Passus* v Avarice, *e.g.* (spelling modernised) " Wickedly to weigh was my first lesson." *Cf.* also *The Devillis Inquest* in Poems of William Dunbar. In England in the fifteenth century " the standard of commercial morality was very low " (*Social England in the Fifteenth Century*, A. Abram, p. 207). Examples are given, pp. 207-8. For France see *Life in Mediæval France*, Joan Evans, p. 72. In France as in Scotland in order to secure satisfactory workmanship " the same prohibitions had to be repeated because artisans continually (*sans cesse*) infringed them " (Levasseur, as cited, i, 325). On such " fraudes et abus " see *ibid.*, ii, 93.

[2] Maitland, p. 307.

[3] *Edinburgh Guilds and Crafts*, Sir James Marwick, p. 48 ; *Records*, i, 33.

[4] *Merchant and Craft Guilds*, Ebenezer Bain, pp. 198, 216: The seals of cause issued in Aberdeen are given under the respective crafts.

[5] *Local Reports*, ii, 361.

magistrates, which, as in that of Canongate, might be confirmed by the Crown.[1]

Even on such terms it was not a case of co-operating happily ever afterwards. In 1493 Parliament again pronounced the activities of deacons of crafts " richt dangerous " and oppressive, and suspended them for a year.[2] They had made a rule that craftsmen like masons and wrights should be paid for holy days, on which work was not done[3]—in modern terms " holidays with pay "—and that a man could leave a job, that is go on strike—presumably if his terms were not agreed to—whereupon no other would dare to finish it. Those making or observing such statutes were to be subject to punishment by the royal courts. There followed next year and on into the middle of the sixteenth century Acts dealing with the standard evils of (alleged) defective workmanship and rising prices, which in 1551-2 are described as doubled and tripled by many crafts. At this stage blame is laid upon the provosts and bailies of the burghs who had the oversight of the deacons but took no action. An Act of 1540-1 provided for breaking a strike by allowing the introduction of workmen from elsewhere to complete an unfinished job, which was a grave infraction of local privilege.[4]

The long conflict reached a climax in 1555 when a drastic Act was passed, the preamble of which stressed the public danger and local commotions due to the practice of crafts making leagues and bands between themselves and between burgh and burgh. Accordingly the choosing of deacons, meetings of the crafts and the making of laws for the crafts were forbidden. They were to be subject to the magistrates and council of the burgh, who were to appoint " visitoures " to test the quality of work. No craftsman for the future was

---

[1] *Lib. S. Crucis*, pp. 290-2, 293-4 ; *Reg. Sec. Sig.*, ii, No. 3948.

[2] There was similar trouble in England as expressed by an Act of 1503-4 directed against the " wardens and people of gilds " making ordinances for the crafts in prices and other things " to the common hurt and damage of the people " (Ashley, *Economic History*, ii, Pt. ii, 159-60).

[3] The number of " holy days " reduced the total earnings of workers. The Church prescribed about fifty saints' days besides Sundays.

[4] For a case under this Act involving the employment of " unfree " masons and wrights where the " free " burgess craftsmen would not get their price, see *Records, Edinburgh*, 1577, p. 58.

to hold office in the burgh, except for two chosen yearly to sit upon the council. This would seem to spell the doom of all craft organisation, but that, as a legal commentator points out, " the Act was never in observance." [1] It was nullified in fact by what may be called the unconstitutional use of the dispensing power under the Great Seal in the very next year and subsequently in 1565 and 1581,[2] whereby, too, all the pre-existing privileges granted to the crafts were ratified. Moreover the dispensation of March 1564-5 declared that the Act had been passed without any pressing reason therefor (*absque urgente causa*) and with no observable advantage, and the last of the series professed to aim at obviating the dissensions and public hatreds between merchants and craftsmen. It seems likely that on each occasion the concession had a political motive in the wish to secure the support of the now numerous and therefore powerful bodies of craftsmen.

Possibly, however, the Queen Regent in her dispensation may not have been immune to the fact that in January 1555-6 commissioners of the burghs determined to collect for her a gift (" propine ") of money on condition she would secure the discharge of certain restrictions on their trade, the magistrates and council of Edinburgh adding a request to dispense with the recent Act, so that " the craftsmen," as they claimed, " may brouke (enjoy) thair auld privilege," otherwise, said the crafts, " thai wald tak the addres that thai mycht get for tham selffis," whatever this vague threat might imply.[3]

That the craftsmen were a force to be reckoned with is suggested by the comment of James VI in his *Basilicon Doron*, of the late sixteenth century, where he wrote : " The craftesmen thinke we should be content with their worke, howe bad and deare soever it be, and if they in any thing be controlled, up goeth the blew-blanket," that is the flag of the trades preluding a demonstration in force, such as indeed is

---

[1] Sir George Mackenzie, *Observations on the Acts of Parliament*, p. 157.

[2] *R.M.S.*, s.d., Nos. 1054 ; 1583 ; 233. Mackenzie raises the point whether an Act of the Estates could be so discharged without their consent, replying " that matters of Government doe not concern them directly " but are " the interest of the King " (*Observations*, as cited).

[3] *Records, Edinburgh*, ii (1528-57), 235-6. For the communication of the dispensations to Perth see *The Burgh Laws of Dundee*, A. J. Warden, p. 236.

suggested in the preamble to the Act of 1555. In the King's judgment, however, the merchants were no better : " The merchants," he writes, " think the whole common-weale ordayned for making them up, and accounting it their lawfull game and trade to enriche themselves upon the losse of all the rest of the people. . . . They buy for us the worst wares and sell them at the dearest prices." Anyhow, the crafts had at last triumphed in this phase of the conflict, " and from this period they may be held as having assumed that form in which they have ever since remained." [1]

In Edinburgh—and it would therefore probably apply to other burghs—it was recognised that " everie industrie is nocht of lyke valour and substance," and they were therefore graded by the amount payable on entering apprenticeship and on its completion. The result is as follows :—

1. Apprentice to merchants, 30s. and £5.
2. Apprentice to a skinner, surgeon, goldsmith, flesher, shoemaker, tailor, baker, hammerman, 20s. and £5.
3. To mason or wright, 13s. 4d. and £3, 6s. 8d.
4. To a weaver, fuller, bonnet-maker, furrier, 10s. and £2, 10s.

Such was considered the relative importance of the merchants and fourteen trades as expressed in the royal Decreet-Arbitral of 1583.[2]

The crafts, growing in numbers and having been by their " seals of cause " made subordinate to the municipal authorities, were inevitably led to seek adequate representation in the magistracy and council. The constitution of the burgh became the field of battle between merchants and craftsmen, in which the merchants succeeded in acquiring a predominance in the functions of government. Craftsmen no doubt contributed to the " multitud and clamor of commonis sympil personis " in the " gret truble and contensione " that had come to characterise the yearly election of burgh officials, and resulted in the Act of 1469, which eliminated popular control from local elections and was to run a troubled course until the Municipal Reform Acts of 1833. It laid down that officials and council should not continue in office for longer

[1] *Report*, 1835, p. 81.   [2] *Extracts, Records*, v (1573-89), 273.

than a year, that the old council should choose the new,[1] which was to be of a number corresponding to the size of the town, that the new council and that of the year before should choose all the officers of the town, and that a representative of each of the crafts should have a vote in the election of these officers. An Act of five years later added the rider that four members of the council of the year before should be chosen to sit upon the new council "and have power withe thame to do justice."

Observance of these Acts came but slowly and disjointedly, never universally or wholly in their simplicity, and more in the spirit of their exclusiveness than in the letter of their procedure. Indeed their application was immediately confused by the practice, which also began in 1469, of inserting in charters, new or regranted, actual clauses of election, which in most cases prescribe a more popular mode of conducting the business.[2] Add to this a local preference for their old fashion of election, and confusion and conflict became inevitable. An additional Act of 1503 had to insist that all having jurisdiction within a burgh should be changed yearly, and in 1552 the Convention of Burghs could regretfully note the great variance in divers burghs in the manner of choosing their officials, adding the instruction to take as an example the method of Edinburgh,[3] which, however, thirty years later was itself to be reconstituted by a royal decreet-arbitral as the result of a violent election controversy between merchants and craftsmen.[4]

The other burghs continued, in Mr Podsnap's words, to " do *as* they do." At Peebles in 1561 the council was elected by " the baillies and haill communite," as, we may conclude,

[1] A parallel practice had already developed in the Belgian towns in the thirteenth century (Pirenne, *Hist. de Belgique* (1902), i, 271). At Montpellier by Statute of 1205 the new councillors were to be elected annually by the old council with the addition of seven representatives from the seven crafts (P. Viollet, *Les communes françaises*, p. 87).

[2] " There is no instance of a Clause of Election being introduced into any charter before 1469, and even after that period it appears that some Charters do, and others do not contain Clauses of Election, though granted in favour of the same Burgh " (*Report*, 1793, p. 4. *Cf.* pp. 29-37). Of course there had long been elections, but not by charter warrant.

[3] *Rec. Conv.*, i, 3.

[4] *Records*, iv (1573-89), 250-5, 264 ; Marwick, *Edinb. Guilds and Crafts*, pp. 126-7.

the custom was, and not till 1578 did the burgh take its first step towards observance of the statute by restricting its officials to one year " conforme to the burro lawis and actis of parliament " ;[1] a fuller conformity with the Acts of Parliament came in the course of subsequent years.[2]

The " differences and debates," legal actions and popular tumults, which could follow on the varying and uncertain powers of election led burghs to secure an authoritative decision on their " sett " or constitution, some by submission to an external arbiter, others from the Convention of Burghs.[3] The Convention worked for uniformity in the observance of the Acts of Parliament and their own Acts in agreement therewith.[4] But the report of their commissioners of 1708 on the prevailing setts of the royal burghs [5] shows anomalies still flourishing. At Cupar the practice was that the magistrates could not continue for more than two successive years. At Inverkeithing, when election was made, those of the old council " who are desirous of ane ease " gave up office and the rest chose " as many new councillors in their room to keep up the number." Selkirk, already noted for its avoidance of a provost, had its own manner of election— the council and magistrates were not " chosen yearly but continued, and as they decrease in their substance are turned out from being councillers and always these of the greatest substance brought in." Wealth was the qualification and there was no time limit for office, only a limit of means. Aberdeen was one of the places in which the Act of 1469 had not taken effect, and the old fashion of electing the magistrates [6] had continued for more than 120 years.[7] The result was what is described in the judgment of the Convention

---

[1] *Charters &c. and Records, Peebles,* pp. 274, 355.

[2] Renwick, *Extracts, Records of Peebles,* 1652-1714, p. xvii.

[3] Pagan, *Convention of Royal Burghs,* pp. 79-105 ; *Report,* 1793, p. 15.

[4] Pagan, p. 75.

[5] In *Miscellany of Scot. Burgh Recs. Socy.,* pp. 161-295.   [6] See p. 131.

[7] For following details, except where otherwise stated, see *Report of Committee of House of Commons,* 1793, pp. 6-12. Fortrose has its own simple way, as on 8th June, 1654 : " In ane unanimous meeting of the inhabitants they made choice of the persons undernamit to be councillors in the said toune, giving them full power to nominate and elect Magistrates for ruling of the said toune." *Trans. Inverness Scientific Socy. and Field Clmb,* vol. ix, p. 232.

(1592) as "intestein varience . . . within the bowellis of the said burgh."[1] It had come to a head in 1590 when the "haill communitie, burgessis and craftismen" complained to the Privy Council against the "unlawful usurpation" of the magistracy of the burgh by "the race of Menzeissis" their friends and allies, for the past eighty years.[2] More adequately the complainers are described in their "protestation" to the Convention as twenty-one persons named, all burgesses, councillors, deacons, and craftsmen "in name and behalff of the remanent afflictit memberis of the pure common welthe of this burgh."[3] The officials indicted attributed such opposition to "persouns provokit to bauld raschnes, namelye to the rascall multitude" seeking change and innovation, and point out that there is no uniformity among the burghs in the choosing of their officers.[4] All very dignified but off the mark. In the same year an action was raised in the Court of Session on the ground that the Magistrates and Council had, without lawful election, continued to sit for thirty years, son succeeding father. A writ of 1591 under the Privy Seal admits the continuance of the same council for forty or fifty years, according to the custom of the burgh for 100 years before,[5] a member being removable only for fault or crime, but to avoid "annual disorder" acquiesces in the practice, dispensing with the provision for annual election in the Act of 1469. Contrariwise, the decision of the Court of Session in 1592 was "that in all time coming the election should be in terms of the Acts of Parliament."[6]

This result was not satisfactory to the burgesses, who apparently saw no escape from abuse in what would simply be a form for prolonging the same conditions, and dissatisfaction was shown by assembly in arms and the election of a rival council. Recourse was then had to a court of arbitration presided over by the King, which declared both elections void and decreed that for the future the Acts of Parliament were to be "precisely observed," but providing for a fuller share by the craftsmen in the election of magistrates.[7]

[1] Recs. of Convention, i, 384.   [2] Reg. Pr. Co., iv, 533.
[3] R.C.B., i, 313.   [4] Ibid., pp. 324, 325.
[5] Report, 1793, p. 7.   [6] Ibid., p. 9.
[7] Report, 1793, p. 9.   Cf. "Philopoliteius," as cited, pp. 226-8.

That the strictly legal provisions as to election could not meet the case of monopoly of office is shown by the plea of certain merchants and inhabitants of Cupar (Fife) to the Privy Council in 1567 to the effect that the old council having always power to elect the new " they cheis men of thair factioun, and swa haldis the publict offices and counsale amangis a certane of particular men fra hand to hand," thereby secluding from office the other burgesses and inhabitants of the burgh " being nevirtheles the mair and bettir part thairof." [1] The matter was settled by an agreed-upon election for the present term with the significant proviso that " Johnne Lindsay, allegit to be ane craftisman of the saidlar craft, befoir he be admittit on the said counsale, renunce his craft and be admittit gild bruther ; and that the ancient custom observit of befoir in that behalf be alwayis inviolabillie kept heireftir." [2] As to the Acts complained of, it is the judgment of the Committee of 1793 that by these " a principle of self-election appears to have been introduced," which, to a greater or less degree, pervaded the setts of all the burghs,[3] " a leading principle," repeats the Commission of 1835, which " with scarcely an exception " excluded " any near approach to popular suffrage." [4]

The working of these Acts of election might rouse, we see, resentment in the community generally, but the terms of settlement in the protest from Cupar expose a special disability on the part of craftsmen. By the Act of 1503 followed by that of 1535 none might " have jurisdiction within burgh " but such as " use merchandice " there. The merchant class was thus confirmed in its hold upon local administration. There was, however, a way round this restriction, as shown in the Cupar settlement : a craftsman might be admitted to office provided he renounced his craft ; in Edinburgh, however, also on condition that he should not return to it thereafter without leave of the magistrates and council.[5] This discrimination is found elsewhere. The free city of Lübeck

[1] *Reg. P. C.*, i, pp. 582-3   [2] *Ibid.*, p. 584.   [3] *Report*, p. 13.
[4] *Ibid.*, p. 27. Or, as it was put in a Court of Session case of 1749, " an aristocratical form of election being introduced in place of the democratical " (Morison, *Decisions &c.*, p. 1842).
[5] *Records*, 1573-89, p. 266.

had a rule excluding craftsmen from the council. Hamburg, though without such a rule, observed it in practice. A similar spirit of exclusiveness developed in French towns.[1] Only members of the merchant class would be accepted in the Convention of Royal Burghs, and the Convention applied the same restriction to burgh representatives in Parliament, with a fine for any breach of these rules.[2] In 1581 Dundee backed a plea for precedence with the boast that the burgh was " governit be the merchandis, excluding the craftismen from all office of governament within the samyn," the implication being that its rival Perth, and presumably some other burghs, were not in this noble position.[3] Edinburgh, at this stage, drew its own line, rejecting as craft representatives on the council bakers, fleshers, and maltsters, who, being occupied with victuals, might work and vote in their business interest, also shoemakers and dyers or any others of " rude occupatioun." [4] No such discrimination finds place in the new constitution of the burgh in 1583.[5] According to a sett given to Inverness in 1676 the trades were excluded from the town council, but in 1722, after an application for redress, they were given three members, a concession opposed by the Convention as being, for one thing, an encroachment on the rights of the guildry.[6]

No such delicacy of feeling would seem to have existed at Haddington. At a meeting in 1574 the Convention of Royal Burghs was shocked to find that one having a commission to attend was a mere shoemaker or leather worker (" cordiner "), John Douglas, " alledgit proveist of Hadingtoun." A crafts-man member had never been known before nor ought to be, and Douglas was therefore ordered " to remove himself fra thair society," a Haddington bailie was chosen in his place, and the town warned that a repetition of the offence would bring a fine of £100.[7] In the following year the Privy Council received a complaint by the council, merchants, and burgesses of that town. The provost, it was explained, was a craftsman

[1] *Les communes françaises*, Paul Viollet, pp. 101-2, 103.

[2] Pagan, as cited, pp. 32-33 ; Mackie and Pryde, *The Estate of the Burgesses in the Scots Parliament*, p. 39. [3] *A.P.S.*, iii, 232.

[4] *Records* (1569), iii, 263-4. [5] See p. 153.

[6] *S.H.R.*, xiii, 268 ; *R.C.B.*, v, 312, 319-20. [7] *R.C.B.*, i, 31.

who had persuaded all the deacons of trades to support him, these being the majority of the council. On any legal issues involved in this state of affairs nothing is said. The provost had gone on to appoint deacons to the shoemaker (" cordinar ") and weaver (" wobstar ") crafts, neither of which had more than two members or ever had a deacon, solely for the purpose of continuing himself, by their vote, as provost in time to come and securing the appointment of others as bailies, etc. Apparently craftsmen were ready to follow and even better the example of merchants in engrossing administrative functions. The Privy Council, in view of the few members of the crafts in question, " discharged " the present deacons and any others set in their places.[1] By countering these tactics, however, the Privy Council did not secure a cessation of " debates . . . betwixt the counsell and craftsmen " and in 1658 a new sett for the burgh was contrived by accepting the decision of the Convention of Burghs in 1655, giving a council of sixteen merchants and nine " tradsmen," composed of seven deacons, one bailie, and one councillor. There is a complicated procedure for the choice of magistrates and new members, in which the old council plays a determining part,[2] in recognition of the Act of 1469.

In the setts of the burghs, however, the number and powers of the craftsmen vary radically. From the report on the enquiry set on foot in 1708 [3] it appears that on the Glasgow council there were then 13 members of merchant rank with 12 of the trades. Dunfermline had 9 merchants and 7 craftsmen, but the officials were chosen from the merchants. Of 17 councillors at Crail 6 were tradesmen, but Dysart returned a council of 21 consisting, apparently without discrimination, of " maltmen, merchants, seamen, and tradesmen."

The general attitude of conservatism and the force of custom find illustration in what happened in the case of Stirling. In the spring of 1615 the deacons and the whole body of craftsmen made a supplication to the King in respect of his recent direction (1610) that all burghs should elect their magistrates from burgesses who were at once merchants

[1] *R.P.C.*, ii (1569-78), 472.

[2] *R.C.B.*, iii, 412 ; *Miscellany, Burgh Records Socy.*, p. 175.

[3] See p. 123. Some returns had not come in by 1711,

and indwellers, and choose their council in the manner prescribed by the Act of Parliament. So much for the degree of adherence given to long-existing legislation under both heads ! The craftsmen claim that unquietness would arise from such a change in any " lovabill (praiseworthy) auld governament " of a burgh, and therefore beg the King to dispense with the precise observance of the laws in question, lest he lose the affection of the burghs by " imbracing ony novatioun and change of thair auld and wounted formes of governament," which they had peacefully enjoyed for so long a time. In particular they ask that they may have the conditions restored to what they had been four years earlier, namely that they may have all their deacons on the council and one of their number a bailie.[1]

This supplication would seem to have been ineffective, but equally so the King's direction, since in 1620 the burgh was fined £100 by the Convention for having chosen a crafts-man as bailie. Further, the Convention ordained a sett for Stirling, the council to consist of twenty-one persons, of whom the seven magistrates must be merchants and guild-brethren, while the rest were to be seven other merchants and seven deacons of crafts. The new and the old council together were to choose the magistrates. This was in conformity with the royal instruction, and so the craftsmen lost their bailie. The Convention declared, however, that this order was only for the peace of the particular burgh and not a law for other burghs, and was without prejudice to any Act of Parliament to the contrary, as to which the burghs forming the Con-vention " dispenssis for thair pairt." [2] The claim to be able to dispense with any obstruction in an Act of Parliament is an invasion of what was held to be a royal prerogative. And many as were the cases in which, during the seventeenth and eighteenth centuries, the Convention amended the sett of a burgh or substituted a new one,[3] when at last the issue was raised in the law courts, a case arising in 1778 with respect to Edinburgh town council brought from the Court of Session the judgment that " the Convention had no powers to alter

---

[1] *Records*, i (1519-1666), 138-9.
[2] *R.C.B.*, iii (1615-76), 110-1.
[3] See Miscellany, *Burgh Records Socy.*, pp. lxxii, lxxv.

the set of the burgh." [1] They had in fact no more standing than that pertaining to any outside arbitrator accepted by the parties in dispute, who might just as lawfully be a nobleman.[2]

In these contentions one is not bound to accept literally the descriptions of the rival parties by each other, or the picture on record of the particular circumstances of the dispute. It may be that for many years there had been in Dundee " ane christeane harmony, love and societie inter- tenyit amangis the haill inhabitantis " till shortly before 1605 a few persons " of ambitious and restles humouris and dispositionis " disturbed the halcyon days of the burgh. The leader of this faction was " Mr Robert Howie, thair pastour," who from the pulpit charged the provost with violating the sett of the burgh, and even committed himself to what must have sounded a revolting proposition, that " it wes mair aggrieable with reason that ane who had come in at the toun end with a creill on his back a year syne [since] should be provost nor any gentleman." Howie was banished from Dundee for life.[3] But it is possible to see the root of the trouble in a dispute over the provostship.

The next year saw a different sort of election trouble in Glasgow. The superiority of that episcopal burgh of regality after the Reformation passed to the Duke of Lennox, which meant his control of its government. Now the provost, Sir George Elphinstone of Blythswood, and the council secured from the King and the Duke full liberty of election of their magistrates, just as in any other burgh. This concession was distasteful to Sir Matthew Minto and his friends, who, under Lennox, had had the town offices at their disposal, and who now managed to persuade the craftsmen, many in number " and for the maist pairt rude and ignorant men," that the new arrangement would be to their disadvantage. The outcome was a scuffle in the streets between the two knights, their servants and partisans, with some bloodshed, followed by investigation by the Privy Council. Elphinstone

---

[1] Morison, *Decisions of the Court of Session*, p. 1863 ; *Miscellany*, as cited, p. lxxix.

[2] *Miscellany*, p. lxxi. On the doubtful judgments exercised by the Convention see further here pp. 78, 171, 179.

[3] *R.P.C.*, vii, 94-7.

I

and Minto were warded in different towns and had to find heavy securities to keep the peace.[1] By the close of the century, however, Glasgow was winning commendation for the " publick spiritidness " of its people.[2]

Canongate, another burgh of regality, with an ecclesiastical superior in the Abbot of Holyrood, had a different history. The superior had conceded to the burgesses the right to elect their own magistrates and council, and this privilege was continued after the Reformation by the lay lords of the Abbey lands. Then in 1612 the deacons of seven crafts in the burgh complained to the Privy Council of " abuse and corruption " in the elections, in which the Act of 1469 was not observed, so that for twelve years nine maltmen had engrossed " the absolute government of the burgh." A new election was ordered and observance of the Act in future.[3] Apparently the Act applied to all burghs in which there were elections, whatever the standing of the burgh.

Variety and individuality, indeed, are the dominant notes of burghal administration. To the Committee of 1793 it did not appear " that any of the setts, except Aberdeen, and perhaps Cupar, and one or two more, are according to the Acts of Parliament mentioned in the papers produced ; neither do they appear to be in conformity with the Charters

---

[1] *R.P.C.*, vii, 241-2, 247.

[2] " Philopoliteius," p. 178. In 1611 Glasgow was made a royal burgh without prejudice to the existing right of the Archbishop to elect magistrates and officers (*Charters and Docts.*, ii, 282-3). On subsequent provisions see Murray, as cited, i, 170 ff.

[3] *R.C.P.*, ix, pp. 462-3. In 1676 Arbroath raised an action in the supreme court for a declaration that the Earl of Panmure as lord of the regality was no longer entitled to nominate a bailie, Arbroath having been made a royal burgh in 1599 with power to elect its magistrates (*R.M.S.*, s.d., No. 977, but *cf.* s.d., 1642, No. 1255) and therefore now holding of the king not of the lord of the regality. Against this it was pleaded that the grant of appointment preceded the erection to royalty, which could not " evacuate the same." The decision was in favour of the Earl (Stair, *Decisions &c.*, ii, 448-9). Paisley was made a burgh of barony in 1488, the abbot to have the power of electing all officials and removing or changing them at his pleasure without any other election by the burgesses or the community (*Reg. Passelet*, pp. 263-4 ; confirmation in the same terms, pp. 269-70). In 1665 the burgh secured the abrogation of the rights of superiority continued by the lords of erection in succession to the abbots (*Chart. and Docts., Paisley*, W. M. Metcalfe, No. 42).

which contain clauses of election ; and it is evident, that neither in the Acts of Parliament nor in the Charters is there any foundation or authority for many of the local usages that have been introduced respecting the modes of election in particular Burghs." [1] Analysis of the systems of election in sixty burghs showed that in thirteen of these " the majority of the council either may or must be continued without change or re-election " ; that in one case, Kinghorn, " one half of the Council are continued without election, and that there is no restriction against re-electing the majority of the remainder " ; that in two burghs " one less than half of the Council is continued, and that with that number a majority of the Council may be re-elected " ; that in thirty-four " The Council or a part of the Council, elect the majority of the new Council, without there being any restrictions in the Sett against their re-electing a majority of themselves " ; and that in four burghs " the old council elect the new but a majority of the Counsellors for the ensuing year must be different persons." At Aberdeen, however, as one of the last group, the apparent righteousness had been compounded by the contrivance that " the persons who go out of the Council one year, may be re-elected at the distance of a year, by the persons they themselves had elected for that year." [2] This method of continuing " ane certane number of persones " in office at Aberdeen, *alteriis termis et vicibus*, was an old custom even in 1592 when it figured in a complaint to the Convention.[3] The picture given in the report of 1793 is in essence repeated by the Commissioners of 1835, who write that " from local influences, which it would be vain to attempt to trace, the constitutions of burghs royal, or their setts, as technically denominated, came to exhibit an endless variety in their details, although agreeing, with scarcely any exception, in their leading principle of what has been usually termed self-election, to the exclusion of any near approach to popular suffrage." [4] Modern investigators have expressed conclusions

---

[1] *Report*, 1793, p. 15.　　　[2] *Report*, 1793, p. 13.
[3] *Recs. Conv. of Burghs*, i, 384-5.
[4] *Report*, 1835, pp. 26-7 ; " In England each town council had a history of its own as regards the principle of self-election " (Gross, *Gild Merchant*, p. 200).

in the language of this report.[1] Strange as this medley may seem, it was not a condition peculiar to Scotland. For different reasons a similar confusion prevailed also in England, where, it has been said, "nothing is more surprising than the variety and intricacy of political systems with which the mediæval burghers were familiar," adding a note on "the complexity and apparently inexhaustible confusion of their methods." "Every borough," it is pointed out, "had its own fashion of choosing its mayor."[2] In England, indeed, conditions were probably more involved than in Scotland,[3] where operated a steady drag towards two basic principles, that of election of the new by the old council and that of limiting craft representation along with the exclusion of craftsmen from the magistracy.

III

The election Act of 1535 disclosed a fundamental abuse, already hinted at by implication in that of 1503, when it forbade the choosing of "outlandis" men to be magistrates, these outsiders, it is affirmed in the Act, being concerned with their own advantage and profit, such as could be served in dealing with the common good. Rightly, as expressed in the earlier Act, none but resident merchants should be eligible for office. This qualification was now being disregarded, so that an Act of 1609 had to repeat that no man was to be capable of being provost or any other magistrate except merchants and actual traffickers living in the burgh.[4] But, on the one side, the attraction of securing a neighbouring nobleman as provost, whether to assist or dignify the burgh, and, on the other, the openings for personal advantage in

[1] Cf. Marwick, Miscellany, as cited, p. lxvii : " endless variety beyond the recognition of the principle of self election established by the Act of 1469."

[2] Town Life in the Fifteenth Century, Mrs J. R. Green, ii, p. 274.

[3] " In Scotland there was considerable national legislation concerning burghs in general, and hence more uniformity of constitution than in England " (Gross, i, 200).

[4] Court of Session conclusion in 1736 : " The acts of Parliament providing, that officers in burghs shall be traffickers, concern only the office bearers not the counsellors " (Morison, Decisions &c., p. 1840).

having a share in the administration of burgh property, overrode Acts of Parliament, and this new element in the burgh life must henceforward be taken into account.

It was thus in defiance both of law and precedent that Lord Ruthven in 1559 could be provost of Perth.[1] His grandson, the second Earl of Gowrie, filled the same office at the time of the notorious affair of 1600. In that year the town was fined by the Convention for acknowledging as its provost Lord Scone, " he being ane noble man and not ane merchand trafficquer of the said burgh," [2] and three years later fined again more heavily for the same offence.[3]

But there was no stopping the practice. In addition to other possibilities there was also that of being chosen a commissioner to represent the burgh in Parliament, and political support by the burghs was on occasion to be desired. Politics complicated the legal issue. So much is indicated by an English agent writing of Scotland in 1580 when he says " the boroughs and burgess towns are wholly at the devotion of some nobleman or other (very few excepted), as Cupar in Fife at the Earl of Rothes' command, St Johnstones at the Earl of Montrose's, Dundee at the Earl of Crawford's ; the northern towns all at the Earl of Huntly's, etc., whereby they have both their own and the commons' voices in Parliament, and nothing can pass that may prejudice the state of the nobility or enlarge the Prince's." [4] In the years following the Reformation the Privy Council endeavoured to enforce the Acts about magistrates being resident traders, but overlooked cases where the religious advantage was the other way. In 1590 the Convention protested in vain against Royal letters ordering the election of " lordis, erlis, barrounis, and utheris gentilmen " as magistrates of divers burghs.[5] Charles II on the contrary sought in 1674 to enforce the residence qualification upon commissioners of burghs in order to exclude

---

[1] Knox, *History of the Reformation.*

[2] *R.C.B.*, ii, 411.

[3] *Miscellany*, as cited, p. 175. But the Court of Session found in 1749 " that it is not necessary the provost, or any of the counsellors, should be resident burgesses " (Morison, *Decisions &c.*, p. 1848, *cf.* p. 1857).

[4] *State of the Scottish Commonwealth* in *Calendar of Scottish Papers*, v, No. 638, p. 564.

[5] *R.C.B.*, i, 340 ; Rait's *Parliament*, etc., p. 302.

country gentlemen who had shown themselves "factious." [1]
His successor, "because the burrowes were the brazen wall
the Papists found hardest," [2] took the opposite line of having
the trafficking and residential qualification removed in order
" to make way to the gentlemen and others now the King's
magistrats," [3] that is the royal nominees. James VII, however,
did not last long enough to benefit by such manipulation.
Edinburgh, generally regarded as the model for other burghs,
had shown a liking for a Preston of Craigmillar as its provost,
and by 1672 had been " govern'd most tyrannically " for
ten years by Sir Andrew Ramsay of Abbotshall,[4] who was
finally ousted as the result of a riotous protest by " the citizens
weary of this yoke." By the next century such an outside
appointment had come to be accepted, the constitution of
Burntisland, as returned, in 1709, actually contemplating the
possibility of the provost being a nobleman, in which case
" he is supernumary of the sett." [5]

By such accession of men not answering to the old
qualifications of a burgess the strictly urban idea of a burgh
was being weakened, but still more by the practice of burgesses
taking up occupation and residence outside the burgh, thereby
adding a class of " outland burgesses." This was another
breach in the burghal barrier. In the beginning a burgess
had to be the resident holder of a burgage tenement as property
within the burgh. Then with the development of self-government and the rise of the craftsmen as a separate class, this
ceased to be the sole qualification. Membership of an
incorporated craft became a title to " burgesry," and the
fees for the privilege an important part of the burgh income.
This in time virtually came to acquisition by purchase. Indeed
in 1587 there is an Act forbidding the sale of the freedom and
privilege of one burgh to another without consent of the
King and the Estates in Parliament. As already noticed, a
burgess was a freeman only of his own burgh ; for other

---

[1] Mackenzie, *Memoirs*, etc., p. 274. "The publick interest of the
Burghs Royal had been prejudg'd, by their choosing gentlemen or noblemen's servants to represent their burghs."

[2] Fountainhall, *Historical Notices*, ii, 727.   [3] *Ibid.*, p. 806.

[4] Sir George Mackenzie, *Memoirs*, etc. (1821), p. 247 ; *R.P.C.*, 3rd
series, iii, 605. Sir George offers evidence against there having been a
tumult.   [5] *Miscellany*, as cited, p. 192.

burghs he was unfree. Thus in 1628 the Burgh Court of Banff took action against " Archibald Nobill, merchant, burgess of Edinburgh, for keeping an open booth, not being a burgess of Banff." He was ordained to pay £20 if he did so in future.[1] But a non-resident burgess was almost a contradiction in terms : he could exercise the privileges of a burgess but avoid the appropriate burdens. Edinburgh in 1517 was dealing with this problem of burgesses who, not being resident, escaped the taxation and responsibilities that fell upon the burgh households, but the problem was still there in 1568 when all non-resident burgesses were required to make their " remanyng " in the burgh or lose their freedom.[2] Even those who lived in Leith had by 1662 to conform to this regulation or suffer a heavy fine.[3] The Convention, also, in the seventeenth century, repeated in successive years their Act against outland burgesses, and were taking measures to enforce upon individual burghs their objections to all " outlandis " or " alegeit " burgesses, classifying them with regrators, forestallers and unfreemen.[4] This " outland " tendency so alarmed the authorities of Peebles that in 1555 a definite effort was made to stop it with such an ordinance as that " all merchandices utouth (outside) the town and outland burgessis " were to be warned " to cum within burgh and mak thair change, merchandice, and residence, or ellis to be dischargit of thair fredome and liberte in tyme cuming." [5] Seven years later the council laid down that in future no burgesses were to be admitted " except thai be induellaris and inhabitaris within the toune and mak residence thairintill baith day and nycht," further, that if after being made burgesses they should remove from the town, they were forthwith to be deprived of their freedom.[6] At Banff in 1682 the Town Council ordered " All land burgesses to be charged to come in and make their actual residence in the burgh, or to desist from all trading." [7] Whatever the degree of success following such measures, landward burgesses continued generally as

[1] *Annals of Banff* (New Spalding Club), i, 60.
[2] *Edinburgh Guilds and Crafts*, pp. 63, 104.   [3] *Ibid.*, p. 181.
[4] *R.C.B.*, ii (1597-1614), 250, 273-4, 288, 310, 342.
[5] *Records, Peebles*, p. 219. *Cf.* p. 208.
[6] *Ibid.*, p. 286.   [7] *Annals of Banff*, i, 161.

an accompaniment to burghs proper. Probably the burghs could not face the sacrifice of burgess fees.

A reason for insisting upon renewing the old obligation upon residence was given as the necessity " to tak part with the toune in thair commoun effairis," [1] among these being the burden of scot, lot, watch and ward (" scottyn, lottyn, wakyn and wardyn "),[2] the two former being hallowed terms for municipal taxation, the latter police duties. But there was no escaping " burgess silver," where such was levied on admission as a burgess, which does not seem to have been universal. At Peebles the fee on that occasion was at least ten shillings but might be twice or three times that amount. Stirling in 1563 fixed the fee for a new burgess at forty shillings,[3] while he had also to show his equipment of hagbut or firearm, steel bonnet, and sword.[4] The Commissioners of 1835 include such payments in their table of burghal revenue and expenditure, where the rates for admission vary according as the new member is an apprentice, a son, a son-in-law, or a " stranger." In the last case the fee for admission at Edinburgh was £12, 10s. for a burgess but double that amount for entry as a guild brother. At Aberdeen the fee for a stranger becoming a guild brother was £50.[5] " In some cases," say the Commissioners, an entry into the community has been made " perhaps, an engine of extortion." [6] Several of the smaller burghs on the list show no charge for admission under any heading. At Stirling, too, in the sixteenth century a burgess, and even a guild brother, for good reason might be admitted " gratis." [7] Edinburgh also

[1] *Annals, of Banff*, p. 286.   [2] *Ibid.*, p. 185. *Cf.* 286 ; and here p. 20.
[3] *Charters &c. Stirling*, p. 214.
[4] See p. 89. Burgesses had to take their part in " weapon-showings " as liable to a levy in time of war, but the custom was to do so of themselves, not as part of the shire display (*R.M.S.*, A.D. 1690, No. 190, a charter of ratification to Dumbarton, in which is incorporated a letter of 1488 under the Privy Seal, dealing with this point).
[5] *Report*, 1835, *Appendix*, pp. 82-7.
[6] *Report*, p. 73.
[7] *Charters &c. Stirling*, pp. 217, 219, etc. In 1681 " John Murray in Banff is made a burgess gratis, he giving a musket and bandalier gratis to the town " (*Annals*, i, 160). In Canongate, a burgh of regality, five men were made burgesses *gratis* in 1583 (*Miscellany*, Maitland Club, ii, Pt. 2, 351).

had its " gratis " admissions,[1] going in time beyond ordinary burgesses to guild brethren. Gavin Douglas, the poet and provost of St Giles, was made a burgess " gratis " in 1513 " for the common good of the town " (*pro communi bono ville*). In the year 1613 we have the Lord President and the bishops of St Andrews and Glasgow made burgesses and guild brethren, when they were regaled with " dry confections, wine, and cherries " ; and three years later certain noblemen, including the Duke of Lennox,[2] were given the same honour. Less commendable, perhaps, is the conferring of a similar compliment in 1656 upon General Monk with the army commanders and the judges of the Cromwellian occupation.[3] By 1767, however, the council came to the conclusion that this " giving the freedom of the city " had been done somewhat indiscriminately and enacted that for the future it should be granted only to " such as are invested with public character, or shall have signalized himself in the service of his country or this city." [4] Thus originated and so was generally delimited the honour of conferring the freedom of a burgh on one who may be neither resident, nor merchant, nor craftsman, nor owner of burgh property.

[1] *Edin. Guilds and Crafts*, pp. 84, 87 and *passim*.
[2] *Ibid.*, p. 165.
[3] *Ibid.*, p. 174.
[4] *Ibid.*, p. 211. " Which privilege " says Lord Bankton, " is merely personal, and does not entitle them to any concern in the affairs of the Burgh." (*Institute of the Laws of Scotland*, i, p. 56).

CHAPTER IX

TRADE AS NATIONAL NOT BURGHAL

Glimpses of Burgh Life. The Scottish merchant. Royal burghs and
"unfree" trading. Trade as a national not a burghal interest.
Breaches in burgh monopoly. A revolutionary Act. Negotiations with
"unfree" burghs. Conditions in burghs down to the Act of 1846.

OPPORTUNITY may now be taken for some glimpses of burgh
life in general. In the first place burghs were by our standard
small, many no more than what we would account a large
village ; those which grew did so slowly and to no great
extent, so that the view of Forres in the late eighteenth century
(Fig. 1) presents pretty much what it had been for centuries
before. Not until the eighteenth century was well advanced,
and the industrial revolution had got under way, did population increase to a notable extent and particularly so in the
more adaptable towns. Not, however, in the Border towns,
which, when the Union dried up smuggling to and from
England, suffered a decrease. The population of Jedburgh
before 1707 was 6000 to 8000 ; by 1784 it was 2000.[1] But
Edinburgh of the fourteenth century contained according to
Froissart only 400 houses.[2] In Stirling about the middle
of the sixteenth century there were resident within the burgh,
according to the original summation, 405 male adults.[3] By
the latter half of the same century Aberdeen is reckoned to
have had a population of about 4000.[4] It was one of the
foremost cities. Glasgow in 1450 is credited with a population
of about 1500.[5] By the Union of 1707 this had expanded

---

[1] Cited by W. Law Mathieson, *The Awakening of Scotland*, p. 273.

[2] This need not mean that he had counted them. The mediæval
historian had not the statistical mind. All it conveys is Froissart's impression
that it was a small place. 400 not 4000 is the reading of the best MS.

[3] *Extracts from Records, 1519-1666*, p. 59.

[4] *The Book of Bon-Accord*, Joseph Robertson, i, 104 ; E. Bain, *Merchant
and Craft Guilds*, p. 144.

[5] Murray, as cited, i, 51, 118. In 1604 merchant burgesses numbered
213, burgess craftsmen 361 (*Ibid.*, p. 484).

to 12,700 and by 1800 to over 80,000.[1] Glasgow, of course, highly favoured by new economic circumstances, was an exceptional case ; it was due to these and not to its burghal privileges that Defoe in his *Tour* could speak of it as " one of the cleanliest, most beautiful, and best built cities in Great Britain," where, runs another record, " since the year 1750 . . . every person is employed, not a beggar is to be seen in the streets, the very children are busy." [2]

In early days houses in the towns were constructed wholly of wood. Thus in 1244 " almost all the burghs of Scotland," of which eight are named, were burned to ashes.[3] As late as the beginning of the sixteenth century probably every private house in Aberdeen was a timber building.[4] By the first quarter of the eighteenth century, however, most towns were built in stone.[5] The main street or " hie gait," at least, was usually set with cobbles in a causeway, as described by John Galt : " in those days the streets were not paved at the sides, but only in the middle, or, as it was called, the crown of the causey ; which was raised and backed upward, to let the rain-water run off into the gutters." [6] The condition of the sidewalks was a matter for the householders, and " in Scotland," writes a contemporary, " you walk generally in the middle of the street." [7] The gutters were about the only means of drainage. Refuse of every kind was got rid of where convenient, even upon the street, where it was routed amongst by wandering swine. In 1462 and again in 1471 it was ordained at Peebles that no middings should lie upon the " calsay " longer than eight days,[8] under penalty of a fine of eight shillings. On the later date, too, a similar

---

[1] A. Macgeorge, *Old Glasgow*, p. 154.

[2] *History of Glasgow* (1777), John Gibson, p. 120.

[3] *Scotich.*, ix, cap. lxi. Haddington, Roxburgh, Lanark, Stirling, Perth, Forfar, Montrose, Aberdeen.

[4] *The Book of Bon Accord*, pp. 105-6.

[5] Burt's *Letters from a Gentleman &c.*, Letter iii. Dr Johnson in his *Journey &c.*, of 1773 remarks that the ancient towns of Scotland had " generally an appearance unusual to Englishmen," the houses being " for the most part built of stones," but with their ends " now and then next the streets " and " very often " an outside stair to the upper floor.

[6] *The Provost*, chap. xv.

[7] Burt, as cited, Letter iv.   [8] *Records, Peebles*, pp. 146, 167.

penalty was to be imposed upon those who allowed their swine to go loose upon the street. At Stirling, however, they turned their muck into money, rouping it as manure with the rest of the common good. In 1562 the " geitt swoippingis " (street sweepings) were set for fifty-two and a half marks but in 1595 for eight score and eight marks,[1] which suggests that Stirling had grown three times dirtier. At Banff " Before the year 1784, the streets had not been cleaned, by order of the magistrates, for time immemorial. This office was left to be performed by the rains of heaven." [2] The poet Dunbar in the later fifteenth century gives a vividly remonstrative picture of the streets of Edinburgh, which was in particular cases recommended as an example to other burghs, dwelling upon the stink, the cries and clamour, and the plague of beggars, such things being derogatory to a capital. But what is said of Edinburgh could be repeated for every town in Europe.[3] The pestilence that from time to time scourged the insanitary towns could be accounted for as the admonition of an offended deity. The water supply was from wells or streams. Lighting, where imposed, was by each shopkeeper and dwellers in side streets hanging out a lantern for so many hours at night.[4]

Within burghs there was the sharp delimitation between burgesses and the class of non-burgesses, the latter made up of servants, apprentices, and dependents, or the unemployed and unfit of one kind or another. Women were regularly admitted to burgess rank.[5] Burgesses, again, had their own

[1] *Charters, Stirling*, pp. 211, 219.

[2] *Reports of Grievances*, p. 72.

[3] Of Germany, " Die Strassen waren schmutzig und von Dungestätten unsäumt," *i.e.* dirty and bordered with middens (Dr Heil, *Die deutschen Städte*, p. 104).

[4] *Records, Edinburgh*, s.d., 1554, pp. 204-5.

[5] Marwick, *Edinb. Guilds and Crafts*, p. 8 ; *Charters &c., Peebles*, pp. 113, 133, etc. ; Thus the Baroness Burdett Coutts could be made an honorary burgess of Edinburgh. *Cf.* " *Libertas Mariote Myller*, Nov. 6, 1497. The quhilk day, the ballies, ourisman [provost] and the communite has gevin ande grantit the fredome of the burghe in moss & mure & aile brewin & bakin for hir lyfftyme, kepand the statutis of the toune before writtin. Apone the quhilk scho has gevin hir gret aitht " (*Burgh Records of Prestwick*, p. 34). Prestwick was a burgh of barony, but in that character unique (See p. 110 n.). " Moss " was for fuel ; " moor " for pasture.

division into merchants proper and craftsmen, while the former category had its inner circle in the members of the merchant guild. All merchants were burgesses, but not all were brethren of the guild ; every craftsman, however, should be a burgess and a member of his guild or incorporation.[1] Nor were all merchants of equal standing. There were those who could retail their goods within their liberty on packhorses or in waggons, as we have seen at Kelso ; [2] others who were but poor packmen who carried their stock upon their back.[3] In the summer of 1581 Peter Lymburner, a burgess of Glasgow " travelling in the Isle of Mull in his vocatioun and trade of mercheandice," was set upon by two Maclean gentlemen and their accomplices, wounded and put in peril of his life, and robbed of his whole pack of merchant wares worth three thousand merks.[4] That was one end of the scale. At the other were such merchants engaged in foreign trade as, in the last quarter of the fourteenth century, the Mercers of Perth, who are credited with great riches (*divitias multas*) ; [5] or in the following century the two merchant burgesses of Edinburgh who successively married the daughter of the sister of James III, before the lady took the Earl of Rothes as her third husband ; [6] and, in the seventeenth century, Sir William Dick, for a time Provost of Edinburgh, who in Scots money was a millionaire twice over, was, from his continental business and financial standing, perhaps the chief source of equipment for the Covenanting armies, and ended as a bankrupted creditor of the Commonwealth.[7]

---

[1] *Records, Edinburgh,* 1403-1528, pp. 65, 116-7. " There are three sorts of burgesses, burgesses *in sua arte,* who are members of one or of other of the corporations ; burgesses who are guild-brothers ; and a third sort, who are simply burgesses, and neither guild-brothers nor members of any corporation " (Morison, *Decisions of the Court of Session,* p. 1928, s.d., 1743).

[2] See p. 91.

[3] See p. 90.

[4] *R.P.C.,* vi, 141.

[5] Walsingham, *Historia Anglicana* (R.S.), i, 369 ; *cf. Exch. Rolls,* i, 116, 597.

[6] See *Accts. Lord High Treasurer,* i, pp. ccxc-xci.

[7] See *Domestic Annals of Scotland,* R. Chambers, ii, 236-40.

It was not considered proper that merchants with but little capital, who could adventure but a small part of a cargo, should take part in foreign trade. Such men could be no credit to the country, particularly when their dress bore witness to their limited means. On this matter the ruling powers were very sensitive. There was a succession of Acts of Parliament prescribing the minimum value of goods allowed for export, with a fine for any transgression. In 1551 the Town Council of Edinburgh, recapitulating these Acts, which as usual were not being observed, was further distressed at information from abroad as to the " lichtleing " of the country's reputation in parts of Flanders and France by the activities of Scottish merchants there " clad in vyle array." [1] The petty dealings of these small merchants were also made an objection by English business men to the proposals for free trade between the countries after the Union of the Crowns. The Scots, they pointed out, " trade after a meaner sort and condition in foreign parts than we, as by retailing parcels and remnants of cloth and other commodities up and down the countries as we cannot do because of the honour of our country." Such remnant merchants and artificers like them would flock into England and by their parsimony and industry beggar the people in their neighbourhood. [2] Apparently it was within the province of the Merchant Guilds to supervise the conduct of merchants and restrain abuses of this character, but by 1672 it could be pleaded that " there are no where poorer traders than within burghs ; to which ordinarily the meanest and poorest amongst the people retire, when they cannot live elsewhere ; and, when they are once settled there, they, because of the easy conveniences of trading, do indiscreetly run upon it." [3] The " mean and peddling " manner of Scottish merchants continued to be a source of English contempt, and the Scottish " pedlar with his pack " was also a grievance to Ireland. [4]

[1] *Records, Edinburgh*, ii, 152.
[2] Cited in *Commercial Relations of England and Scotland, 1603-1707*, Theodora Keith, pp. 11-12.
[3] Sir George Mackenzie, *Pleadings &c.*, Works 1716, i, 65.
[4] *Commercial Relations of England and Scotland, 1603-1707*, Theodora Keith, pp. 141, 111.

II

It was the practice to renew with each reign the Acts on the privileges of royal burghs, and sometimes more than once in a single reign. For all that, transgression or evasion was habitual, to which local inconvenience and prospect of profit were the contributory causes. The royal burghs, of course, did what they could to suppress these encroachments by unfreemen on both their local privileges and that of foreign trade. Individual offenders could be dealt with in the burgh court, but to take action against a community meant a suit in the Court of Session, which took time and was expensive. The Convention of Royal Burghs, however, was always ready to help in the good work. Irvine in 1602 pleaded the great expenses with which it was burdened in proceeding against unfree burghs before the lords and was promised financial assistance while encouraged " to insist eirnestly in the said action." [1] Such measures were not very effective. In 1657 the merchants of Edinburgh for themselves and in name of all the merchants of free burghs represented to the Convention that " the whole tread onlie competent to merchandis of free burrowis, beareris of the burdines thairof, wes inhanced be unfreemen, induelloris in burghis of barronis, clauchanis, and villages throughout the whole natione, to the utter ruyne of the whole free burrowis." [2] Dealing with this complaint the Convention pointed out " that this abuse does for the most part arys through the default of the saidis burrowis thair not puting of the actis of parliament and burrowis to dew executione, but the samyn have bein for thir many yearis bypast so vilified, neglectit, and contemned, as if the samyn had nevir bein maid." There is more than a hint, too, that burghs had themselves been guilty of sharing in the activities of the unfree, the Convention ordaining that they should not grant their freedom to any but such as would reside and trade within the burgh, and that none of their merchants should buy any foreign commodity from an unfree man or in an unfree place, or sell " free goodis " in quantity to unfree traders but only enough to serve their immediate use. All this with serious penalties attached for non-observance.[3]

---

[1] R.C.B., ii, 113, 130.   [2] R.C.B., iii, 440.   [3] Ibid., pp. 445-6.

The truth is that throughout the seventeenth century the burghs with their privileges went increasingly out of step with the new commercial aims and developments. As already observed, the principle of trade as a national concern was overshadowing the individual and partial interests of the burghs. An Act of 1661 constituted a Council of Trade to be appointed by each successive parliament with seven members from each Estate, " for ordering of trade within this kingdom," and " regulating, improveing, and advancing of trade, naviga-tion and manufactories." The burghal interest was thus represented as but a third of the whole, and no longer the primary consideration. This subversive idea underlies the economic legislation of the century, particularly after the Restoration. An Act was passed in the same year for the establishment of companies and societies to undertake and improve the manufacture of linen and woollen cloths and for the encouragement of " skilful artizans " to come from abroad to serve as instructors. Such men were to be " free to set up and work in burghs and landwart where the companies shall think fit, without paying any thing whatsoever to any person or persons, under whatsoever colour or pretext for their freedom " and to be " free of taxes and publick burdens or exactions during their lifetime." These provisions struck at the very heart of burghal privilege. The national point of view finds formal expression in an Act of 1663 which lays down that " the ordering and disposal of trade with foreign countries " was a prerogative of the Crown, and annuls all statutes and customs to the contrary. Obviously a new conception of industry was at work, overriding alike the monopoly and restrictions of the incorporated crafts and the monopoly of foreign trade cherished by the royal burghs. Both interested parties, however, could only continue on the old lines. Of the parliament of 1661 Principal Baillie wrote that " there were many brave designs for fishing and more use of trade ; but after much toome-talk, all seems to be vanished, the burroughs sticking absolutely to their old job-trot for their own hurt." [1]

As Baillie suggests not much came, for the time being, of these " designs " for trade. The country had not had time to

[1] *Letters*, etc., Robert Baillie, iii, 469 : " toome " = empty.

recover from a series of wars and its financial bleedings by the Protectorate. The burghs were not helpful. A Fishing Company initiated in 1669, in which the King himself was a large shareholder, failed to make good because, for one thing, the merchants feared that they would be overawed by the noble partners, and these believed they would be cheated by the merchants.[1] But the idea of joint-stock companies for the expansion of industry and trade, which was in this century the outstanding feature of English commerce, was at last to establish itself in Scotland, when the Act of 1681 put the coping-stone upon a policy of economic protection for industries, an expedient which had made a beginning in 1645. " Manufactories " for articles such as linen, soap, sugar, paper, fine cloth and other new industries,[2] were buttressed with special privileges, such as freedom from taxation, the prohibition of the export of the necessary raw materials, with the exclusion of competitive imports, and so gave rise to about fifty such enterprises, most of them public companies, but some due to private capitalists, who received the privileges accorded to the companies. The monopolistic privileges of these undertakings were established by statute just as were those of the burghs, but all that was necessary to share in their trading profits was to have enough money to be a shareholder. But the very fact that it was confined to shareholders made the joint-stock company a more rigid institution than the merchant class of the burghs, which was always receiving new members. The movement, indeed, was one towards a system of capitalism promoted by the State and based on the privileges and reliefs granted at first in individual patents and subsequently to company promoters.

Meantime, in face of all this new policy the royal burghs continued, in Baillie's words, on their old job-trot, being mightily active, under direction and encouragement by their Convention, against outland burgesses, unfree burghs, and unfree traders in general. Stirling in 1649 had the

[1] Mackenzie, *Memoirs &c.*, p. 184. Yet the stock did reach £25,000 sterling.

[2] See list of these before and after the Revolution in *Joint-Stock Companies*, W. R. Scott, Litt.D., iii, 128-9. They included after 1681 silk, sail-cloth, white paper, glass, ropes, pottery, hardware, etc.

concurrence of the agent of the Convention in taking action against unfree traders in Falkirk, Alloa, and other places.[1] In 1664 the Convention was concurring in the proceedings of five burghs against unfree traders within their bounds and encroachers upon their privileges.[2] Opposition to new erections also continued. Glasgow and Dumbarton thus united in opposing the effort of Sir John Shaw of Greenock in 1633 and 1634 to have that promising port raised to the rank of a burgh of barony, and, when this end was secured, subjected the place to vexatious attentions as exceeding its rights.[3] In 1662 there was a proposal to erect Borrowstounness (Bo'ness), a similarly advantageous port on the Firth of Forth, into a royal burgh, which in turn was considered inimical to Linlithgow, which had its own port on that shore at Blackness, and the agent of the Convention was instructed to co-operate with Linlithgow in carrying the business to the law courts, while advancing money towards the expenses.[4] Bo'ness was created a burgh of regality by charter in 1668.[5] It was also a standing grievance with the craftsmen that they should be barred from importing themselves the raw materials of their manufacture and themselves selling their finished products abroad, being in both cases bound to have recourse to the merchants of royal burghs. Of course such restrictions were being constantly infringed, but always with the risk of prosecution for illegal trading and a heavy penalty upon conviction.

The general issue as to " free " and " unfree " trade came to a head in a case before the Court of Session in 1672, when " The burgh of Stirling had charged the unfreemen of Falkirk to desist from trading, they being but a burgh of regality, belonging to the Earl of Callendar." [6] As an advocate for Falkirk, Sir George Mackenzie challenged the laws " that none but the indwellers of burghs-royal can trade with foreigners " as " far from being advantagious either to the public or to private persons." The pursuers, he claimed, " who desire to lessen the freedom of trade are the sixth part

---

[1] *R.C.B.*, iii, 334.   [2] *Ibid.*, p. 574.   [3] Pagan, as cited, p. 137.
[4] *R.C.B.*, iii, 551, 558, 577, etc.
[5] *Borrowstounness and District*, T. J. Salmon, p. 78 ; *A.P.S.*, vii, 580 (1669).   [6] Sir George Mackenzie, *Memoirs &c*, (1821), p. 226.

only of Scotland, who desire to retrench the privileges of the other five parts." The result was that many places well situated for trading were prevented from exploiting their natural advantages " to the great prejudice of the nation." The royal burghs, he pointed out, could not deny that most of the Acts " limiting [*i.e.* defining] their trade and government " were " gone into desuetude." Moreover, the King had " the sole prerogative of ordering and disposing trade with foreigners," [1] and so in this way there had been granted to " all burghs of regality and many burghs of barony " full liberty of such trade, and this, too, in spite of protests to his Majesty by the royal burghs and their agents at Court as " a concession contrary to the privileges granted to them by Parliament." As for the plea of the royal burghs that they enjoyed their special privileges because they contributed a sixth part of the public taxation, he argued that now they could bear a much larger proportion, since " the burghs are six times more numerous [2] and each particular burgh six times more rich and populous " than they were when it was determined at one-sixth, and " little moncy is bestowed upon food or raiment in Scotland except only in burgh." The evidence he offers for these estimates is only in general observations, as that " now the nobility and gentry only toil to get money, to buy from burgesses what they import from foreign countries." [3]

The decision of the Supreme Court was that as this was a matter of general policy, it should be referred to Parliament, where the outcome was the sweeping Act of 1672. This Act sums up the existing state of things as to burgh privileges, citing expressly the statement of these in the Act of 1633 [4] and continuing : " Which priviledges soe extended wer never in use, and are highlie prejudiciall to the common interest and good of the kingdome, and are by the said statute extended far beyond the ancient priviledges of burrowes

---

[1] See p. 144.
[2] The royal burghs numbered at most 67, at least 65. See p. 154. Green's *Encyclopædia of Scots Law*, ii, 355-60, lists 70, in reference to burgage registers.
[3] *Pleadings before the Supreme Court* in Mackenzie's *Works* (1716), i, 63-8.
[4] See p. 69.

repeated and confirmed therein ; applying the priviledges granted to burrowes generally to royall burrowes onlie, to the prejudice of the burghs of regallities and barony, and extending of the sale of imported commodities, which could onlie be understood of wholesale to the topping [*i.e.* breaking bulk] and retailing of the saids commodities."

It is admitted, however, that " the just priviledges of the royall burrowes have bein encroached upon by uthers " in the export and import, of staple commodities without sharing the burden of public taxation laid upon the royal burghs. To meet this part of the case, therefore, it was to continue the privilege of the freemen of royal burghs " to buy or sell, in great or whole sale," wine, wax, silks, spiceries, woad and other materials for dyeing, with the ancient exemption in favour of noblemen, prelates, barons and certain others to import such goods for the personal use of themselves and their families only. But it was now made lawful for any of his Majesty's subjects to export by sea or land all sorts of corn grown in the country, cattle, sheep, horses, coal, salt, wool, skins, hides and all other native commodities ; burghs of regality or barony and factories to export their own manufactures and to import timber, iron, tar, soap, lint, lintseed, hemp, onions, or other things necessary for tillage or building or for the use of their manufactures, and sell in retail all commodities whatsoever.[1]

This measure legalised practices which had long prevailed more or less surreptitiously, and which the Convention had duly striven to suppress. It was also a sore disappointment. The royal burghs kept an agent at Court to watch over their interests, and the occupant of that post since the Restoration had been he who was now Duke of Lauderdale and who had been the more ready to serve as he knew " it would secure him that third estate of Parliament." [2] He apparently also

---

[1] Sir Robert Rait writes that, as a result of this Act, three royal burghs sought to resign their status, one of these being Cromarty. But Cromarty's application was due not to the Act but to the fact that two years earlier its extensive landed property had, by plain chicanery, been acquired by the Sheriff, Sir John Urquhart, who then manœuvred the petition for the removal of the place from the list of royal burghs, which indeed was not given effect to till 1685 (*R.C.B.*, iv, 54).

[2] Mackenzie, *Memoirs*, p. 227.

drew a salary from the Convention of £1600 Scots a year.[1]
Unluckily for the burghs he owned the regality of Musselburgh,
which would share in the advantages of the Act, and so gave
it his active support, whereby he " lost the affection of the
burghs royal." [2]   There remained the question how far the
Act would be strictly observed, and three years after its
passing the Convention was proposing to take legal advice
on this [3] and to commit the burghs as a whole to meet the
expenses of actions in the Court of Session which it was .
understood certain of them were prepared to undertake.

A more hopeful way, however, of minimising the Act of
1672 was by securing Court influence to that purpose,
wherefore the burghs " yeilded to every demand of the Duke
of York " ; [4] but all the Parliament of 1681 would do was to
enact that the burghs of barony and regality should retail
their imported commodities only " for the use of the inhabitants " of these burghs and not to any others coming to these
burghs and offering to buy such goods.   This was far short
of what the royal burghs had drafted on their own part, in
their hope of recovering their ancient privileges as before
the Act of 1672,[5] but, threatened with even worse treatment,
they " ware glad to put up ther pipes, and hold them as
they ware." [6]

On the accession of James VII the Convention renewed
its efforts, drafting another Act for " the reponing of the
royall burrows " in their privileges and representing to the
Secretary of State how they " charged with a very great
share of publict taxes, have of late suffered and does still
suffer unspecable prejudice and loss " by the Act of 1672,
which had communicated their privileges " to the burghs of
barronie and regality, who being free of any pairt of the said
taxes are able and will infalliblie in tyme ingros the whole
trade to themselves, to our utter ruine." [7]   Nothing came of

---

[1] R.C.B., iii, 569.

[2] Mackenzie, p. 227.

[3] R.C.B., iii, 656-7.   " burghs of regalities and barronies invaides
upon many priviledges which are only competent by the said act to royall
burrows."

[4] Fountainhall, *Historical Notices*, i, 323.   [5] R.C.B., iv, p. 27.

[6] Fountainhall, as cited, i, 323.

[7] R.C.B., iv, 59, 60 ; *cf.* " Philopoliteius " (1685), pp. 106-9.

this appeal to a King for whom the royal burghs were the toughest part of the opposition to his designs.[1] On the other hand, this very fact would be a recommendation to King William to whom the commissioners of the Convention explained that " it wes the undoubted and unquestionable priviledge of your royal borrowes, by a constant and uninterrupted series of lawes and acts of parliament for many hundreds of years in their favores to have the trade both of export and import within this kingdom," until " of late, whyll arbitrary government wes creiping in upon us, by one strock," namely the Act of 1672, all these laws and Acts " wer whollie cut of " and their trade communicated to the other burghs.[2] There was the usual reminder that the royal burghs bore a sixth part of national taxation as well as other burdens, such as the " building of prison houses for the benefit and advantadge of the wholl subjects of the Kingdome," a particular plea which might have been expressed more felicitously. There followed the Act of 1690 pretty much on the lines the burghs had laid down, though less restrictive than might have been expected. Importation by sea or land was to be confined to freemen of royal burghs except that of cattle, horses, sheep, and other beasts, and excepting the privilege granted to noblemen and barons, also all export by sea except of corn, cattle, etc., metals, minerals, coals, salt, lime, and stone, but all lieges to have liberty to transport by land the native commodities of the kingdom. Further, inhabitants of burghs of regality and barony could retail all foreign commodities, provided they bought these from freemen of the royal burghs. The Act of 1672 was abrogated in so far as it was inconsistent with this one. The net result in contrast with the Act of 1681 appears to be that the liberty of import and export was severely restricted in the case of unfree burghs and that of retail given greater freedom.

However, in view of the long controversy, the possibilities still open of evading the Act, and the expense of legal

---

[1] See p. 134.

[2] *R.C.B.*, iv, 100-1. An Act of 1597 ordered all burghs to provide within three years, at their own expense, " sure " jails for the detention of offenders against both criminal and civil laws, whether within the burgh or handed over by the sheriff of the shire.

proceedings against infringement, it is perhaps not surprising to find later in the same year an approach to the burghs of barony asking for " satisfieing proposalls " on their part as to " communication of trade " with the royal burghs.[1] There was no response in kind, but the idea of an accommodation between the rival groups was not abandoned. The royal burghs now concentrated on the principle that the unfree burghs could share their privileges as to foreign trade in importing and retailing such goods directly, provided they paid a specified proportion of the taxation laid upon the royal burghs. Negotiations on these lines were backed by Acts of Parliament in 1693 and 1698. Some of the larger burghs of regality and barony took advantage of this compromise, but on the whole little agreement was achieved. There was no very obvious gain for the unfree burghs, which could continue on the old evasive lines, while prosecution was an expensive business, and the law uncertain. " Time and the hour " was on their side. By 1706 the Convention was reduced to considering whether it would not be to their interest that the burghs should be taxed not separately but " completely with the land rent of the rest of the kingdome . . . and that the haill kingdome have the benefite and priviledge of trade." [2] By the Act of Union, however, the royal burghs were confirmed in their rights and privileges, but without any specification of these—the last in the long tale of legislative measures until 1846. Meantime, throughout the eighteenth century and into the next, the offer of communication of trade on a declining scale of payment was being dangled before the unfree burghs with little return, despite occasional prosecutions, chiefly of the smaller burghs concerned.[3] " But the unfree trade increased and the quota paid by the unfree traders decreased." [4] By 1708 no more than nineteen of these had been brought into the taxable fold, and those which then and later conformed " did not always pay their share,

---

[1] *R.C.B.*, iv, 123. The issue was complicated by the practice of burgesses in royal burghs becoming " partners " with " unfreemen inhabitants in the burghs of regalities and barronies and uther unfree places, both in poynt of trade and shipping," which the Convention in 1691 sought to stop by heavy fines on their offending freemen (*Ibid.*, pp. 133-4).

[2] *R.C.B.*, iv, 390-1.   [3] *Report*, 1835, p. 77.   [4] Pagan, p. 147.

and it was difficult or impossible to make them do so if they declined. Some burghs renounced the privilege and the payment ; other towns which had made no agreement with the royal burghs, grew up and carried on foreign trade." [1] The Commission of 1835 found that for more than fifty years the burghs of regality and barony which had come in to share the privilege of foreign trade, had contributed no more than £200 yearly to the full burgh taxation of £8000. [2]

All along, too, the law courts were more inclined to the removal than the enforcement of restrictions. The Convention was particularly disturbed by the result of an action before the Court of Session in 1757. The guildry of Inverness had seized and confiscated the goods of a John Smith landed at the harbour as having been imported contrary to the Acts of 1672 and 1690. It was argued for Smith, as pursuer, that he was a burgess of Annan and therefore entitled to deal in foreign trade in any burgh of the kingdom ; further that the goods had been bought in London and could not therefore, by an article of the Treaty of Union, be considered as foreign goods. For the guildry it was pleaded that, though Smith had a burgess ticket from Annan, it did not appear that he ever paid scot and lot as a burgess there, and that he did not claim to have any residence or carry on any trade there. His ticket, therefore, gave him no right to any privilege in another burgh of which he had not the freedom. Though the Union established freedom of trade between the countries, that trade, it would be understood, was to be carried on in a regular manner, and " by the immemorial laws " of Scotland that could only be done by freemen residing in the royal burghs, whose privileges indeed were expressly reserved by an article of the Treaty. The decision of the Court was that goods brought from London were not to be reckoned foreign goods, and that the defenders were liable to Mr Smith for the value of the goods confiscated as also for damages and expenses. [3] As part of the goods in dispute had come from the plantations this decision opened a way to several possibilities.

---

[1] Keith, as cited, *Eng. Hist. Rev.*, 1913, pp. 687-8.

[2] *Appendix to Report*, p. 10. See *Local Taxation in Scotland*, S. Horsfall Turner, pp. 155-6, 268, and *Miscellany, Burgh Recs. Socy.*, pp. xxv-lx.

[3] Morison, *Decisions &c.*, pp. 1952-3.

Provided the goods were bought in London in the way of trade, it would seem the question of their ultimate origin did not arise ; London would be a back door for any sort of foreign trade. That issue, however, was not tried. But in 1823 there did come a further opening of the door, when it was judicially decided that craftsmen might import and sell goods manufactured in England, provided these were of the class of goods which they had the privilege of manufacturing themselves.[1]

The obvious way out of the dilemma was to abolish the distinction between royal burghs and the rest. But this step would have involved other issues than those of trade, problems of local and national administration. Before the Union of 1707 the royal burghs provided the Third Estate in the Scottish Parliament, and that part could not be allowed to lapse. After the union the Scottish members were elected by the royal burghs in groups, and as a body were to prove too serviceable and amenable to party methods of securing a majority in the House of Commons [2] for any attack on the system to win encouragement. And so for political ends the burghal system with its trade and industrial division, already shaken almost into ruin in practice and destined to sink commercially into desuetude, was kept in being.

III

All round, the seventeenth century, in circumstances as well as in commercial policy and practice, was inimical to the burghal system. Successive wars, civil and foreign, had depressing effects on trade in general. Dysart in 1691 was still emphasising the " decay " to which it had been brought by the civil war of rather less than fifty years before, when " the most pairt of the skippers and traffiquers were killed and destroyed," it being now " altogether without trade." [3]

[1] *Report*, 1835, p. 77. Already, in 1793, the Court of Session had unanimously decided that the incorporated trades of Aberdeen were " entitled to import the materials of their respective trades, crafts, and manufactures, and to export the produce thereof " (Morison, *Decisions,* p. 1981).

[2] See *The Awakening of Scotland*, W. Law Mathieson, pp. 21-2.

[3] Report as over.

Other factors, however, were peculiar to the burghs themselves. The joint-stock company had given trade a new outlook and a wider field of enterprise. By the lavish creation of burghs of regality and barony supplemented by so many market-towns and fairs the butter of internal monopoly had been spread very thin. Above all the burghs had a canker in the mismanagement, waste, and private peculation of their property in the common good, the fruit of which was gathered in debts and local taxation, on all of which something must be said later in fuller detail.

Thus it happened that in the summer of 1691 [1] the Convention of Royal Burghs, influenced by the universal complaints of these for years past as to " ther poverty, want and decay of trade," was moved to institute an enquiry into the condition and state of every royal burgh, providing their " visitors " with a list of fifteen points for investigation, the replies to be furnished upon oath by the magistrates and town clerk. Fifty-nine burghs out of sixty-four were thus inspected, Kirkwall, Wick, Inverary, and " Rothesay in Boot " to be omitted " because of the difficulty of access to these places," but Rothesay was actually visited, while three others, including Dornoch and Bervie in Mearns, were omitted. All the information required was not necessarily forthcoming in full, since, for example, Rothesay, Jedburgh and Whithorn had no treasurer's books, at North Berwick the magistrates were absent and no account could be got of the treasurer's books, and at Queensferry only a bailie attended to supply the answers, the rest of the magistrates and the town clerk being absent and no treasurer's books kept. In some cases the returns are very summary and abrupt.[2] That for Kirkcaldy consists only of a list of ships in being at the port and another of those lost within recent years.

As a whole the picture painted is a dark one, illustrating in detail the original complaints which gave rise to the enquiry. So far as the royal burghs are concerned, home and foreign trade are in decay. Haddington protests that

---

[1] *R.C.B.*, iv, 129-30.

[2] The returns for all the burghs are given complete in an Appendix (1836) to the Report of the Commissioners of 1835. and in the Miscellany volume of the Burgh Records Society.

its inland trade is not worth noticing, a depreciation which
is echoed by Selkirk, Peebles, Annan, and Lauder, while
Renfrew is in the same position, Dumbarton only retails
small goods from Glasgow and other royal burghs, Rutherglen
has no trade, foreign or inland, and Dingwall no trade at all.
On the Fife coast, where the little royal burghs had suffered
particularly, Anstruther Wester had no fairs, no markets,
no ships, no merchants, no trade, and but one fishing boat.
Overseas trade in terms of shipping would seem to have been
equally stagnant, the port of Leith having 29 ships, though
there is also a list of independent voyages on behalf of Edinburgh merchants, Dundee returning 21 vessels, and Glasgow
8 at home with 7 abroad and uncertain to return. Inhabitants
of Perth, to encourage trade, had a new ship built at
Rotterdam, naming it the *Eagle of Perth* ; it was cast away
at Taymouth on its first voyage with its cargo, worth £20,000
Scots, a total loss. Still to encourage trade they had another
built at Leith, which also was called the *Eagle of Perth*, but
after two or three voyages her skipper " runne away with her "
and her cargo worth at least £10,000, and she never returned
from Virginia. By English laws she should never have gone
there : Scottish trade with the plantations was contraband.

There is much about burgh finances, but while revenues
are usually given, even if only an estimate, there is often no
record of expenditure. Revenue comes from the petty customs,
feu-duties, mills, fishings and other elements in the common
good ; the discharge goes to officials, ministers, schoolmasters,
in some cases to a doctor, to repair of streets, the tolbooth,
bridges, the expense of commissioners to Parliament and
Convention of Burghs, etc. At Inverness and Ayr salaries
were paid to provost and bailies, and Dundee debited itself
with a comparatively large sum " for maintaining the honor
of the good town in waiting on noblemen and others in whom
the burgh is concerned." So far as can be made out, every
burgh was living beyond its means, except perhaps—and
only perhaps—Arbroath and Forres. That meant a growing
debt, with interest to be found, at 6 per cent. for the main
sum at Dunfermline, 5 per cent. for the balance. Deficits in
the accounts had then to be met by a " stent " or tax upon
the inhabitants. The burden of debt ranged from £771,000

Scots at Edinburgh with a common good of £85,464 some shillings, to Dingwall which had no public debt because it would get no credit. Aberdeen, too, " can not have credit," because it had " already borrowed so much " and with accumulating debts could only expect to be, in a short time, " utterly ruined." Glasgow was due " vast sowmes " in addition to its ordinary expenditure, and under such expense " this poor place cannot subsist." The little burgh of Fortrose was in this respect on the same footing. It carried a debt of £800 " and noway under heaven to pay it, unless the inhabitants be stented," in which case most of them would " run away," as some for that reason had already done " being brock." Ayr was contracting debt yearly.

One particularly important subject of enquiry related to the number and the effect of burghs of regality and barony within the precinct of the royal burgh. With a few exceptions the existence of such neighbours is recorded as disastrous to the senior community. Stirling, for example, reported seven " who have a considerable trade and are very prejudiciall to them " ; Linlithgow " within their precinct and adjacent to them " had five " all which are highly prejudiciall to ther trade both outland and inland, particularly Borrow-stounes and Grangepans [Grangemouth] whose houses are in better conditione and sett at a higher rate then many of ther burgh," while the place further suffered from " a number of villages and kirktowns," which dealt in staple commodities. Glasgow specifies four unfree burghs as " highly prejudiciall to ther trade," including Hamilton " with a great inland trade and in a flourishing condition," Paisley the same, and particularly Greenock, with a very great trade both foreign and inland. Annan singles out four such burghs as having taken " all there trade from them " ; while Haddington lists more than ten burghs of barony " round about . . . which are now more frequented and more buying and selling therein than in Haddingtoun," whereby, along with the public burdens, has come decay of trade in the burgh. Several burghs have no contribution to make on this line, and Stranraer notes only Portpatrick within its precinct but does not suffer any prejudice, as Portpatrick had no trade ; while North Berwick is not worried about Dirleton, a mile away,

where the merchants " they conceave are of no great value."
Dunbar is a special case, its only adjacent burgh of barony
being Eyemouth, where, however, the principal traders had
become burgesses and took an equal share in the burdens
with the rest—were, in fact, outland burgesses. Another
special case was Crail, which had no burgh of regality or
barony near it, but pointed out that four royal burghs, erected
on its privileges, existed within four miles of it. No conclusion
is drawn, but the present condition of the burgh was that
the two fairs of a day each were in value " worth nothing at
all " and that a very great number of the houses were " all-
together ruinous, and not inhabited."

The suggestion so far is that the only really thriving
places are some unfree burghs. It happens, however, that
seven years later we get descriptions of such of these burghs
as have been mentioned, arising out of the negotiations
regarding communication of trade.[1] The result so far as
these are concerned, is a very different picture. Grangepans,
which had been represented as one of the places so harmful
to Linlithgow and with superior housing, now appears as
" a small and inconsiderable burgh of barronie," its inhabitants
for the most part " poor work people " employed about the
coal and salt-works, and the place as a whole " mean and
poor " ; Borrowstounness, another reputed drag on Linlithgow, as suffering from decay of trade, by which nearly a
hundred families were being supported on the charity of their
neighbours, who indeed were in want themselves. Paisley,
that was claimed to be " flourishing " at the expense of
Glasgow, professes to be " very low and in a poor condition,"
never having had any other trade than that of retailing foreign
goods bought from the freemen of royal burghs and dealing
in the native commodities of the kingdom ; while Kilmarnock,
named as another handicap, lived on charity—" the greatest
part of that town is wast." Prestonpans, a supposed parasite
on Haddington, was " much depoperat [impoverished] by
[beyond] what it was 10 or 12 years ago, and there is nothing
now but ruinous houses, where there lived formerly persons
of a considerable trade."

[1] *A.P.S.*, x, Appendix, pp. 107-48. *Miscellany Scot. Burghs Rec. Socy.*,
pp. li-lvi.

In both these pictures the shadows may have been deepened by the hope, frankly expressed, of securing some financial relief. Of such relief, however, there is little or no evidence in the roll of public taxation as adjusted in 1692 by the Convention of Burghs, as compared with that of twenty-two years before. In the earlier list Edinburgh continues to head the list in the proportion of £100 tax allotted to each burgh, being assessed at £33, 6s. 8d., while Glasgow has to pay £12, and these are the only two burghs out of sixty-four which run to double figures. Including Aberdeen at £7 these three account for over one-half of the total sum. After a small group at lesser amounts down to Elgin at £1 there follow forty-seven burghs below that figure, with three at one shilling.[1] In 1692 there is no striking difference, except that £20 are paid in the name of burghs of regality and barony, apparently to be recovered by an agent employed in conducting the negotiations over the communication of trade as explained above. But Edinburgh is still at almost its previous figure in £32, 6s. 8d., Glasgow goes up to £15, Aberdeen is at £6, 1s. so that these three continue to supply just over half of the taxation of each £100. There are fifty-one out of the sixty-five burghs at below the £1, 3s. of Elgin and five at one shilling, all per £100 of tax.[2] As we have seen, the compromise measures for communication of trade brought little relief.[3] It was still possible, however, under the law of 1690, to cite unfree traders before the court of the royal burgh affected and have their questionable goods forfeited, as in the Inverness case of 1757,[4] whereupon, as in that case, the issue might be carried to a higher court, with considerable expense and uncertainty of judgment, there being much occasion for legal

[1] R.C.B., iii, 622-3.   [2] R.C.B., iv, 161.

[3] See pp. 152-2. In 1886 it could be complained that under the Act of Union the burghal proportion of cess or land tax was " leviable only from royal burghs, in respect of their ancient exclusive privileges of trade," privileges which had been abolished (Sir James Marwick, *Observations on Early Guilds of Merchants and Craftsmen*, Glasgow, 1886, p. 16). The amount was the old sixth part of £48,000. " Costly to collect and vexatious in method, and partly redeemed by a few burghs, it was desirable to get rid of it." A rearrangement was come to under the Agricultural Rates Act of 1896 (See S. H. Turner, *History of Local Taxation in Scotland* (1908), pp. 153, 268).   [4] P. 152.

debate as to the precise effects of the statutory provisions.
All this severely discouraged prosecutions, particularly since
the Union, and particularly, for more general reasons, " on
the part of the larger and more prosperous towns," [1] especially
after the oncoming of the industrial revolution from the
middle of the eighteenth century.   A veritable landmark in
the process was the Act of 1752, which, contrary to all earlier
principle, especially as regards the weaving crafts, authorised
those engaged in industries connected with the making of
linen, Scotland's foremost manufacture, to practise their trade
in any " city, town, corporation, burgh or place in Scotland
without any let or hindrance from any person or persons
whatsoever," and without any preliminary payment.   That
worked out to the end of the monopoly of the weaving crafts.
Individuals might still, in other connections, invoke the law
" as an instrument of vexation, or as the means of extorting
advantageous compromises from unfree traders," [2] but the
general system, it is claimed by the Royal Commissioners,
" has been gradually subsiding into desuetude," which in
Scotland meant that it was on the point of death, for which,
and other reasons, they recommend " the entire Abolition
of this class of exclusive privileges."   Yet another eleven
years were to pass before, in 1846, came the " Act for the
abolition of exclusive privilege of trading in Scotland."   All
that was left to the corporations was " their corporate
character " and to those which had been subject to land tax
the inconsistent privilege of still paying it.[3]   Thus the domination of the burghs, which had been maintained, not without
difficulty, down so many centuries till it had become of only
nuisance value, ended at last without " a bang " or " a
whimper."

[1] *Report*, 1835, p. 77.   [2] *Ibid.*, p. 138.   [3] See p. 158 *n*.

CHAPTER X

FATE OF BURGH PROPERTY

The burgh property. Fate of the petty customs. Use of burgh land. Disappearance of control by the Chamberlain. Setting land in feu-farm and consequences in loss of property. Ineffectual laws to check dilapidation of burgh possessions. Cases of alienation of lands. Impoverishment of burghs. Further ineffectual measures. Failure of appeals to Courts. Continuing mismanagement and alienation. Rise of burgh reformers. Parliamentary Committee, 1819. Politics and the burghs. Municipal Reform Acts.

MUCH comment has been made on the way in which Church property was dispersed after the Reformation, comparatively little on the fate of the considerable property once possessed by royal burghs. That in general included lands, fishings, mills, and the right to levy tolls on articles brought for sale to their markets and fairs, where also non-burgesses had to pay fees for the privilege of setting up stalls for the disposal of their goods. All such possessions and rights constituted the " common good," a property held in trust by the community to enable the burgh to discharge its local and national obligations. The first grant of land to Inverness by William the Lion declares it to be " for the support of the burgh " (*ad sustentamentum burgi*) ; the next in the time of Alexander II is similarly defined (*ad sustentationem burgi*). At Inverkeithing the land was conferred by the same King for " the common ease or advantage of the burgh." [1] An Act of 1535, dealing with this matter, describes " the commoun gudis of burrowis " as granted " for the uphald of honestie and policy within burgh." Or, as it is put in a royal commission of 1684, " grants and concessions wholly sufficient for the payment of these liabilities." [2]

Obviously it was understood that there need be no taxation to cover the cost of administration in burghs so

[1] *ad commune asiamentum burgi*. Local Reports, 1835, App., p. 8 ; *B.B.C.*, ii, 378.

[2] *ad debita illa persolvenda omnino sufficientes* (Cited, *Report*, 1835, p. 25).

endowed. There should be no demand for municipal rates. The only assessment that could legally be laid upon a royal burgh was that for cess or land-tax, in origin an occasional but latterly a yearly levy, which was not allowed to be paid from the common good. There was no statutory authority for the imposition of any other rate, until an Act of 1574, supplemented by another of 1579, imposed one for the support of " the aigit, impotent, and puyr people." Owing, however, to the development of burghs and the shrinkage or even liquidation of their common good in ways to be dealt with presently, that endowment became insufficient to meet local charges. This defect gave rise to the expedient of adding something to the nett tax or " stent " for cess and using the overcharge to balance the burgh accounts.[1] The legality of this course, however, was questioned in an action brought by John Forbes of Culloden, a holder of burgess lands from Inverness, before the Court of Session in 1663, when it was pleaded that the burgh burdens should be satisfied from the common good, but that the magistrates were imposing an excessive stent in order to meet particular expenses and debts incurred without authority.[2] The Court laid down that before a stent was imposed (i.e. beyond the regular cess) the burgesses and inhabitants should be publicly summoned to a meeting, where they would be fully instructed in the cir-cumstances necessitating such a levy and give the necessary approval.[3] That course made it a voluntary or quasi-voluntary contribution. Burghs adopted this procedure but its weakness lay in the fact that those who might refuse to pay could not be compelled to do so by any process of law.[4] Thus the

[1] Cullen was still doing this at the time of the Report of 1835 : " There is levied about one-half more cess than is paid into the public revenue, and the surplus goes to the general funds of the burgh " (Local Reports, i, 166). This was not the only case.

[2] Collection of Decisions &c., Sir John Gilmour (1701), No. xcii, p. 70. Cf. Stair, Decisions &c., ii, 69.

[3] Cf. Aberdeen case in Morison, p. 1896, under date 1678.

[4] Thus at Macduff this usage had " existed for upwards of 40 years," but " for upwards of 10 years many of the inhabitants have refused to pay on the ground of alleged illegality." Thus there were " considerable arrears," but " No attempt has been made to enforce payment by diligence or action " (Local Reports, 1835, Pt. i, p. 119). At Banff there was acquies-cence in enforcement without any question of its legality (Ibid., p. 107).

L

Royal Commission reported in 1835 that for more than a century the practice of taxation by magistrates and town councils had fallen into disuse. In the meantime, however, had come the resource of securing a special Act for levying an assessment. Edinburgh took the lead, when in 1690 it was empowered to impose a rate for the expense of a military company to take the place of the now totally inadequate " watch " by citizens in the old fashion, instituting what the poet Fergusson called " that black banditti, the City Guard."

In the latter part of the eighteenth century such Acts were procured by many towns, making similar provision by rates for lighting, cleansing, and water-supply, but, town councils being such as will hereafter appear, the application of these measures was placed for the most part in the hands of commissioners, the term " police " used in this connection covering, in the Scottish fashion, as in the manner of France, all the amenities just mentioned. Other burghs avoided Parliamentary expenses and the burden of rates [1] by relying upon purely voluntary subscriptions to provide these elementary requisites of town life, in some cases with the help of a grant from the common good, where that was available.[2] On the reform of burgh administration, however, came general legislation to establish the elaborate system of municipal imposts under which we live.[3] Things might well have been different had the common good survived in its entirety to play the part for which it was devised. The Royal Commission of 1835 regretfully remarks that " if the large possessions which were bestowed on the Scottish burghs had been

---

[1] Aberdeen " very heavily taxed under their Police Act " (*Local Reports*, 1835, i, 19).

[2] As for the lighting of Elgin. At Cupar " The lighting of the town is defrayed by subscription among the inhabitants, who appoint committees to manage their subscriptions." At Jedburgh the magistrates had " been in the habit of assessing the inhabitants . . . for water and lighting. Last year, however, the inhabitants refused to pay for lighting the streets, and this assessment is accordingly discontinued. It has been stated, however, that a considerable portion of them continue to pay for their supply of water." It was proposed to introduce a Police Bill (See *Local Reports* under names).

[3] On the earlier conditions see *Report*, 1835, pp. 43-6, and *History of Local Taxation in Scotland*, S. Horsfall Turner, pp. 168-186.

managed with common prudence and honesty, the taxes and burdens by which almost all of them are now weighed down would have been nearly unknown." [1] These possessions were diverted to other ends.

Parts of the common good were destined to die what may be called a natural death. Town mills suffered the freeing and displacing fate of all mills after the Act of 1799 providing for relief from their exactions. Petty customs the Commission of 1835 was inclined to leave optional between their continuance and an assessment to meet the loss by their cessation.[2] They lingered long in several places, though always tending to fall into disuse or be abolished. In 1870 Parliament gave authority to town councils to levy a rate in lieu of the petty customs, if these were removed, the rate to be no more than the equivalent of the loss, and no new customs to be imposed or any increased. A number took advantage of the Act,[3] but in 1900 petty customs were still being exacted in twenty-four burghs, five of them baronial.[4] The institution of the parcel post in 1883 overrode such an obstacle, and the Town Council Act of 1900 repeated the provision of 1870. Returns from petty customs and mills had made a considerable contribution to the common good and shared in its fortunes. The more substantial, however, and, as it should have been, the more lasting part of that endowment was the real property, the " extensive possessions " in land of the royal burghs " of which the far greater portion is now lost to the community." [5]

This connection with property in land has led to some confusion of ideas. It has been taken to signify that burgesses at the beginning and generally to some degree were farmers, thus harking back to the conception of the burgh as an agricultural unit [6] and obscuring or diminishing the fact, patent in all the charters, that it was in origin and nature essentially a trading community.[7] Hence burghs were not

---

[1] *Report*, p. 39.   [2] *Report*, p. 50.

[3] Banff abolished them in 1888 (*Annals*, i, 380).

[4] *Juridical Review*, xii (1900), 175.   [5] *Report*, 1835, p. 30.

[6] Whence the picture of Glasgow as " the little community of cultivating burgesses " by one change after another " gradually transformed into the great municipality which we now know " (Murray, as cited, i, 284).

[7] " Traffic is the very essence, and by it the being and vitalls of a Burgh or City is maintained " (" Philopoliteius," as cited (1685), p. 94).

ipso facto in possession of land ; that had to come by a special grant. They did not enter upon a heritage of pre-existing farm land. No doubt burgesses would require pasture for their milk-cows and the horses that were their transport, also the timber that was both their building material and, with peat, where that was present, their fuel.[1] But we have seen burghs in existence, as at Inverness and Dumbarton, before grants of land came their way, and that such a grant was for the support of the burgh, was in fact an endowment, the only sort of endowment possible. For such land no royal rent was exacted ; the burghs held it free of charge to make what they could of it, so that no question arose of increasing the return from the property, which belonged to the community as a body, not to individuals. And small-scale agriculture on apportioned rigs in the " burgh roods " no more made the burgess substantially a farmer than the raising of vegetables and fruit by the modern town-dweller on his plot makes him a market-gardener. The burgess could stack his crop beside his " kaill " (cabbage) in the " yard " within the dikes of his holding.[2] It was for his household consumption. His part in the " common " beyond cultivated land has been referred to above.

The case at Ayr,[3] where there was a distribution of rough land to those who cleared it, was quite exceptional, and it does not follow that the burgesses did all the work themselves, then or after : there was labour to hire and tenantry for lease, the burgh affording a handy market for produce. So long as it was imperative for burgesses to be resident within the burgh, occupation in farming was necessarily limited. In time we do find some of them, singly or as joint tenants, so engaged upon burgh land. The " Newtoun of Cromarty," adjacent to the burgh and still as a large farm preserving the name, was thus brought into cultivation by four burgesses as joint tenants after 1449.[4] Of such may well have been some of the outland burgesses whom we have seen to have caused

---

[1] Brechin " was at one time possessed of very extensive landed property," but " it was all muirland," most of which had been feued out before 1770 (*Local Reports*, i, 126).

[2] See *History of Arbroath*, George Hay, p. 112.

[3] See p. 34.　　　　[4] Fraser's *Earls of Cromarty*, ii, 324.

so much question and trouble in the later stages of burgh history. The Inverness charter of King William, however, in granting land to the burgh clearly contemplates the possibility of non-burgess tenants, since it lays down that none should have tillage or pasture on this land except with consent of the burgesses. In 1536 we have a royal licence to the bailies, burgesses, and community of Selkirk empowering them to break up (" ryve ") and till yearly 1000 acres of the common lands of the burgh in what part they pleased, and either to occupy this land themselves or lease it to tenants, as shall seem most expedient for the good of the burgh.[1] In 1681 the " vast bounds of ground called the Common of Selkirk " are described as having lain unprofitable " for these many ages past." [2] Tain had about 3000 acres of moor, used only for pasture and cutting turf. They were feued at sixpence an acre principally to councillors " or their near connexions." [3] When the lands of Inverkeithing, extending for about four miles, were feued out for " very small duties " about or previous to the beginning of the eighteenth century, they were " in a state of nature." [4]

But whatever the way in which burgh land was utilised, the law, as expressed in Acts of 1491 and 1593 crystallising current practice, laid down that " all the rentis of burrowis, as landis, fischingis, fermes, myllis and utheris yerely reveneuiis," should be allotted annually by public " roup " or auction for three years only, presumably to the highest bidder. Thus the petty custom at Peebles was to be set in 1571 " to maist hieast availl," [5] that is, to the greatest advantage. No lease of any item was to be for longer than three years, and the proceeds were to be applied to the " common and necessar thingis of the burgh." For the observance of these conditions responsibility lay with the magistrates and council, who in their turn had to answer to the Lord Chamberlain, the financial minister of the Crown, one of whose duties was to supervise burgh administration in yearly visits either by himself personally or by his deputies. Of the records of these courts " we have little or nothing," [6]

---

[1] *R.M.S.*, s.d., No. 1773.   [2] *A.P.S.*, viii, 420.   [3] *Local Reports*, ii, 422.
[4] *Local Reports*, ii, 91.   [5] *Records*, etc., p. 333.
[6] *Public Records of Scotland*, Maitland Thomson, p. 136.

but there are two lists of the matters to be enquired into at the Chamberlain's Ayre or Circuit. The first of these (*Articuli Inquirendi in Itinere Camerarii*) is dated in the second half of the reign of Robert I, who died in 1329,[1] or in the reign of his successor,[2] the second (*Iter Camerarii*) apparently of the end of the fourteenth century,[3] or of the age of James III (1460-88), but embodying earlier material.[4] In the former one " article " is an enquiry as to whether there has been a just setting and return (*levacio*) of the common good and a faithful account made to the community, and if not, as to whose hands the product has come, and whether the common good is bestowed on the affairs (*negotiis*) of the community. Nothing of this appears in the later document, though it is much fuller in detail than the other.[5]

The power and prestige of the Chamberlain, which had been very great, suffered a serious diminution when King James I introduced the offices of Treasurer and Comptroller to deal with all financial business, the latter to receive the revenues of the burghs. The Chamberlain retained his other duties but had now sunk to being a minor or less significant official. His supervision of the burghs continued, but there are things which suggest that this was becoming less close and effective.[6] It has already been noticed how negligibly the burghs treated the 1469 election Act, and it might be expected that the Chamberlain would take action for its observance, but there is no record of his having done anything.

[1] Cosmo Innes, *Ancient Laws and Customs of the Burghs*, 1124-1424, p. iv.
[2] *Report*, 1835, p. 22.   [3] Cosmo Innes, *ibid.*
[4] *Report, ibid.* Lord Bankton says the *Iter Camerarii* " seems not to be authentick " (*Institute of the Laws of Scotland*, i, 32). *Cf.* Stair, on p. 77 *n*.
[5] It has five sections dealing with the powers and procedure of the court, ten on the nature of possible charges (" chalances " = challenges) against burgh officials, and fourteen against illegal trading and dishonest tradesmen using defective material or otherwise transgressing, such as shoemakers, saddlers, tailors, weavers, millers, fishers, etc. Strangely enough there is one section (xii) on the collectors of small customs who take more custom than is granted by the King and the people and contained in the law, but " there is no indication that there were such officers in the fourteenth century," the petty customs being levied by the *prepositi* of the burghs (*Exch. Rolls*, i, p. xcvi). By whom compiled, from what source, with what intention, or why there should be two schedules, are questions which cannot be answered.   [6] *Report*, 1835, p. 22.

By 1491 we find the legislature intervening with the reminder, which should have been unnecessary, that the common good must be devoted to the common and necessary things of the burgh, and that the expenditure and disposal of the same was a matter for yearly inquisition by the Chamberlain's Ayre. The implication of such a measure is that there had been neglect in this department. An Act of 1503-4 prescribed that appeal from a decision of the burgh court of provost and bailies should be presented to the Chamberlain, who was to summon a court of the Four Burghs for its consideration. With the formation of the Court of Session in 1535 that body became the court of appeal in all civil causes, " and the Chamberlain's regulative functions seem simply to have ceased to be exercised." [1]

The parliament of 1503-4 was responsible for another measure which, in the long run, was to affect the royal burghs vitally, though that, no doubt, was neither premeditated nor foreseen. This Act removed the restriction of leases to short terms which was characteristic of Scottish estate management. It gave sanction, even encouragement, to the setting of lands in feu-farm, that is, on a lease in perpetuity for a definite payment, substantially a form of ownership, in respect of Crown property and that of barons and freeholders, lay and clerical. That relative values might change, that an estate in land might in time appreciate in value out of all proportion to its feu-duty, so as to make that return little more than nominal—such a possibility was beyond recognition by the mediæval economist. The provision of a stabilised revenue in ready money would, at this stage, figure as an advantage, and the feu-farm might well mean, at the time, an increase on what would accrue from a short lease, just as was the case when the burghs secured their establishment on similar terms.[2]

Burghal property was not mentioned in the Act, and so far the setting of such in feu-farm, as amounting to alienation,

---

[1] Maitland Thomson, *Public Records of Scotland*, p. 137. On the Chamberlain see also Theodora Keith in *S.H.R.*, x, 397-402. *Cf.* " the very great extent of the jurisdiction of the High Chamberlain in many other respects, rendered his office, it has been said, dangerous to the government. For reasons of state, therefore, it was abolished some time after the year 1503 " (*Memoir on Royal Burghs*, Archibald Fletcher, p. 4).

[2] See p. 113.

remained illegal. But that omission could be bridged. Edinburgh in 1508 secured by royal charter liberty to set in feu-farm the common lands of the burgh to anyone it thought expedient, as a means of augmenting the common revenue. The feuars were to be under the jurisdiction of the burgh, but were to hold their land in fee and heritage and in free burgage of the King, though the rental was to go to the town.[1] This was the normal relationship. The lands could not be held of the magistrates, since they, strictly subject to yearly election, were a transient body, while the burgh itself was not yet, at least, a true corporation, a legal *persona ficta*. So in a case of 1688 it could be pleaded by the defendant against the magistrates of Arbroath that the lands in question being held in burgage, "the town was not his superior but only the King, whose bailies and commissioners they were," [2] a principle we shall find successfully maintained also on a subsequent occasion.[3]

It seems safe to conjecture that in securing the right to set their land in feu-farm Edinburgh itself had taken the initiative and did so in good faith, satisfied, as the charter says, that in this way an increase of revenue would accrue. But even under the earlier system there might be misuse. In 1528 Perth raised an action to get rid of Patrick Charteris as provost, a position he had usurped from year to year "without fre electioune," while he and his accomplices disposed of the common good at their pleasure.[4] Feu-farm or perpetual feu was to prove the most effective means of alienating public property. There were others, but this device was final in its consequences; land so distributed became private property beyond recovery so long as the feu was paid. Other burghs, first apparently the greater and then all alike, followed the example of Edinburgh in feuing their land, not in all cases, it can be judged, first securing the permission of the superior. In the long run the results were disastrous. In 1551 Aberdeen had a licence from the government of Queen Mary's minority to set burgh property in feu-farm. It then possessed lands "which extended many miles in circuit round Aberdeen,"

---

[1] *Charters &c. Edinburgh*, No. lxii. [2] Fountainhall, as cited, ii, p.879.
[3] See p. 174. [4] *Acts of Lords of Council*, i, 281, 291. See further p. 179.

but " at different remote periods, the greater part of them have been alienated by the magistrates and council, with the reservation of small feu duties." In particular, the fishings of the Dee and Don had gone for a yearly feu-duty of £27, 7s. 8d. sterling, whereas at the time of the report of 1819 they were producing about £10,000 a year. The greater part of the lands had been feued out immediately after the licence of 1551 ; by the eighteenth century the feus themselves were being sold at so many years' purchase ; in 1819 the burgh was found to be insolvent.[1]

In 1581 Banff was given power to set its lands and salmon-fishings in feu-farm, the reason given being that neighbouring noblemen (*proceres circumjacentes*) sought to acquire leases of the properties as those held by burgesses expired and so caused great disquiet.[2] Accordingly, in 1595, the provost, bailies, council, and community appointed commissioners to dispose of the common lands and salmon-fishings in feu-farm to their present occupiers in order to provide means of relieving the heavy taxation now being incurred by the burgh.[3] The charter of 1581 had laid down that this should be done only to resident burgesses and their heirs-male, transference to other than a resident burgess involving reversion to the burgh. This limitation ceased to be operative, and " the greater part of the property was acquired by neighbouring proprietors, including the families of Fife, Findlater, and Banff." [4]

Ayr was in possession of land practically covering the old parish of that name, but in the course of the sixteenth century at least, much of it and finally the whole was disposed of in feu.[5] The council of Kinghorn put on record in 1818

---

[1] *Report, Select Committee, House of Commons,* 1819, p. 23 ; Evidence, pp. 287, 340.

[2] *ac sic rempublicam ejusdem disturbant* (*Annals of Banff* (New Spalding Club), ii, 386).

[3] *Annals of Banff,* ii, 403-5.

[4] *Report,* 1835, Local Reports, Pt. i, p. 102 ; *Reports of Grievances, Committees of Burgesses* (1788), p. 51. In 1700 the town council complained of " our salmond fishing, which was the suport of the burgh, inhansed in the hands of private countrey gentlemen " (*Annals* i, 171).

[5] *Ayr Burgh Records,* ed. G. S. Pryde (*S.H.S.*), p. xxxiv ; *Report,* 1835, p. 31, " nearly the whole."

that a great part of the heritable property of the town had
been " at different times alienated by sales, feus, or otherwise,
for trifling considerations," and that " the town council have
been known to set various parts of the common good by
private bargain to themselves or to their friends . . . at an
under value," and then allowed even that to " run greatly
in arrear." [1] Dumbarton was " nearly altogether divested
of its landed property." [2] " A large part of the landed
property " of Inverness was alienated at different times, and
" in some instances," say the Commissioners of 1835, " the
alienations were highly censurable, by reason of having been
made privately, for an inadequate value, and to members of
council." [3] In their report of 1691 the magistrates of Dingwall
informed the investigators that the burgh had " no kind of
publict good belonging to it, by reasone ther predecessors
did few and sell the little thing they hade many years for the
payment of ther publict debts," all left being £29 Scots of
feu-duties, of which the town clerk drew £20 as salary.[4]
For some places there is no precise information. Thus the
town clerk of Kintore " had always understood that the burgh
had, at one time, been possessed of lands ; but that they
had all been disposed of to the family of Keith, Earls Marischal
. . . at different times between the years 1511 and 1609." [5]

To sell was going a step further than to feu, but seems
to have been done with the same modest sense of value. In
1691 the Provost of Glasgow in name of the burgh supplicated
the Convention to warrant the sale of part of their lands in
order to pay off debt incurred in the " vast soumes " borrowed
by the late magistrates and " the misapplying and dilapidation
of the tounes patrimony in suffering their debt to swell, and
employing the common stock for their own sinistrous ends
and uses." [6] Thus was sold " at a low price " an estate which,
at its value in 1835 would, according to the Commissioners,

[1] *Local Reports*, 1835, Pt. ii, p. 149.
[2] *Ibid.*, p. 197. " The present free rent does not exceed £15 Sterling
although the present real rent of these lands cannot possibly be less than
£1000 Sterling " (*Reports of Grievances*, 1788, as cited, p. 46).
[3] *Local Reports*, ii, 98.
[4] *Report*, 1835, Appendix, p. 75.
[5] *Local Reports*, ii, 153.
[6] Cited *Report of Committee of House of Commons*, 1793, pp. 21-2.

" have relieved the inhabitants of almost all the burghal taxes that now press on them." [1] As Glasgow had been a royal burgh since 1611, saving the right of the archbishop, but there was now no such personage, it is not apparent how the Convention could grant such a liberty where royal property was concerned.[2] But the Convention did at times assume a power not legally within its scope, as in authorising feu-farm tenure,[3] or imposing, as of their own decision, a " sett " or constitution upon a burgh.[4] For the Glasgow magistrates the authority was good enough.[5] And Dingwall—as also no doubt other places—did not, so far as is known, seek authority to sell from any source.

The consequences to the royal burghs of this and other forms of mishandling their property are set forth in an Act of 1535, which pictures them as all " putt to povertie, waistit and distroyit in ther gudis and polecy, and almaist ruynous." This lamentable state is traced in part to a failing of trade, and partly to the presence among the magistrates of " outlandismen " concerned with " thare awine particular wele in consumyng of the commoun gudis of burrowis." To deal with the latter contingency it was now provided that magistrates should present a yearly statement of their accounts to Exchequer, where also anyone concerned could appear to question these accounts. This arrangement, it was hopefully expected, would put an end to complaints. Accordingly it appears that " during the latter half of the sixteenth and the earlier part of the seventeenth centuries . . . accounts from at least a great many burghs were rendered in exchequer," but the predominant business of that body was with national

[1] *Report*, 1835, pp. 26, 31.

[2] *Cf.* p. 129. On this practice see Pagan, pp. 114-5. " However illegal and incompetent it was. for the Convention of Royal Burghs to authorize a sale of the common property of any individual Burgh, etc." (Fletcher, *Memoir &c.*, p. 11).

[3] *Report*, 1835, p. 25.

[4] Pagan, as cited, p. 93. The Court of Exchequer pronounced in the Dumbarton case of 1787 (see pp. 178-9) " that the jurisdiction of the Convention was private, of consent, or prorogation, self-created and illlegal " (Cited in *Memoir*, etc., Arch. Fletcher, p. 57).

[5] An Act of the Convention empowering Glasgow in 1676 to feu its Common Muir was ratified by Parliament in 1681 (viii, p. 431) apparently as considered legally desirable.

not burghal finance, and the burghal share cannot have
received a very close scrutiny, while there is no trace of the
appearance before it of any representative of the " murmurers "
against the municipal mal-administration of which they
complained.   Such attendance indeed was but an empty
concession in view of distance, expense, and no provision in
the statute of penalty for offenders or compensation to those
responsible for any correction or exposure.[1]   Thus the yearly
rendering of accounts in Exchequer was never more than a
" barren formality." [2]   Indeed it was claimed that " a Burgh
can scarcely be named, whose accounts were audited in
Exchequer, excepting during a short period between 1660
and 1680." [3]   The Royal Commissioners, we have just seen,
found reason to assign an earlier date for this very restricted
practice.

II

These legislative measures therefore could not avail to
stop the waste of burgh resources, for which opportunity was
made by the method of electing magistrates and council
whereby a mere coterie acting together could secure control.
In 1567 " certane marchandis and inhabitantis " of Cupar
entered a protest against men who were keeping the public
offices among themselves and " usand and disposand the
commoun gude of the said burgh at thair plesour " in detriment
of the common weal.[4]   In 1590 there was the case of Aberdeen,
already introduced,[5] in which a set of individuals were
monopolising offices with the effect of " delapidating, spending,
and waisting of the commoun gude," [6] as if " it war thair
awin particular heritages," and so for many years " in thairis
and thair freyndis handis, onropit [not rouped] " contrary to
the custom in other burghs.[7]

Following on such complaints came the Act of 1593, as
ineffective materially as its predecessors.   Again the burghs
are described as greatly decayed.   Again one reason is lack

---

[1] *Report*, 1835, pp. 23-4.   [2] *Ibid.*, p. 27.
[3] Archibald Fletcher, *Memoir on the Royal Burghs*, p. 7
[4] *Reg. Pr. Council*, i, 582.   See further p. 125.   *Cf.* also the case at
Peebles, 1571 (*Records*, etc., p. 329).
[5] See pp. 124, 131.   [6] *R.P.C.*, iv, 533.   [7] *R.C.B.*, i, 313, 314.

of trade. Again it is noted how particular persons have
converted the patrimony of the burgh to personal use. And
once more it is prescribed that the common good be put to
public auction yearly, and be devoted to the common affairs
of the burgh only. The Convention, too, did its best to
impose the legislative restrictions, fining in 1603 eleven burghs
£20 each for not producing evidence of the rouping of their
common good " and perambulating of their mercheis " ; [1]
and threatening Inverkeithing in 1619 with heavy penalties
on discovering there " ane gritt pairt of thair commoun guid
to be restan in thair magistrats hands, quhairby the samin
wes verie evill imployet and no compt maid thairof." [2] Four
years later it deplores how " the burgh of Cullen is utterlie
ruined and almost altogidder left desolate be ressoun that the
common guid of the said burgh and landis appertening
thairto ar sett in few to gentlemen throw the cuntrey for
such small dewtie as the samin ar altogidder unprofittable,"
numbering this calamity among the grievances to be laid
before the royal commissioners with the suggestion that, if
these acquisitions were taken out of the hands of their unjust
possessors, means might be found to restore its lands and
" former beauty " to the burgh. Alas ! the royal commissioners on grievances found they had no warrant to pronounce upon heritable titles or call them in question.[3]

This rebuttal may have been justified, but the fundamental
facts are that municipal abuses were made possible and
even prompted by the restricted methods of electing council
and magistrates, and that the ideas of the government during
the seventeenth century increasingly discountenanced any
popular movement against constituted authority. Aberdeen,
as already noted,[4] had tried the device of electing a rival
council. The same step was taken in the small but ancient
burgh of Cromarty, where the extensive burgh lands were in
danger of becoming the prey of the local sheriff, Sir John

[1] *R.C.B.*, ii, 160. " It being an antient custom in Scotland, for the
several Boroughs of the Kingdome, to survey the boundaries of their
respective jurisdictions, which is called Riding the Marches. This custom
is still performed yearly by many of the said Boroughs. But the Edin-
burghers seem to have been very backward in this affair." In two hundred
years it had been done only twice (Maitland, *Hist. of Edinb.*, p. 178).

[2] *Ibid.*, iii, p. 82.   [3] *Ibid.*, iii, 149-50, 152.   [4] P. 124.

Urquhart, cousin of the famous Sir Thomas. Sir John had acted as provost of the burgh for some years before 1669, though possessing all the legal disqualifications but in accordance with the policy of Charles II of getting country gentlemen introduced as magistrates.[1] His support came from the small heritors on the burgh lands and the lesser burgesses of the town. The councillors of the past year within the burgh met on a day and elected the new body of men opposed to Urquhart's schemes. A few days later the Urquhart party met and elected their own council and magistrates. The issue between these two bodies was taken before the Privy Council, which pronounced in favour of what was Urquhart's council on the ground that it had been chosen on the legal day, the other council not.[2] Then in the summer of 1670 this council transferred the whole lands and revenues of the burgh to Sir John Urquhart on the ground that they and their predecessors were in his debt for a considerable loan,[3] and for an immediate payment of 5000 merks Scots, that is about £278 sterling, dirt cheap as it has turned out to be.

This transaction came under review in a case before the Court of Session in 1756, when another Urquhart claimed that he was feudal superior of the heritors on what had been burgh lands. It was then argued that the disposition of these lands to Sir John Urquhart was " intrinsically void," which, as the statutory procedure had not been followed, was certainly the case. The Court, however, avoided this issue by founding upon a later charter of 1685 to Viscount Tarbat, afterwards Earl of Cromarty, who had acquired the sheriffdom, and whose charter was held to be not merely " a charter of progress," but " an original grant of these burrow-lands." The heritors, then, were declared to be vassals of the Crown, as we saw in the case of the Edinburgh feus in 1508,[4] while the burgh was constituted a burgh of barony, but remained the head burgh of the shire. The

---

[1] See pp. 133-4.

[2] For the details see *R.P.C.* (Third Series), iii, 106-11.

[3] The deed of disposition in three sheets pasted end to end and measuring nearly five feet in length is in H.M. Register House, where it was entered for registration in 1747.

[4] P. 168.

point of it all is that the lands were appropriated to private ownership, and the burgh was a shorn lamb. This was perhaps the most complete swoop on record. Magistrates, councillors, and burgesses sign the deed of disposition.[1]

How far popular claims were distasteful to government policy and to the courts was made clear in other cases. Relying on Acts of Parliament a merchant of Edinburgh in 1683 appealed to Exchequer to enforce the Act of 1535 by compelling two late provosts and the other magistrates to produce their accounts to show that they had applied the common good to its proper uses. The Court of Exchequer, however, found it improper to take such action at the instance of a private burgess,[2] "it looking too popular and democratic,"[3] or, as Sir George Mackenzie puts it, " would have given too great occasion to faction, and would have discourag'd magistracy too much, nor are such popular actions in matters of government to be easily allowed under monarchy."[4] Only the High Treasurer, it was held, as coming in the place of the old-time Chamberlain, was entitled to call a burgh to account. In the particular case, however, the Edinburgh magistrates in office were ordered to produce their account books by a specified date, and in the examination of these the assistance of any citizen was declared to be welcome.

In fact the continuing impoverishment of the royal burghs, which threatened to render them unable to meet their share of public taxation, was a problem that could not be ignored. Following upon an ineffective effort to impose control a special commission was issued in June 1684 to the Treasurer and his depute, which proceeded upon a very frank narrative of the circumstances. It affirmed that in many of the royal burghs the property and revenues of the common good were being either extravagantly wasted or privately consumed (*privatim decoquuntur*). Accordingly debts, which should have been unnecessary, were incurred, and assessments laid upon

---

[1] *Session Papers* in Signet Library, Nos. 39, 58 (1756) ; Morison's *Decisions of the Court of Session*, p. 15079 ff. (1758) ; *The Royal Burgh of Cromarty*, W. Mackay Mackenzie, pp. 24-7.

[2] *Cf.* p. 171.

[3] Fountainhall, *Decisions of the Lords of Session*, i, 231.

[4] *Observations on the Acts of Parliament*, p. 131.

the inhabitants to pay off these, which, in most of the burghs, were nevertheless left unpaid. The result was much murmuring and complaint, directed against men who formed parties and factions to have themselves elected and continued as magistrates, that they might apply the public good to the advantage of themselves and their friends, " every Bird taking a Fether," as Bacon has it in another connection. The Commission therefore empowered the officers named to summon all magistrates and their representatives since 1660 to submit accounts of their dealings with the common good down to the present time, and to hold them personally liable for all undue and unjustifiable expenditure.[1] An heroic measure, but between the idea and the reality fell the shadow, when Charles II died six months later, and the commission with him.

It is just at this time that we get a dissenting note struck by an Aberdeen writer in repudiation of the charges of misappropriation of public property by magistrates. " To which I can say," he affirms, " (having severall years born office in our own Town,) I never knew any cause for such a thought, nor that ever a Magistrat was so base as to be guilty of such a Crime, which the Romans called, *Crimen Peculatus* : when Magistrats or others took of the Publick Money to make their personal gain " : continuing in moral denunciation of " such baseness." [2] If this repudiation by a municipal administrator, who in his treatise on the government of the royal burghs quotes freely from classical authors and the Scriptures, is to be accepted, then he must have been fortunate to flourish at a time of civic purity not always exemplified in his native city,[3] not to speak of the contrary record as to other burghs to be gathered from official sources.

Following, apparently, on the revelations of the enquiry by the Convention in 1691-2 [4] an Act of Parliament in 1693 proceeded on much the same lines as the abortive commission, repeating the familiar complaints as to mal-administration. Commissioners were to be appointed to enquire into the

[1] *Report*, 1793, App. F ; *Report*, 1835, p. 25.
[2] *Memorialls &c. Royall Burghs*, " Philopoliteius," Aberdeen, 1685, p. 180. The author was Alexander Skene, bailie of Aberdeen.
[3] *Cf.* here pp. 124, 172. [4] See pp. 154-5.

condition and state of the common good and revenues in all royal burghs and how these had been " imployed or mis-imployed " before or hereafter.   Stress is laid upon the practice of borrowing, which is not to be valid except for reasons held adequate and on the authority of the town council. Unless the " causes and uses " are found to be " just, true, and reale " those responsible, or their heirs and successors, would be held liable " in their private fortunes " to relieve the town of the burden so incurred.   In conformity, however, with the judicial gloss upon the Act of 1535,[1] action at law could be taken only by a burgess who had held office as a provost, bailie, or dean of guild.   Thus action against offenders could be taken only by those who may well have been guilty themselves.   It mattered less as no evidence has been found of the Commission having ever done anything.[2]   On all these legislative provisions since the cessation of the Chamberlain Ayres the Commissioners of 1835 pronounce the judgment " that they were practically inoperative, and, in their effects, even worse than useless." [3]   The judgment of the later burgh reformers was that " while the chamberlain continued to exercise this power, we meet with few or no complaints of the malversation of magistrates.   But when the chamberlain ceased to carry the ensigns and the terrors of justice to the burghs, their magistrates no longer confined themselves within the line of their duty.   They appear to have broke loose like felons from their fetters, and to have committed the most enormous waste and dilapidation of the property of burghs." [4]

III

In addition to these obvious ways of diverting public funds into private pockets there were others more indirect. Sir Andrew Ramsay, provost of Edinburgh, was accused in a court case of 1672 of having in that office " govern'd most tyrannically for ten years, applying the common good to himself and friends," which was a too familiar accusation, but also of " inventing new though unnecessary employments

---

[1] See pp. 125,167.   [2] *Report*, 1835, p. 27.   [3] *Ibid.*, p. 27.
[4] *Illustrations of the Bill to be submitted to Parliament*, Archibald Fletcher (1787), ed. 1819, p. 247.

M

within the town, to oblige those who depended upon him." [1] Further, he had induced the council to appoint his own son " while he was yet a meer child " to be town-clerk. Father of course " lifted the profit annexed." [2] Such patronage was familiar also in other burghs.[3] At Forfar the son of a leading member of council was appointed town-clerk in 1803. An action for his removal nineteen years later produced proof that he " laboured under mental imbecility," yet, having been appointed *ad vitam aut culpam*, he could not be removed.[4] Imbecility was not a legal misdemeanour.

The appeal to the Court of Exchequer in 1683 for production of the accounts of the common good having been turned down, the eighteenth-century reformers had recourse to the Court of Session on the same issue, based on the Acts of 1535 and 1693, but with no more success. An action from Selkirk in 1748 was inconclusive in a hostile atmosphere.[5] Another effort was made in 1771 by burgesses and inhabitants of Kinghorn, who entered a claim for a general inspection of the accounts of the common good. The Court decided that an action at the instance of private burgesses was incompetent and that such accounting could take place only in Exchequer.[6] To Exchequer, then, in 1787 burgesses of Dumbarton presented a petition that the accounts of the burgh might be inspected according to the Act of 1535.[7] The Court, however, pronounced that the Act had never been in observance and had fallen into desuetude, in which assertions they were clearly mistaken, and that in any case

[1] Sir George Mackenzie, *Memoirs of the Affairs of Scotland*, etc., p. 247.

[2] Fountainhall, *Historical Notices*, i, 58.

[3] *Report*, 1835, p. 67. Of Banff it was said that " Sinecure offices have been created, without the shadow of necessity, and salaries annexed to them, in order to pension some poor dependant or relation of the ruler or of the junto " (*Reports of Grievances*, etc., p. 88).

[4] *Report*, 1835, p. 67. This clerk " never acted and cannot act." The work was done by a deputy, who received a fourth of the fees (*Local Reports*, 1835, i, 443).

[5] *Report*, 1835, p. 29. Elchies *Decisions*, i, App. ii, No. 27.

[6] Morison's *Decisions*, pp. 7373-7374.

[7] The Commissioners of 1835 record of Dumbarton that " Its management for many years has exhibited most reckless borrowing and an equally prodigal expenditure . . . the credit of the burgh is now entirely gone " (*Local Reports*, Pt. i, p. 200).

the change in the constitution of Exchequer after the Union
had foreclosed that jurisdiction.[1] The plea that it pertained
to the Convention of Burghs was peremptorily denied as
without legal sanction either in statute or common law.[2]
The case for a general accounting being thus ruled out,
burgesses of Inverury in 1820 approached the Court of
Session with specific acts of malversation on the part of the
magistrates, only to be met with the judgment, based on the
previous cases, that the Court had no jurisdiction on such
questions.[3] The sum total of these proceedings had been
expressed in 1787 to Pitt, as prime minister, in a letter on
behalf of the Committee of Burgh Delegates, to the effect
that " as the law of Scotland is now understood there does not
exist a power to controul the administration of burghs," [4]
an opinion confirmed in the Inverury case of 1820.
For Exchequer the law of 1535 was dead and that of 1693
outwith their power ; the Court of Session had no jurisdiction ;
and the Convention of Royal Burghs had no legal right to
impose any judgment in the matter.

There was, then, no prospect of relief from proceedings in
the courts, and through the eighteenth century mismanagement and alienation of burgh property, or what was left,
continued on the old lines.[5] Four transactions at Renfrew
during 1798-1802 impressed the Royal Commission as
deserving " particular notice." Each was a sale in the
interest of the provost, as indeed the minute of the first
transaction frankly states, not for any advantage to the
burgh. Each was proposed by the provost himself, who
presided and collaborated at each meeting that gave effect
to his own proposal and thereafter signed the minutes
authorizing the particular sales to himself, sales for which,
so far as concerned the burgh, there was no necessity.[6] Perth
was fortunate in that alienations of its property did not begin

---

[1] *Report*, 1835, p. 29 ; Fletcher's *Memoir*, p. 55.
[2] Pagan, *C.R.B.*, p. 98 : Fletcher, pp. 56-7 : As Baron Sir John
Dalrymple put it : " is a body made up of the defaulters themselves to try
these defaulters ? " (p. 56). *Cf.* p. 145.
[3] *Decisions, Court of Session*, No. lviii, pp. 218-20.
[4] In Fletcher volume of 1819, pp. 145, 148.
[5] Pagan, as cited, p. 94.
[6] *Report*, 1835, p. 31, and *Local Reports*, ii, pp. 358-60.

until 1746, after which down to 1830 they were "numerous and extensive," nevertheless leaving the town in 1835 "still possessed of large heritable property," at which time, too, the administration is reported as "in general correct."[1] At Irvine and Jedburgh feuing for the previous forty years is declared to have been fair and adequate, while Kirkcaldy is commended for the "care and ability" shown in its management.[2]

Such cases, however, were exceptional. More general is the long record of peculation, great and small. It is perhaps difficult now to account for this practice on the part of public men, but what Gibbon would call "secondary causes" may have operated. The Privy Council in 1619 had a particular reason to point out to James VI that in England public officials "hes goode allowance and fees able to raimburs [reimburse] thair haill chargeis . . . whereas the magistratis and counsell of the burrows of this kingdome . . . serve freelie without fee or allowance."[3]

The sequel is to be found in the words attributed to the Provost in John Galt's novel of that name how "it seemed to be the use and wont of men in public trusts to think they were free to indemnify themselves in a left-handed way for the time and trouble they bestowed on the same. But the thing was not so far wrong in principle as in the hugger-muggering way in which it was done." This provost, having first had his share in such misdoing, ultimately "became conscious of being raised into public life for a better purpose than to prey upon the leaves and flourishes of the commonwealth."[4] But by this time leaves and flourishes were mostly gone ; what the locust laird left, the councillor cankerworm had eaten, or the other way round.

Thus increasingly impoverished in their resources the royal burghs, in order to meet their local and public burdens, had already for some time had recourse to borrowing, in

[1] *Local Reports*, ii, 300, 305.
[2] *Ibid*, pp. 128, 134, 158.
[3] *Melrose Papers* (Abbotsford Club), ii, 349. But in the return to the Convention in 1691 Inverness shows a payment of "sallaries" to the provost and four bailies, the sum total, however, amounting to less than the salary of the town drummer.
[4] *The Provost*, chap. xxiii. "Flourishes = blossoms."

some cases, however, without real justification, and not always properly accounted for. Aberdeen in 1810 obtained an Act of Parliament authorising the magistrates and council to raise money mainly for the provision of wet and graving docks, and to increase shore dues to pay the interest and principal of the debt. A Committee of the House of Commons investigating in 1819 found that £127,000 had been borrowed and spent and the additional dues levied, but, it blandly remarks, "the wet and graving docks contemplated by the Act have not been executed;" [1] "nor are likely to be so" add the Commissioners of 1835. [2]

The appointment of this Committee, on the motion of a Scottish member, to enquire into burgh affairs was an unexpected triumph for the advocates of reform—" by a miracle," says Lord Cockburn. [3] The affairs of Edinburgh, Aberdeen, Dundee, and Dunfermline were investigated, and it appeared that, as the result of municipal mismanagement, all four burghs were bankrupt. At Edinburgh present and late officials and councillors professed themselves to be " wholly uninformed " on the financial situation in the burgh. [4] Aberdeen had for some time been "in a state of manifest and declared insolvency." [5] The revenues of Dundee were " altogether insufficient," parts of the public property having been set to members of council or their friends " below their fair value and for long periods," in

---

[1] *Report*, 1819, p. 22. For evidence see pp. 278, 302.

[2] *Local Reports*, i, 46.

[3] *Memorials*, etc., ed. 1910, p. 308. " Loud were the rejoicings on the one side, and sad the dismay on the other, when the tidings of this scarcely credible vote reached Scotland."

[4] *Cf.* the case of Aberdeen in the examination of the chamberlain : " Have you brought any cash books of intromissions of public money from the year 1793 to the time you took charge in 1812 ?—I have not ; not having any such in my possession."
" Are any such books in existence ?—I never saw them " (*Report*, 1819, Evidence, pp. 340-1).

[5] Yet the funds of charities of which the magistrates were trustees had been lent to the town " without heritable security," and by 1833 the magistrates and council had " sold above £34,000 of heritable property belonging to the charities of which they were sole trustees, not for the purpose of the trust, but to be applied to the relief of the town treasury or its creditors " (*Report*, 1819, Evidence, p. 273 ; *Local Reports*, 1835, i, 23-4).

one case for only a sixth of the rent which it fetched when put up to public auction three years before the date of the Committee. The annual expenditure of Dundee exceeded its income.[1] This exposure was a strengthening of the position of the burgh reformers, and the activities of the Committee were brought to a close.[2] But the refusal of jurisdiction by existing courts, and the growing force of public opinion, led to an Act in 1822, the terms of which virtually repeated so much earlier legislation : the accounts of the magistrates to be submitted for public inspection ; burgesses to be entitled to make written representations on these to the Court of Exchequer, which was now empowered to pronounce on them ; alienations and leases to be by public auction ; and no debts to be contracted without authority of the council. The result, too, followed precedent : " the provisions of the Act have proved nearly useless." [3] Of six cases under it the burgesses were successful in just one. Exchequer proved still fertile in legal demurrers.

For example, certain burgesses of Nairn in 1823 raised a case under this Act against the magistrates as having sold certain lands without following the statutory procedure. The prosecutors had to prove their standing as burgesses, and this they did in a manner valid under Scottish law by presenting their burgess tickets, which were, as usual, in the form of extracts from the town council records certified by the town-clerk. But the Court of Exchequer professed to follow English law, which did not accept even authenticated extracts so long as the principal record was in existence. Because this record when called for was not produced, a verdict was given against the complainers with heavy costs. The Royal Commissioners of 1835 significantly add to their narrative, " It is understood that, had this objection been unsuccessful, numerous other technical objections, derived from English practice, were in reserve, some of which must have been sustained." [4]

The whole problem of the burghs, however, was now occupying a wider field. Since the last decade of the eighteenth

[1] *Report*, 1819, pp. 19, 4, 29, 34.

[2] Cockburn, as cited, p. 309 : " the enquiry was suddenly quashed."

[3] *Report*, 1835, p. 30.   [4] *Report*, p. 30.

century it had grown from a matter of local interest to one of national policy and general discussion as involved in the spreading movement towards constitutional reform.[1] It may well seem extraordinary that in spite of public condemnation and the wholly new urban conditions set up by the industrial revolution, such a close, incongruous, and corrupt procedure should persist. The reason is that in their final phase, as in their beginning, the burghs were serving also a political end. A government was formed of ministers of state directly appointed by and solely responsible to the Crown, who had then to improvise a majority in Parliament. Scotland returned forty-five members to the House of Commons, of which fifteen were burgh representatives, who were elected by groups of three, four, or five burgh constituencies,[2] where the method was for each town council to choose a delegate and these to elect the member. Within so narrow a field the political expedients of the time could be operated with ease and certainty—personal influence, social and pecuniary advantage, and particularly the patronage of many posts in the services and branches of administration at home and abroad. By the prevailing methods of election, too, the town councils themselves could be packed or purged so as to secure the return of the desirable parliamentary representative.[3] On such lines, laid down in the conditions following on the Union of the Parliaments, was framed the system carried to perfection by Henry Dundas, first Lord Melville, " the Pharos of Scotland," by whom alone could one safely direct his political course since to him " every man owed what he had got and looked

[1] " the proposed reform of the abuses in the internal government of the Royal Burghs of Scotland was first brought under public discussion in 1782 " (*Memoir on Royal Burghs*, Archibald Fletcher, p. 1).

[2] Edinburgh alone returned a member for itself.

[3] Consider the evidence as to Edinburgh given by the deacon of the Goldsmiths' Incorporation : " Have you ever known any pledges exacted from persons, before they were admitted into the council ?—I have frequently heard it stated by individuals themselves, both before and after they had been admitted, that such pledges were required and given."

" By whom were they required, and what was the nature of them, as you have understood ?—By one or two of the leading members at the time, it was understood that they were to support a particular system of politics, and to avoid being troublesome while they were there " (*Report*, 1819 ; evidence, p. 219.

for what he wished." [1] All this of course favoured already existing practices of burgh corruption, and such political needs undoubtedly influenced the judgments of the courts in appeals against burgh misrule. Dundas, Scotland's uncrowned King,[2] was inevitably as flint against all municipal reform.[3] Any change was held to be linked up with revolution in another field,[4] though in fact the burgh reformers considered parliamentary reform "infinitely less" important than their own cause.[5] The outspoken denunciation of magistrates seemed to prefigure the excesses of the French Revolution. Then with the outbreak of the war with France "all proceedings in burgh reform were for the time suspended . . . to be resumed at a more auspicious period." [6] Burghal and national politics were thus closely intermingled, as expressed in Cockburn's caustic comment on the town councils, " In general they were sinks of political and municipal iniquity, steeped in the baseness which they propagated, and types and causes of the corruption that surrounded them." [7]

The burgh reformers had concentrated their attack on " the self-electing power of the Town Councils as the original fountain from which all the other grievances and abuses were naturally and necessarily derived." [8] To their scheme of reform the Convention of Royal Burghs showed no good will, denouncing it on the grounds that " it would unhinge a constitution which has stood the test of ages . . . and has

---

[1] Cockburn, as cited, p. 201.

[2] Hume Brown, *History of Scotland*, iii, p. 379.

[3] *Ibid.*, p. 357.

[4] There were assertions in the House of Commons that the burgh reformers from 1784 to 1794 were the same description of men " ' who not long since contributed to crowd the table with petitions for radical reform ' that is, a reform by universal suffrage and annual parliaments " (Arch. Fletcher, *Memoir*, etc., p. 128).

[5] Cockburn, p. 306. They opposed annual parliaments and universal suffrage (Fletcher, as cited, pp. 128-9).

[6] Arch. Fletcher, *Memoir*, etc., p. 126.

[7] *Memoir*, p. 91. For England the poet Cowper has it :

> " Hence charter'd boroughs are such public plagues,
> And burghers, men immaculate perhaps
> In all their private functions, once combined,
> Become a loathsome body."   *The Task*, Bk. iv.

[8] Fletcher, *Memoir*, etc., p. 85.

been attended with as many advantages as could have been expected from any institution whatever."[1] In 1787 the Convention resolved " to grant a sum not exceeding £200 for the purpose of opposing the Reform of the Royal Boroughs," though it could be claimed that the same body had virtually acknowledged " that the opposition to the Reform was not supported by almost a single Burgess out of the Town Councils."[2] On the close of the Napoleonic war the reform movement was vigorously revived and attained success in the Municipal Reform Acts of 1833, under which town councils were to be elected by qualified householders.[3]

The case of the burghs of regality and barony had its own complications. The jurisdiction of a lord of regality was " almost abolished " by the Act of 1747 removing heritable jurisdictions while the baronial jurisdiction in a burgh was made " cumulative with the jurisdiction of the district." There remained burghs with " a modified right of election of their magistrates," others where " the dependence upon the superior subsists unqualified," and some which, by various measures, had come to " enjoy the elective constitution."[4] The varying constitutions of these burghs were ultimately regularised by bringing them, according to their state, into line with the general constitution of burghs.

The exclusive economic privileges of the burghs lingered on, but really received a death blow in the Report of the Royal Commission of 1833-5, which had no hesitation in recommending that they " should be directly and completely abolished." This was done in 1846,[5] removing the last outworn relics of the mediæval economic age. Whether the freer factory age, which had already established itself, was a wholly advantageous substitute is a question which does not concern us here.

[1] *Ibid.*, pp. 148-9.

[2] *The Caledonian Mercury*, No. 10,297, 8th Sept. 1787. At Banff in 1784 " It was resolved by the Head Court . . . that no money be paid out of the Burgh Funds in opposing the Bill intended to be brought into Parliament for reform in the burghs " (*Annals of Banff*, i, 276).

[3] In nine royal burghs the number of £10 householders was smaller than the number of the council. These meantime retained the old system.

[4] *Report*, 1835, pp. 97-9. *Cf.* here p. 81-2.

[5] See p. 1.

AUTHORS QUOTED

[Where number is followed by italic *n* the reference is to the footnote.]

187

GENERAL INDEX

See also chapter headings

[Where number is followed by italic *n* the reference is to the footnote.]

PRINTED IN GREAT BRITAIN BY OLIVER AND BOYD LTD., EDINBURGH

KINTYRE

IN THE 17th CENTURY

by

ANDREW McKERRAL
C.I.E., M.A., F.S.A.Scot.

Kintyre was the original home of the Scots of Dalriada. This book gives a short summary of its early history, and then deals in greater detail with the events of one of its most important centuries — the seventeenth. It relates the causes of the fall of the Macdonalds of the Isles, the rise of the great family of Argyll, the foundation of the burgh of Lochhead or Campbeltown, the stirring events of the Colkitto raids, the campaign of General David Leslie, the massacre of Dunaverty, and the visitation of Plague. Perhaps most important of all, it gives for the first time, the real causes and circumstances of the plantation of the district by Covenanters from Ayrshire and Renfrewshire directed by the Marquis of Argyll.

The author is a native of Kintyre and has long been interested in its history. He is a member of the Kintyre Club and Kintyre Antiquarian Society, a member of the Scottish History Society and Fellow of the Scottish Society of Antiquarians.

Demy 8vo.   15s. net.

OLIVER AND BOYD LTD.
EDINBURGH AND LONDON

EARLY SOURCES
OF SCOTTISH HISTORY

A.D. 500-1286

collected and translated by

Allan Orr Anderson

Summary of Contents

Volume I, clvii+604 pages

Preface. Abbreviations. Bibliographical Notes. Calendar Notes. Orthographical Notes. Tables of the Succession of Kings in Northumbria, Dalriata, Pictland, Scotland, and England. Introduction. Kings' Reigns, Districts, and Pedigrees, with a collation of the unexpanded Chronicles of the Kings. Establishment of the Kingdoms of Dalriata and Northumbria. Kings of Bernicia. Christianisation of the Picts. Life of Columba. Affairs before and after the Council of Druimm-Ceta. Death of Columba. Zenith and Decline of Dalriata. Zenith and Decline of Northumbria. Domination of the Picts over Dalriata. Recovery of Dalriata. Norwegian Invasions. Union of the Kingdoms of the Scots and the Picts. Scandinavian Settlements. Harold Fairhair. Orkney and the Hebrides. Iceland and the Hebrides. Ketil Flatnose establishes Scandinavian Rule in the Hebrides. Thorstein the Red becomes master of Caithness and Sutherland. Turf-Einar in the Orkneys. Harold Fairhair's Invasion. Reign of Constantine II. Battle of Vin-heath. End of Constantine's Reign. Reign of Malcolm. Eric's Sons. Reigns of Indulf, Dub, and Culen. Reign of Kenneth II. Reigns of Constantine III and Kenneth III. Reign of Malcolm II and the Danish Conquest. Reigns of Duncan, Macbeth, and Lulach. History of Northumbria.

Volume II, vii+806 pages

Reign of Malcolm III and the Norman Conquest. Life of Queen Margaret. Reigns of Donald Ban, Duncan II, and Edgar. First invasion of Magnus. Second Invasion of Magnus and the end of Edgar's Reign. Reign of Alexander I. History of Huntingdon. Reign of David and the Wars of Stephen. Reign of Malcolm IV. Reign of William and the Wars of Henry. Scotland in feudal subjection to England, 1175 to 1189. Latter part of William's Reign. Reign of Alexander II and the Invasion of Louis. Reign of Alexander III to the year 1263. The Invasion of Hakon. End of Alexander's Reign and Extinction of the Royal Family. Appendix. Religious Houses. Index.

Two volumes.   Medium 8vo.   Price £3, 10s. net.

OLIVER AND BOYD LTD.
EDINBURGH AND LONDON